A Political Companion to
Henry Adams

POLITICAL COMPANIONS TO GREAT AMERICAN AUTHORS

Series Editor: Patrick J. Deneen, Georgetown University

The Political Companions to Great American Authors series illuminates the complex political thought of the nation's most celebrated writers from the founding era to the present. The goals of the series are to demonstrate how American political thought is understood and represented by great American writers and to describe how our polity's understanding of fundamental principles such as democracy, equality, freedom, toleration, and fraternity has been influenced by these canonical authors.

The series features a broad spectrum of political theorists, philosophers, and literary critics and scholars whose work examines classic authors and seeks to explain their continuing influence on American political, social, intellectual, and cultural life. This series reappraises esteemed American authors and evaluates their writings as lasting works of art that continue to inform and guide the American democratic experiment.

A POLITICAL COMPANION TO
Henry Adams

Edited by Natalie Fuehrer Taylor

THE UNIVERSITY PRESS OF KENTUCKY

Scholarly publisher for the Commonwealth,
serving Bellarmine University, Berea College, Centre
College of Kentucky, Eastern Kentucky University,
The Filson Historical Society, Georgetown College,
Kentucky Historical Society, Kentucky State University,
Morehead State University, Murray State University,
Northern Kentucky University, Transylvania University,
University of Kentucky, University of Louisville,
and Western Kentucky University.
All rights reserved.

Editorial and Sales Offices: The University Press of Kentucky
663 South Limestone Street, Lexington, Kentucky 40508-4008
www.kentuckypress.com

14 13 12 11 10   5 4 3 2 1

Library of Congress Cataloging-in-Publication Data

A political companion to Henry Adams / edited by Natalie Fuehrer Taylor.
       p.   cm. — (Political companions to great American authors)
    Includes bibliographical references and index.
    ISBN 978-0-8131-2590-9 (hardcover : alk. paper)
    1. Adams, Henry, 1838–1918—Political and social views. I. Taylor,
Natalie Fuehrer.
    PS1004.A4Z8 2010
    818'.409—dc22

                          2010013912

This book is printed on acid-free recycled paper meeting
the requirements of the American National Standard
for Permanence in Paper for Printed Library Materials.

∞ ⊛

Manufactured in the United States of America.

 Member of the Association of
American University Presses

Contents

PART II. THE SEARCH FOR LOST FAITH

Series Foreword

THOSE WHO UNDERTAKE A study of American political thought must attend to the great theorists, philosophers, and essayists. But such a study is incomplete, however, if it neglects American literature, one of the greatest repositories of the nation's political thought and teachings.

America's literature is distinctive because it is, above all, intended for a democratic citizenry. In contrast to eras when an author would aim to inform or influence a select aristocratic audience, in democratic times, public influence and education must resonate with a more expansive, less leisured, and diverse audience to be effective. The great works of America's literary tradition are the natural locus of democratic political teaching. Invoking the interest and attention of citizens through the pleasures afforded by the literary form, many of America's great thinkers sought to forge a democratic public philosophy with subtle and often challenging teachings that unfolded in narrative, plot, and character development. Perhaps more than any other nation's literary tradition, American literature is ineluctably political—shaped by democracy as much as it has in turn shaped democracy.

The Political Companions to Great American Authors series highlights the teachings of the great authors in America's literary and belletristic tradition. An astute political interpretation of America's literary tradition requires careful, patient, and attentive readers who approach the text with a view to understanding its underlying messages about citizenship and democracy. Essayists in this series approach the classic texts not with a "hermeneutics of suspicion" but with the curiosity of fellow citizens who believe that the great authors have something of value to teach their readers. The series brings together essays from varied approaches and viewpoints for the common purpose of elucidating the political teachings of the nation's greatest authors for those seeking a better understanding of American democracy.

Patrick J. Deneen
Series Editor

Acknowledgments

ABOVE ALL I AM INDEBTED to the late Wilson Carey McWilliams for introducing me to Henry Adams in a graduate course that he taught at Fordham University several years ago. Once a week, Professor McWilliams traveled from Rutgers to Fordham, taking the train to Manhattan and then riding the D train to the Bronx. He always had time for a stop at a local diner or pizzeria with students before walking back up Fordham Road to his subway stop and returning home. This example bore witness to Professor McWilliams's esteem for American political thought and his commitment to his profession. Seemingly amused by Adams's curmudgeonly posture, Professor McWilliams indulged it. But knowing that Adams's subtle mind and the American experiment that occupied it deserve serious contemplation, he did not allow Adams to be easily dismissed by simple characterization. My study of Henry Adams, which began so many years ago in Professor McWilliams's class, continues to be profoundly rewarding. I believe a volume on Henry Adams without a contribution from Carey McWilliams would be incomplete and impoverished. I am very grateful to Nancy McWilliams for the permission to publish Professor McWilliams's essay in this volume.

I am thankful to the many people who helped bring *A Political Companion to Henry Adams* to publication. Patrick J. Deneen, a contributor to this volume as well as the series editor, was an enthusiastic and thoughtful collaborator on this project from its beginning. The authors of the new essays were a pleasure to work with. My own thinking about Henry Adams has profited from their lively minds. As we wrote and revised our essays, we benefited from the insightful comments of several people, including the anonymous reviewers, David Alvis, Susan McWilliams, James P. Young, and

Lauren Weiner. I am also proud to include in this volume so many excellent previously published essays on Henry Adams, and I am grateful for the permissions to reprint them. Acknowledgments for the reprinted works appear in the essay endnotes.

Skidmore College generously funded a pre-tenure sabbatical for my work. I have enjoyed the support of my friends and colleagues at Skidmore while working on the collection. Jennifer Delton cheerfully indulged many conversations about Adams. I am also very grateful to my research assistants, Kelly Carr and Simone Perez, who gathered previously published essays for consideration. Barbara McDonough's keen attention to detail was essential in compiling the manuscript.

I am very fortunate to have had such a fine editor, Stephen Wrinn, on this project. He always helped me to find my bearings when I felt the project was adrift. And he did so with unfailing good humor. Candace Chaney, Anne Dean Watkins, Ila McEntire, and Susan Murray have also provided invaluable editorial assistance.

I am blessed to have a loving husband, patient children, a loyal sister, devoted parents, and caring in-laws. My scholarly work would not be possible without the support of my family.

Abbreviations for Frequently Cited Works

Chartres	*Mont-Saint-Michel and Chartres*
Degradation	*The Degradation of the Democratic Dogma*
Democracy	*Democracy: An American Novel*
Education	*The Education of Henry Adams*
Great Secession Winter	*The Great Secession Winter of 1860–61 and Other Essays*
History I	*History of the United States during the Administration of Thomas Jefferson*
History II	*History of the United States during the Administration of James Madison*
Letters	*Letters of Henry Adams*
Life of Gallatin	*The Life of Albert Gallatin*
Randolph	*John Randolph*

Introduction: The Literary Statesmanship of Henry Adams

Natalie Fuehrer Taylor

AT THE OUTSET OF *The Education of Henry Adams,* the great-grandson of John Adams and the grandson of John Quincy Adams recalls the assumptions of a small boy: "It was unusual for boys to sit behind a President grandfather, and to read over his head the tablet in memory of a President great-grandfather, who had 'pledged his life, his fortune, and his sacred honor' to secure the independence of his country and so forth; but boys naturally supposed, without much reasoning, that other boys had the equivalent of President grandfathers. . . . What had been would continue to be. He doubted not about Presidents nor about Churches, and no one suggested at that time a doubt whether a system of society which had lasted since Adam would outlast one Adams more."[1] Yet, the system of society taken for granted by the boy seemed to crumble in front of the man. Henry Adams came of age during the Civil War and was an onlooker to the corrupt politics of the Gilded Age. In his declining years, he witnessed the rise of technology and foresaw the profound consequences technology would have on the American character. Throughout his remarkable life, Henry Adams wrote a nine-volume history, biographies, novels, and other works that escape categorization.

The authors who have contributed to this volume believe that Adams, like his famous ancestors, was engaged in political life. However, we do not understand the term "political" in its narrow, modern sense—as the use and abuse of power. For Adams, the political life entailed a consideration of how human beings ought to live and what form of government would best promote human flourishing. As an American and as an Adams, Henry tended toward certain answers to these questions. He shared the belief held by generations of Adams statesmen "that government was a moral agent designed to aid man in realizing the 'good.'"[2] The regime that best promotes the "good" is the republic for a republic fosters the exercise of liberty under the protection of law. A statesman sets aside his own self-interest in order to uphold the principles of the republic. To Charles Francis Adams, "The first and greatest qualification of a statesman . . . is the mastery of the whole theory of morals which makes the foundation of all human society" (Hochfield, introduction to *Great Secession Winter,* xiv). The Constitution provided the moral framework within which statesmen could govern. Yet, a statesman appreciated that in order to govern well, he must do so in accordance with the national mind. The statesman must guide the people in maintaining their theory of morals. On the foundations of the American republic that his ancestors had built, a democracy emerged. Democracy was understood simply to be the rule of the people and therefore vulnerable to the people's narrow self-interest. Disappointed by the changes in American politics, Adams departed from the conventional path of public service that his father had followed and turned instead to a seemingly private life as a man of letters. Writing to his brother Charles in 1867, Henry Adams promised: "I will never make a speech, never run for an office, never belong to a party. I am going to plunge under the stream. For years you will hear nothing of any publication of mine—perhaps never, who knows. . . . I shall probably remain under water for a long time. If you see me come up, it will be with an oyster and a pearl inside. If not, why-so!"[3] Still, Adams continued to ponder the nature of democracy and to strive after the greatest qualification of a statesman, "the mastery of the whole theory of morals." He was, like his famous ancestors, a political animal. Henry Adams is often remembered as the ironic, cynical, sometimes bitter critic of democracy, but he was always an astute observer of American politics. Unwilling to "follow the family go-cart," Henry Adams practiced statesmanship as a man of letters.

Born on February 16, 1838, Henry Adams was the third son of Charles Francis Adams and Abigail Brooks Adams, the daughter of a wealthy Boston merchant. The small boy's life followed a course, at least for a time, that one might expect for a person of such distinguished background. His boyhood, spent in both Boston and Quincy, seems to have been carefree in the manner typical of the privileged. As the boy grew older, his father took him to Washington and to visit President Zachary Taylor in the White

House. Given the number of Adamses who had lived in the White House, Adams recalls that the boy "half thought that he owned it" (*Education*, 46). After attending Harvard, Henry pursued the study of law in Germany and traveled through Europe. Henry sent letters from his travels to the *Boston Daily Courier*, and a career in journalism seemed possible. Yet, what had been would continue to be. Like the generations before him, Henry Adams served as his father's private secretary, first in Washington, where his father served in Congress, and then in London, where his father served as minister to England during the Civil War.

Adams returned to Washington at war's end, and it soon became clear to him that he was not likely to secure public office. Still, the nation's capital offered amusement for a young man with such an impressive political pedigree: "I am prancing and flirting every night more or less, and every morning I am lazily political. The life amuses me as you can imagine it would. It is in fact a brilliant sort of butterfly existence, which cannot last very long, but may pass for some years still" (*Letters*, 2:59–60). Yet, there was more to Adams's life than "prancing and flirting." He pursued a career as a journalist and gained a reputation as a critic of government. Henry Adams's butterfly existence came to an end when he was offered positions as professor of medieval history at Harvard and as editor of the *North American Review*. During this stretch in Boston, Henry married Marian ("Clover") Hooper. It was also during this time that Adams sought to bring reform to American politics through the Liberal Republican Party.

The time he spent in Washington following the Civil War and his efforts on behalf of the Liberal Republicans were demoralizing to the young reform-minded Adams. The Civil War, Henry Adams feared, had wrought irreparable damages to the Constitution. The practice and influence of political parties, the decay of the executive power, and the corruption of the legislature—all topics for Adams's criticism—were evidence of a profound transformation of the American regime from a republic to a democracy. Among the consequences of the transformation was the decline in statesmanship.

> In the brief history of the nation, Adams believed, the statesman had been displaced by the mere politician. The national ideal was being distorted to serve a nation enthralled by scientific and industrial advances, overwhelmed by its own economic and political strength. Careful vision was being displaced by expedient myopia in the service of crude power. Moreover, the idea of democracy had failed. Instead of elevating mankind as many believed it would,

democracy, as a philosophical ideal, had deteriorated to, in Adams' words, "the fundamental principle that one man is as good as another."[1]

Despite his disappointments in the transformation in American politics, Adams returned to Washington in 1877.

Henry explained his decision to return to the nation's capital in a letter to a friend: "[T]he fact is I gravitate to a capital by a primary law of nature. This is the only place in America where society amuses me, or where life offers variety. Here, too, I can fancy that we are of use in the world, for we distinctly occupy niches which ought to be filled" (*Letters,* 2:326). Although political life is still amusing to Adams, he seems to have become more serious in the time spent away from America's capital. Henry Adams expresses a sense of purpose and the start of something new, rather than the end of a life—however beautiful "a brilliant sort of butterfly existence" may be. Living in the shadow of the White House, Henry and Clover Adams hosted many of Washington's most influential political personages, including current and future presidents Rutherford B. Hayes and Teddy Roosevelt. However, public office continued to elude Adams. It was unclear which niche Henry Adams, the fourth generation of a family singularly devoted to the American republic, would distinctly occupy.

Although Adams was not by nature a politician, he did have qualities appropriate for statesmanship, particularly his foresight and his judgment of human beings.[5] The challenge that faced Henry Adams was how to practice statesmanship amidst the forces that were transforming the American regime: "America is increasing so rapidly, and her future is so vast, that one man may reasonably devote his life to the effort at impressing a moral in the national mind, which is now almost void" (*Letters,* 2:371). John Ernest suggests that Adams describes his own manner of "impressing a moral on the national mind" in his description of William Henry Seward's literary statesmanship:

> As Adams once said of the, in his view, rare statesman William Henry Seward, the *literary* statesman needed to guide "by quiet unseen influences those who seemed . . . to act independently on their own ground" (*Great Secession Winter,* 22–23). In effect, the job called for a national confidence-man, duping people out of their public roles to lead them to self-examination and self-recognition. (Ernest, 26)

Taking up his pen and writing in numerous genres, Adams appealed to various segments of the American public—political actors as well as private citizens—quietly leading the American people to ponder what "meaning was to be discerned in politics other than that contained in its superficial aspect, 'the crash and war of jealous and hostile interests?'" (Hochfield, introduction to *Great Secession Winter*, xvi).

Henry Adams distinguished himself from the generations of Adams statesmen who came before him by publishing a variety of works. Adams gained recognition as a historian in 1879 with the publication of *The Life of Albert Gallatin*. His nine-volume historical work, *The History of the United States during the Administrations of Thomas Jefferson and James Madison*, was published between 1889 and 1891. While writing biographies of statesmen and the *History*, Adams also published two novels, *Democracy: An American Novel* (1880) and *Esther* (1884). Adams's first novel takes place in Washington, D.C., and is the story of the political education and the courtship of Madeleine Lightfoot Lee by the powerful, corrupt Senator Silas Ratcliffe. Adams's second novel is also a story of courtship. In this instance, a young New York socialite is wooed by a minister while the minister's friend and competitor, a scientist, looks on. Shortly after the publication of *Esther*, Henry Adams's beloved wife, Clover, committed suicide. Henry survived Clover for more than thirty years and spent his days traveling to Europe, as well as more exotic destinations such as Tahiti, Fiji, and Cuba. In time, Adams also became the confidant of political actors on the world stage, most notably John Hay, William McKinley's secretary of state. Adams described his role as a "stable companion to statesmen." Adams's most widely read and celebrated works, *Mont-Saint-Michel and Chartres* (1905) and *The Education of Henry Adams* (1908), were yet to be written.

The preface of *The Education of Henry Adams* announces that it is a sequel to the author's earlier work *Mont-Saint-Michel and Chartres*. The earlier work, according to the author, is a study of thirteenth-century unity, and the *Education* is a study of twentieth-century multiplicity. These works are linked by their inquiry into the relationship between religion, science, technology, and politics.

Mont-Saint-Michel and Chartres begins with an invitation to his nieces to read what follows and, in so doing, travel to medieval France. The book seems to be part epistolary novel and part travel log. In this work, Adams examines architecture, particularly the great cathedrals, as well as medieval literature and theology. Devotion to the Virgin unified the age. By contrasting the new twentieth century to the medieval world, Adams sought greater understanding of his own complex and troubling age. To add to the complexity of the *Education*, the book is not only a study of twentieth-century multiplicity, but an account of Henry Adams's life. Like *Mont-Saint-Michel and Chartres*, this work does not fit easily into conventional categories. The *Education* was identified as an autobiography by its publisher after Adams's death. Written in the third person and complete with a list of characters, it reads like a novel. With its attention to the social forces gaining momentum throughout Adams's lifetime, it also reads like social commentary. Adams's professed inability to anticipate and affect the rapidly changing social and political circumstances leads him to repeatedly declare that the education of Henry Adams was a failure. By the end of the work, we are left with the impression that Adams was an ironic, cynical man. The *Education* was Adams's last major work before his death in 1918.

The enigmatic works and the figure of Henry Adams captured the attention of literary scholars. Not surprisingly, Adams elicited differing interpretations from them. Van Wyck Brooks diminishes Adams's literary pursuits by arguing that these were neither rewarding to him nor serious efforts: "But, feeling that he should have been a statesman, that he ought to have been a reformer, that he ought to have carried on the Adams name, he could not feel writing justified him."[6] Although Van Wyck Brooks considers Adams an "excellent craftsman" who wrote "admirable books," he argues that "in motive [Adams] was always a dilettante" (Brooks, 275). In his influential book, J. C. Levenson refutes those like Brooks who would dismiss Henry Adams. As a literary scholar, Levenson views Adams as an artist, arguing that it is Adams's artistic talent that warrants serious attention: "Making history into art, transforming the dead records of the past into a living possession for the present, he won a victory over oblivion."[7]

Adams's "dead record of the past" has drawn historians into the debate over Henry Adams. Richard Hofstadter credits the Progressive historians with taking "American history out of the hands of the Brahmins and the satisfied classes and [making] it responsive to the intellectual needs of new types of Americans who were beginning to constitute a productive, insurgent, intelligentsia."[8] Hofstadter points to Adams's *History of the United*

States during the Administrations of Thomas Jefferson and James Madison as an example of the history produced by "the self-satisfied classes." According to Hofstadter, Adams understood Jefferson's and Madison's administrations to be "dreary and unproductive, as an age of slack and derivative culture, of fumbling and small-minded statecraft" (30). Despite Henry Adams's claims to undertake this historical project in order to test a notion of scientific history, Hofstadter insists, "What is visible to the reader who knows Adams and the Adamses is a pilgrimage to the family pieties and a delicate resumption of old family quarrels" (31). Following this logic, Adams's critique of democracy is merely a not-so-veiled grudge against Jefferson and, later, Andrew Jackson, who displaced John Adams and John Quincy Adams respectively.

More recently, Gary Wills has returned to the *History* in his book *Henry Adams and the Making of America*. In this work, Wills seeks to dispel the reasons for neglecting Adams's *History*, which he considers the "non-fiction masterpiece of nineteenth century America."[9] Scholars have been too willing to accept the "family feud" thesis of the *History* (Wills, 4). Furthermore, Wills would also like to correct the negative impressions of Adams by eliminating "the *Education* effect" (5), which he identifies as the tendency to read Adams's other works from the perspective of his last major work and to attribute the pessimism of that volume to his entire life and corpus. Wills distinguishes himself from earlier scholars by reading Henry Adams forward (6). He begins with an account of Adams's biography, noting the influences on Adams that made him especially able to analyze the making of a nation. Wills suggests that Adams's own development mirrors that of America. He then turns his attention to the *History*. Wills's interpretation argues for Adams's admiration of the Virginian presidents, rather than his rekindling of old family grudges.

Henry Adams and the Need to Know, a volume of essays edited by William Merrill Decker and Earl N. Harbert, recently joined the relatively few edited volumes devoted to Henry Adams. The essays in this volume address many and various topics, including Henry Adams's relationship to both John Adams and to Henry Cabot Lodge, the influence of travel on Adams's work, and Adams's models of knowing. The editors rightly observe that "by the evidence of the essays, Adams's work appeals to a wide spectrum of historical and literary inquiry and claims a place in multiple scholarly contexts."[10]

But they neglect Henry Adams's political project. With the exception of a few essays, the volume emphasizes the private, rather than the public, dimensions of Adams's thought.

For the most part, political scientists have been happy to leave Adams to the literary scholars and have not argued for the political character of his works. Judith Shklar is put off by Adams's apparent pessimism. In her 1974 essay on *The Education of Henry Adams*, Shklar points to Adams's failures: "Not only had he failed to meet the standards of public eminence set by his ancestors, but he had not achieved his own intellectual ends either."[11] In the only full-length treatment of Henry Adams by a political scientist, *Henry Adams: The Historian as Political Theorist*, James P. Young demonstrates that Adams's thought is much too sophisticated to be dismissed as bitter regrets. Young reminds us of Richard Hofstadter's observation about the relationship between history and political theory: "While it is no doubt true to some degree everywhere that history doubles for political theory and has even in secular ages taken on some of the work of theology, it is perhaps more keenly true in the United States."[12] Examining Henry Adams's many and various works, Young emphasizes two related theories of history that persist throughout Adams's writings: "The first is his overview of American experience, focusing on what he saw as the early betrayal of the original constitutional understanding by Jeffersonians and the further debasement of American ideals by the rapid development of industrial and financial capitalism following the Civil War" (8). The second theory of history emerges from Adams's understanding of the American experience: "It is an almost Weberian lament for the decline of human values in the wake of capitalist industrialization and the concomitant growth of technological power, a set of forces seen in their most advanced form in the United States" (Young, 8).

The essays gathered in *A Political Companion to Henry Adams* focus on Henry Adams's political inquiries and their implications for American political thought. The essays do not reduce Adams's political inquiries to a mere revival of an old family feud, written by a dilettante or a self-proclaimed failure. Henry Adams's many and various works reveal him to be one of our most profound political thinkers, authors, and even statesmen. Adams claims this place by the merit of his astute understanding of political life in all its complexity. His musings on democracy reappear throughout his writings. Though his clever satire is most often and easily remembered, Adams's thoughts on the emerging democracy should not be discounted as caustic defense of ancestors, who need no defending. Rather, his writings should be considered a sincere and often profound attempt to understand the changing American regime. As a literary statesman, Henry Adams sought to guide the people in upholding their political heritage and realizing the promise of America.

This volume is divided into two parts. Part 1, "Republicanism, Democracy, and the Nature of the American Regime," examines the complex character of American politics, owing to the transformation of the early republic into a large, liberal democracy. This section begins with a well-known and highly regarded piece by Russell L. Hanson and W. Richard Merriman, "Henry Adams and the Decline of the Republican Tradition." Hanson and Merriman begin by refuting Louis Hartz's claim that liberalism has always enjoyed a strong hold on the American mind. Instead, they recognize that the republican tradition has been influential in America's early politics. Republicanism emphasizes civic virtue and condemns the political corruption bred by personal ambition and commercial interests. Hanson and Merriman also remind us that republicanism includes "a style of political action," as well as a theory of government. "The watchful sentinel symbolizes the role of citizens in republican politics, for it is the watchman who alerts others to danger and very often forms the first line of defense." The historian or the man of letters embodies such a style of political action. "It was then the responsibility of the republican historian to sound the alarm, decry the absence of statesmen, and identify remedies for the problem." Hanson and Merriman argue that Henry Adams's *History of the United States during the Administrations of Jefferson and Madison,* as well as his biographies of Albert Gallatin and John Randolph, are histories in this republican tradition. However, "conditions in the nation seemed decidedly to favor the rise of politicians who, in contrast to statesmen, did not lead, but were led by, public opinion." Hanson and Merriman argue that Adams lost confidence in the power of history to do more than record events, including the demise of the republic. Adams had sounded the alarm, but it was not heeded. The republican historian could offer no solutions to the loss of statesmen.

If one of the consequences of the declining republican tradition was the eclipse of statesmen by politicians, the statesman would have to exercise his influence on American politics indirectly or more subtly than had previous generations of Adams statesmen. Adams, the republican historian, was also the literary statesman. During the years that the republican historian was crafting the biography of Gallatin and the *History*, he was also at work on two novels, *Democracy* and *Esther*. Published anonymously or under a pen name, Henry Adams served as a "national confidence man, duping people out of their public roles to lead them to self-examination and self-recognition" (Ernest, 27). The essays on Henry Adams's novels in this collection reveal that Adams continued to sound the alarm and to offer solutions to the problems posed by the fading republican tradition. "*Democracy*: Henry Adams and the Role of Political Leader," by B. H. Gilley, examines the consequences of the decline of republicanism for American statesmanship. It would be too easy to simply describe the post–Civil War politicians as selfish. Adams, Gilley argues, is sensitive to the social and political forces that thwarted the intentions of the Gilded Age's political leaders to serve the public. Michael Colacurcio's essay, "*Democracy* and *Esther*: Henry Adams's Flirtation with Pragmatism," begins with the observation that pragmatism is deeply rooted in the American character, but finds its philosophic expression in the thought of William James. Colacurcio argues that the characters of Adams's two novels give voice to pragmatism, leaving the reader to wonder about the fate of America's ideals. However, Colacurcio concludes that Adams himself does not finally adopt the philosophy, despite its appeal to his generation. The last two essays in this section, "Henry Adams's *Democracy*: Novel Sources of Democratic Virtues," by Denise Dutton, and "The Flowers of Freedom or the New Tyranny: Science, Art, and Religion in Henry Adams's *Esther*," by Natalie Fuehrer Taylor, are new contributions. Like Colacurcio, Dutton and Taylor do not think that Adams adopts the pragmatism of his generation. However, they go beyond Colacurio's essay by demonstrating Adams's hope for the American regime that was made possible by his confidence in the American people. Dutton's piece nicely complements Gilley's piece. In her essay, Dutton devotes her attention to the character of the American citizenry in the wake of the American republic's transformation to a democracy. She looks to the novel's secondary characters to reveal Adams's quiet hopes for American democracy. In the absence of statesmen, it is the American people who safeguard America's moral purpose. Taylor's essay is also concerned with the virtue of American citizens. The threat to Americans comes not from power-seeking politicians, but from what Adams dubs the princes of science, art, and religion. Taylor examines the capacity of the American people to thwart the threat they pose. By novel's end, it is unclear whether the prince of science or religion will prevail in the hearts and minds of Americans. However, it is clear that the faith of the young boy who doubted not "about Presidents nor about Churches" had been shaken. The "system of society which had lasted since Adam" would not "outlast one Adams more." Adams's efforts to regain his lost faith would occupy him through the course of his lifetime and would be the subject of his most widely read works.

Part 2, "The Search for Lost Faith," is dedicated to Henry Adams's attempt to recapture the moral certainty of his ancestors. This section begins with "Henry Adams," written by one of America's most highly regarded historians, Henry Steele Commager. Commager examines Henry Adams's efforts as a historian to make sense of the quickly changing, nearly unrecognizable American republic that should have been so familiar to someone from a family of such long standing. When the standard historical formulas fail Adams, he tries less conventional ways of writing. He formulates a philosophy of history. Adams tries to bring human history into harmony with the laws of the universe. This endeavor also proves dissatisfying to Adams. Commager argues that Adams came to recognize that the person of Henry Adams is left to be the object of our contemplation: "For whether we confine ourselves to the mere outward aspects of Adams's career or embrace the history of the entire family which he recapitulated, or penetrate to his own intellectual and psychological reactions to his generation, we will find that Adams illuminates, better than any of his contemporaries, the course of American history." As a symbol, though perhaps not as a historian or as a philosopher, Adams was able to perform the tasks of the literary statesman, leading the people to self-examination and self-recognition. Henry Adams symbolizes the lost moral certainty of his generation, as well as the despair experienced in the face of an uncertain future. Commager finishes his essay with speculation that the Virgin was attractive to Henry Adams for her unlimited pity, which he and his generation needed.

The essays following Commager's piece revisit Henry Adams's search for his lost faith and that of his generation. In "The Politics of Scientific History," Richard Samuelson considers scientific history as a means of restoring that lost faith. Drawing largely on Adams's 1892 presidential address to the American Historical Association, Samuelson demonstrates the singular capacity of Adams's subtle and ironic mind to appreciate the potential, as well as the limitations, of scientific history to account for human life. Samuelson notes that science had become the religion of modernity and that historians were seduced by the promise of scientific history to explain society's path. Although skeptical, Adams takes this project seriously— more seriously than many historians—and in doing so Adams wished to help his fellow historians to recognize the true nature and purpose of scientific history. Samuelson does not conclude, as Commager does, that Adams simply despaired of the project. On the contrary, he suggests that Adams feared that his "brother historians" would never find the courage to question their own premises, and thereby attain the wisdom they, and society, needed.

"*Mont-Saint-Michel and Chartres*: From Unity to Multiplicity," by Patrick J. Deneen, is a study of Henry Adams's peculiar book on two medieval French cathedrals, a work that fits into no obvious genre and that seems to look beyond Adams's more often preferred subject, America. Deneen argues that this work may be understood as a political-theological treatise. Medieval theology, Deneen argues, offers more to Adams than pity in his search for lost faith. Most scholars have not questioned the claim made by Adams in the *Education* that unity found its most profound expression in devotion to the Virgin during the twelfth century and that unity degenerated into the seemingly unintelligible multiplicity of the twentieth century. If we accept Adams's explanation of the relationship between *Mont-Saint-Michel and Chartres* and the *Education,* the descent into modern multiplicity begins with twelfth- and thirteenth-century scholasticism for it announces the rise of modern science. Deneen does not leave Adams's explanation unexamined and offers a fresh reading of *Mont-Saint-Michel and Chartres.* The unity achieved during the medieval period was distinguished from twentieth-century multiplicity not by the absence of multiplicity, but by the way in which that unity was achieved. The medieval age achieved unity through the multiplicity of various understandings of human beings' relation to God. Deneen argues that the philosophy of Saint Thomas Aquinas is the culmination of unity achieved though multiplicity. Modernity, informed by modern science, is marked by multiplicity and even contradictions that apparently cannot be reconciled. To the extent that unity is realized, it is achieved by the destruction of multiplicity. As Deneen shows us, Adams leads his readers to appreciate that the unity achieved amidst the multiplicity of the medieval period allows for greater liberty and diversity than the modern age.

From Deneen's study of unity in the thirteenth century and multiplicity in the twentieth century, we move to the other major theme of the *Education*, the life of Henry Adams and the life of the American regime. "History, Science, and Politics: A Lifetime's Education" is a chapter reprinted from James P. Young's *Henry Adams: The Historian as Political Theorist*. Young argues: "*The Education of Henry Adams* is both a tale of a lifetime of education and a theory of history. . . . The story Adams tells represents not only his life but also the history of his family, his class, and indeed his country, not to mention, in his later years, the fate of the Western world." Throughout the *Education*, Henry Adams laments his failed education, but Young does not accept Adams's pose of ignorance. He observes that while Adams insists on his ignorance and confusion, Adams quietly claims to know more than the other characters who people Adams's tale. Young offers us a careful consideration of each phase of Henry Adams's education, explaining the well-known and significant passages. He considers the possible lessons that Adams's pose of Socratic ignorance can impart to his readers. Despite Adams's inability to fall back on the old New England certainties and his perplexed ambivalence about science and technology, Young does not find evidence that Adams was ready to give up on America. Though Adams had lost faith in our political institutions, Adams had not lost faith in the American people.

The final essay of part 2, "Henry Adams and the 'Burden of History': Intimations of Fraternity amidst the Ravages of Nature Conquered," was written by Wilson Carey McWilliams, who is also author of the influential book *The Idea of Fraternity in America*. In his essay, originally part of his dissertation, McWilliams argues that fraternity, community, self-sacrifice, and love are central to political life and that American political thought has too often been simply understood as classically liberal. McWilliams eloquently examines these themes in Henry Adams's singular corpus. With McWilliams's meditations on fraternity in Henry Adams's writings, the volume ends with a compelling reminder of Henry Adams's importance as a sentinel for the American regime.

Although he never held public office, Henry Adams remains one of America's great statesmen. Unable or unwilling to practice statesmanship as earlier generations of Adams statesmen had done, Adams recognized the importance of literary statesmanship to America. The statesman with the capacity to "impress a moral on the national mind" had been replaced by the mere politician in the halls of U.S. government. As a literary statesman, Adams could guide public opinion "by quiet unseen influences." Public opinion would in turn lead politicians in restoring America's moral purpose. Since contemporary U.S. politics continue to be peopled by mere politicians, the literary statesmanship of Henry Adams remains an important source of self-examination for our citizens and our nation.

Notes

1. Henry Adams, *The Education of Henry Adams*, with an introduction by Edmund Morris (New York: Modern Library, 1999), 15–16. Hereafter cited parenthetically.

2. Henry Adams, *"The Great Secession Winter of 1860–61" and Other Essays*, edited and with an introduction by George Hochfield (New York: Sagamore Press, 1958), xiii. Hereafter cited parenthetically.

3. Henry Adams, *Letters of Henry Adams Volume I: 1858–1868*, ed. J. C. Levenson, Ernest Samuels, Charles Vandersee, and Viola Hopkins Winner (Cambridge: Belknap Press of Harvard University Press, 1982), 557. Hereafter cited parenthetically.

4. John Ernest, "Henry Adams' Double: Recreating the Philosophical Statesman," *Journal of American Culture* 14, no. 1: 25–26. Hereafter cited parenthetically.

5. Herbert Edwards, "Henry Adams: Politician and Statesman," *New England Quarterly* 22, no. 1 (March 1949): 53–54.

6. Van Wyck Brooks, *New England: Indian Summer* (New York: Dutton, 1940), 275. Hereafter cited parenthetically.

7. J. C. Levenson, *The Mind and Art of Henry Adams* (Boston: Houghton Mifflin, 1957), 2. Hereafter cited parenthetically.

8. Richard Hofstadter, *The Progressive Historians: Turner, Beard, Parrington* (New York: Knopf, 1968), xvi. Hereafter cited parenthetically.

9. Gary Wills, *Henry Adams and the Making of America* (New York: Houghton Mifflin, 2005), 1. Hereafter cited parenthetically.

10. William Merrill Decker and Earl N. Harbert, eds., *Henry Adams and the Need to Know* (Boston: Massachusetts Historical Society, 2005), xii.

11. Judith N. Shklar, *"The Education of Henry Adams* by Henry Adams," in *Redeeming American Political Thought*, ed. Stanley Hoffman and Dennis F. Thompson (Chicago: University of Chicago Press, 1998), 81.

12. James P. Young, *Henry Adams: The Historian as Political Theorist* (Lawrence: University Press of Kansas, 2001), 1. Hereafter cited parenthetically.

PART I

Republicanism, Democracy, and the Nature of the American Regime

CHAPTER 1

Henry Adams and the Decline of the Republican Tradition

Russell L. Hanson and W. Richard Merriman

I

IN *THE LIBERAL TRADITION in America,* Louis Hartz attributed the absence of vibrant socialist or conservative traditions in the United States to Americans' absolute and irrational attachment to the liberal ideas of John Locke. Hartz ultimately concluded this mind-set was so deeply ingrained that our country "must look to its contact with other nations to provide that spark of philosophy, that grain of relative insight that its own history has denied it."[1] Thirty-five years of contact—and conflict—with other nations have failed to break the hegemony of liberalism. Though its premises are no longer accepted without question, liberalism is still the dominant public philosophy of our time and place; *The Liberal Tradition in America* remains an apt characterization of contemporary American culture.

As a reading of American history, however, Hartz's account of liberalism's hegemony has lost much of its credence. Those who insist, as he did, that liberalism always has been the American philosophy par excellence are sailing against the prevailing winds of contemporary historiography, which stresses the early importance of a "republican" tradition different from, and by some accounts opposed to, liberalism. The republican tradition embodied an ethos of political participation rooted in "civic virtue." It was also critical of the corruption of politics by ambitious individuals, commercial interests, and political factions.[2] Evidence of the influence of republicanism in the founding period is pervasive, and militates against Hartz's straightforward description of colonial political thought in terms of liberal categories of understanding.

But if American culture was once heavily republican, when and how did it come to be so thoroughly liberal? Gordon Wood suggests one answer in his enormously influential *The Creation of the American Republic*. He argues that the victory achieved by the Federalists in the campaign for ratification of the Constitution marked the "end of classical politics" in America, and set the stage for the liberal politics that followed. According to Wood, the Federalists invented "an entirely new and original sort of republican government—a republic which did not require a virtuous people for its sustenance."[3] This system of politics assumed that most citizens would not be oriented toward the res publica, but would instead behave according to their self-interest. In fact, such behavior was essential to the proper operation of the system of checks and balances embedded in the Constitution, which was a product of a "new science of politics" that bore a strong resemblance to modern liberalism.

However, this shift from a politics of virtue to one of interest easily can be exaggerated, as Banning warns.[4] Republican notions of virtue were never as self-denying as some commentators have suggested. Virtue meant attending to public matters, which in a democratic commonwealth were necessarily the affair of all. Virtuous citizens took time from private life to tend public business, and once that business was decided, true citizens willingly submitted to the will of the community, whether or not it suited their individual interests. However, in the actual making of political decisions, citizens might reasonably prefer actions that served their individual interests, as long as they accepted the need to accommodate the interests of others. Thus, moderation, not self-abnegation, was the animating spirit of republican virtue.

That was not very far from Madison's position, especially since Federalist conceptions of self-interest and individual rights were themselves limited by considerations of the public good. As Horne shows, there existed in the founding period a prevalent notion of "bourgeois virtue" that linked rights and duties, especially where property was concerned.[5] Individuals might indeed possess property rights, and they could claim them against thieves and trespassers. But they could not rightfully insist upon these rights at the expense of the happiness and prosperity of the community in which they lived; attempts to do so demonstrated a clear lack of virtue.[6] In that sense, liberals agreed with republicans both upon the need for citizens to balance public and private lives, and on the difficulty of maintaining that equilibrium.

Of course, adherents of the two traditions disagreed on where to strike the balance. Republicans were not convinced that bourgeois virtues were strong enough to ensure an adequate defense against invasions from abroad and the enervating effects of commercial development on patriotism, the two principal dangers to commonwealth.[7] They vigorously expressed these fears in postratification disputes over the establishment of a standing army and navy, creation of a national bank, enactment of protective tariffs, and funding of internal improvements, all of which prompted debates over the meaning of the public good and its relation to sectional and class interests.[8] The potency of republican rhetoric in the political discourse of the early nineteenth century strongly suggests that liberalism—at least in Hartz's sense—did not come into its own until much later than the founding period, Wood's suggestion to the contrary notwithstanding.[9]

Indeed, republican ideas were still prominent during the Age of Jackson. Brown and Howe show that republican themes were central elements of nineteenth-century Whig political thought;[10] it was John Quincy Adams, after all, who insisted that Congress not be "palsied by the will" of constituents and prevented thereby from pursuing policies that served the public good. Underlying Adams's injunction was a preference for a deferential style of politics in which officeholders functioned as trustees of the commonwealth. As such, they were expected to demonstrate the requisite attachment to community and independence of judgment that were needed to direct the affairs of state. The freehold requirement for voting and officeholding provided surety for this by materially relating the interests of public stewards to the happiness and prosperity of their community.

Yet many Americans who lacked a freehold nevertheless felt a stake in policy questions concerning commerce, taxation, and banking. They were not willing to remain political spectators, nor were they willing to submit to policies made by men who claimed to be their betters, while pursuing policies that held no benefit for common men—"the bone and sinew of the republic." The attack on deference was led by Andrew Jackson, who insisted in his bank veto message that "[W]hen the laws undertake to . . . grant titles, gratuities, and exclusive privileges, to make the rich richer and the potent more powerful, the humble members of society—the farmers, mechanics, and laborers—who have neither the time nor the means of securing like favors to themselves have a right to complain of the injustice of their Government."[11]

Armed with the recently won right to vote, the "humble members of society" had it within their power to rectify injustice and preserve the republic against monied factions; having the power, they demonstrated virtue by "throwing the rascals out of office" instead of deferring to them. Thus, republican values—frugal and simple government, the virtues of the yeoman farmer, and the vigilance of common citizens—were the rhetorical touchstone of Jacksonian politics. Yet the Jacksonian solution to the corrupt bargain, the minimalist state, actually cleared the path for the ideological triumph of liberalism in America, as Meyers has shown.[12] Jackson vanquished the forces of corruption by dismantling the national bank, just as he ended the threat of foreign invasion by defeating the British at New Orleans in 1814. Once the government of the republic was wrested from the grasp of the Money Power, the need for vigilance dissipated, and there were few other means by which citizens could demonstrate virtue, except by generating wealth.

As the Jacksonians reduced government to a minimum, republican politics apparently required little more of citizens than their dedicated pursuit of self-interest. The achievement of economic independence was no longer a condition for political liberty, as it had been for classical republicans. To a significant degree, economic independence was liberty: in theory, the elimination of public monopolies, e.g., the Bank, freed citizens from dependence on the will of others, and enabled them to secure economic freedom. Those who used their newfound liberty to good effect prospered, and at the same time enlarged the wealth of the republic. Those who failed could blame only themselves, once the yoke of privilege was broken—in the North, at least. So developed the notion of the self-made man, the hero of a free-labor ideology essential to the formation of the Republican Party and the election of Abraham Lincoln.[13]

The very idea of a "republican party" would have offended classical sensibilities, but it was very much in tune with emerging liberal sympathies.[14] Virtue, once synonymous with public-spirited action, became increasingly privatized as citizens of all persuasions strove to obtain wealth. The acquisition of wealth was an outward sign of virtue, industry, frugality, etc.—the key bourgeois virtues of the more attractive versions of nineteenth-century liberalism. Furthermore, the pursuit of happiness, far from being a distraction from public affairs, was itself a valuable contribution to the common good, insofar as it helped realize the "manifest destiny" of the United States.

Hence, Francis Grund, an observer of the period, could truthfully say that Americans pursued business not simply as a means of procuring the necessary comforts of life, but because it was "the fountain of all human felicity" (Meyers, 123).

Clearly, traditional republican values were being absorbed and transformed in mid-nineteenth-century America, but the process was far from complete. The difference between public good and private interest was still ideologically important, even though many believed that both purposes ultimately could be served by one and the same action—the pursuit of wealth. However, the distinction itself began to disappear after the Civil War, or so it seems to us. During the Gilded Age, for example, men such as William Graham Sumner adamantly insisted that reforms intended to serve the public interest were terribly misguided. To the extent that reforms were implemented, they would inevitably retard the development of civilization, which allegedly depended on the "survival of the fittest" members of society. Such Darwinian arguments spawned resolute defenses of the unrestrained pursuit of private interest, and even created doubts about the existence of something so nebulous as the "public good." As a result, laissez-faire became the order of the day, and notions of vigilance and civic action were routed from the field.

Republicanism therefore ceased to be a coherent political tradition in the Gilded Age; as Hartz himself put it, "the taking over by Whiggery of the whole of the Jeffersonian ethos was finally achieved" in the years after Lincoln's presidency (198). The ideological tension between virtue and commerce, the leitmotif of republican thought, vanished in an unbridled celebration of industrial development and the indispensable, if unintended, social contributions of business tycoons. Although elements of republican thought survived the gospel of wealth, they were fragmented, isolated, and provided no basis for political action or effective opposition to the emerging hegemony of liberalism.[15]

Evidence of the decline of republicanism in the Gilded Age is plentiful, but in defense of our interpretation we will emphasize the testimony of republicans of that time. These republicans sensed the increasing obsolescence of ideas about civic virtue, and lamented the passing of republican politics. Among the mourners was Henry Adams, a self-styled man of the eighteenth century with strongly republican convictions, and a shrewd observer of the momentous political, social, and economic changes that were reshaping the nation during the nineteenth century. Adams recognized that such changes made his own sensibilities and skills irrelevant to politics, though they were the very same sensibilities and skills that had served the Adams family—and the republic—so well in the early decades of independence. In trying to account for his own political marginalization and that of others like him, Adams was therefore led to consider the fate of republican politics in the United States.[16]

Thus, in Adams's writings we find an invaluable firsthand account of the meaning of republicanism in America, the causes of its decline, and the forces that propelled liberalism to the fore in American culture. Moreover, his writings are particularly helpful in skirting certain methodological difficulties intrinsic to our claim about the decline of republicanism. If republicanism is no longer a vital tradition, as we aver, then it is only with great difficulty that historians may trace the development of a *Weltanschauung* so different from our own.[17] Banning's discussion of virtue, as well as Wood's complementary treatment of interest, persuade us that contemporary scholars cannot confidently claim to understand the language of republicanism well enough to trace its decline without extraordinary assistance from those who are closer in time and sympathy to republican thought. Hence, we now turn to Henry Adams to improve our understanding of the fate of republicanism in the United States.

II

The republican tradition includes both a theory of government and a style of political action. The former outlines the dangers to liberty posed by corrupt rulers, and warns of the likelihood that rulers will become tyrannical. The latter insists that citizens must be vigilant and ever-prepared to resist corruption in order to preserve their common liberty. The watchful sentinel symbolizes the role of citizens in republican politics, for it is the watchman who alerts others to danger and very often forms the first line of defense.[18]

Historians are among the most important sentinels of the republic, attuned as they are both to the principles of liberty on which the republic was founded and to the subsequent struggle to maintain those principles against the evil of corruption. For this reason, republicanism embraces a particular kind of historiography, which we shall call "republican history."[19] This historiography provides important information about the vitality of republican politics; the waxing and waning of republican historiography mirrors the life and times of the politics it records. Hence, an inspection of republican historiography illuminates the liberal absorption of republicanism in America.

History told from a republican point of view is quintessentially an account of the *vivere civile* of a commonwealth, as Machiavelli so vividly demonstrated.[20] The central events in this story include the enactment of signal legislation, the conduct of crucial diplomatic negotiations, and the prosecution of vital military affairs (presented as patriotic undertakings, rather than as matters of strategy and tactics). The pivotal actors are therefore lawgivers, ministers, generals, and war heroes; citizens figure in the story primarily as foot soldiers and loyal subjects willing to respect the judgment of their superiors. Only with the rise of democratic or popular history do the people assume a more prominent role in determining the outcome of the story.

Because the history of the republic is intimately linked to the deeds of its statesmen, republican historiography often assumes the form of a morality play in which certain statesmen are presented as paragons of virtue, and others as the incarnation of vanity, foolhardiness, cowardice, corruption, or other vices that incapacitate them as makers of history.[21] Leaders learn the art of statecraft from considering these examples, and so the telling of republican history performs an important educational function by preventing "virtuous actions from being forgotten" and ensuring "that evil words and deeds should fear an infamous reputation with posterity" (Tacitus, 3:65).

Henry Adams wrote American history in this vein (Levenson). His *History of the United States during the Administrations of Jefferson and Madison; John Randolph; Life of Albert Gallatin;* early portions of *The Education of Henry Adams;* along with essays on contemporary politics portray the evolution of the American republic during the nineteenth century. Throughout, Adams emphasizes the role of statesmen, individuals who "guided public opinion but were little guided by it."[22] Conspicuously absent from his account are bankers, manufacturers, and other economic movers and shakers—men ill-suited to public service, which required individuals to rise above calculations of self-interest and to exhibit virtues not rewarded, and hence not generally practiced, in commercial exchanges. To the extent that such individuals served the commonweal, it was because they also had talents superior to those needed to succeed in private life.

Adams's preoccupation with politics to the near-exclusion of economics often troubles later historians, accustomed as they are to the evident importance or even primacy of economic forces in political and social development. But in truth Adams was deeply concerned with economic affairs, at least insofar as they raised questions of public policy. He was acutely aware of the impact of public policy on commerce and the way in which economic interests, once mobilized, limited the policy options pursued by statesmen. Adams also grasped, as had his grandfather and great-grandfather before him, that the demands placed upon statesmen were susceptible to improvement and enlargement. Precisely because policies affected the character and ambitions of citizens, statecraft was a kind of "soulcraft," to borrow from George Will. Hence, navigation acts, tariffs, the acquisition and disposition of public lands, and of course public finance were all important themes in his historical writings precisely because they involved both the political and moral economy of the republic.

Yet because Adams insisted on the distinction between wealth and commonwealth, he established a significant role for political leaders in balancing the two. Not surprisingly, in his view the two best models of leadership in American history were secretaries of the treasury: "Washington and Jefferson doubtless stand preeminent as the representatives of what is best in our national character of its aspirations, but Washington depended mainly upon Hamilton, and without Gallatin Mr. Jefferson would have been helpless."[23] Thus, it was Alexander Hamilton and Albert Gallatin who "had at once the breadth of mind to grapple with the machine of government as a whole, and the authority necessary to make it work efficiently for a given object; the practical knowledge of affairs and of politics that enabled them to foresee every movement; the long apprenticeship which had allowed them to educate and discipline their parties; and finally, the good fortune to enjoy power when government was still plastic and capable of receiving a new impulse" (*Gallatin*, 268).[24]

Hamilton's luck was better, and his success at Treasury greater, perhaps because he preceded Gallatin in office, when the government was young and especially "capable of receiving a new impulse." But in a letter to Samuel J. Tilden, Adams concluded that "After long study of the prominent figures in our history, I am more than ever convinced that, for combination of ability, integrity, knowledge, unselfishness, and social fitness, Mr. Gallatin has no equal. He was the most fully and perfectly equipped statesman we can show."[25] Thus, the fortunes of the early republic turned crucially on Gallatin's successes and failures, at least in Adams's telling. For him, as for other republican historians, the biographies of statesmen and the story of the republic were narratively inseparable.

What distinguished Gallatin was his tenacious effort to use his authority to keep the nation free of international embroilments, without succumbing to the temptations and vanity of power that generally attend such ambitions. Gallatin believed that if the Americans "could relieve themselves from debts, taxes, armies, and government interference with industry, they must succeed in outstripping Europe in economy of production" and secure their place in the world.[26] To defer these policies "was to incur the risk, if not the certainty, of following the career of England in debt, corruption, and rottenness" (*Gallatin*, 269). To advance these policies, however, was to ensure the longevity of the republic.

The entire policy presumed peace, which proved elusive. Adams wryly observed that "Few men have dared to legislate as though eternal peace were at hand, in a world torn by wars and convulsions and drowned in blood; but this is what Jefferson aspired to do" (*History*, 107–8). Yet Jefferson's own policies of nonintercourse and embargo attempts against European powers involved the new republic in a global conflict between France and England, much to his dismay. Madison proved singularly unable to unite the nation as it edged inexorably toward a war for which it was militarily unprepared. To Gallatin fell the impossible task of preparing for armed conflict while pursuing economic policies predicated on peace. A recalcitrant Congress impeded his efforts and finally drove him from office and into a diplomatic career that helped end the war on unexpectedly favorable terms.

For Adams, a statesman's response to political adversity was a true test of character. Of Gallatin's successful conduct of peace negotiations with England, he wrote: "Gallatin had abandoned place and power, had thrown himself with all his energy upon the only point where he could make his strength effective, and had actually succeeded, by skill and persistence, in guiding the country back to safe and solid ground." For this, Adams bestowed the supreme republican accolade: "no one had done more than [Gallatin] to serve his country, and no one had acted a more unselfish part" in guiding the nation through such dangerous and troubled times (*Gallatin*, 547).

Gallatin's engagement with history contrasted sharply with that of Jefferson, Madison, and Monroe. For them, "[t]here is no possibility of reconciling their theories with their acts, or their extraordinary foreign policy with dignity." These individuals lacked the qualities of practical statesmen that might have allowed them to master fate. Instead, "they were carried along on a stream which floated them after a fashion without much regard to themselves, like crickets on the Mississippi River" (*Letters,* 2:491).

Adams's sympathy for Gallatin and his reproach of the Virginians suggest his belief that the early history of the republic was to a significant degree open to human intervention. The fate of the young republic was not predetermined; if it had been, differences between individuals would have been unimportant, and the actions of statesmen would not have been the stuff of history. On the other hand, statesmen did not enjoy perfect freedom of action. Men like Gallatin had to contend with circumstances that were not of their own making, even as they set in motion events that unavoidably influenced both the need for, and possibility of, future actions—either of their own doing, or of that of others. True statesmen demonstrated their heroic qualities in this struggle to master fortune.

The later history of the republic, Adams believed, was not so open to the action of statesmen. After 1815, the character of American citizens was relatively fixed, and popular opinion seemed less susceptible to guidance: "For a time the aggressions of England and France forced the United States into a path that seemed to lead toward European methods of government; but the popular resistance, or inertia, was so great that the most popular party leaders failed to overcome it, and no sooner did foreign dangers disappear than the system began to revert to American practices; the national government tried to lay aside its assumed powers. When Madison vetoed the bill for internal improvements he could have had no other motive than that of restoring to the government, as far as possible, its original American character" (*History,* 403).

Once government was restored to its original character and the role of leadership substantially reduced, what would become of the nation? That concern is what inspired the uneasy questions that conclude Adams's *History:* What interests were to vivify a society so vast and uniform? What ideals were to ennoble it? What object, besides territorial expansion, must a democratic continent aspire to attain? What sort of corruptions would their relations bring, and by what means were these corruptions to be purged? For the treatment of such questions, "history required another century of experience"—and Adams lived that century and recorded its answers.

III

The issues posed by Adams at the end of *History of the United States* ultimately turned on the succession of political leaders. For Adams and other republican historiographers, survival of the republic depended upon the existence of a class or stratum of political talent from which successive generations of leaders were drawn into public service. A well-founded republic was one in which conditions favored the continuous production of qualified leaders. Where these conditions did not hold, chronic shortages of leadership arose and contributed to the decline of the republic over time. It was then the responsibility of the republican historian to sound the alarm, decry the absence of statesmen, and identify remedies for the problem.

For Adams, the decline from Washington to Jackson—or better yet, from Hamilton, who created the National Bank, to Roger Taney, the treasury secretary chosen by Jackson to destroy it—was both palpable and alarming. The most distressing aspect of this decline was its apparent inexorability. Conditions in the nation seemed decidedly to favor the rise of politicians who, in contrast to statesmen, did not lead, but were led by, public opinion. This was related to the emergence of mass political parties in the United States during the third decade of the nineteenth century, which was bound to favor politicians over statesmen, as Adams realized. Though true statesmen, like Webster and Seward, had little or nothing to do with party politics, they nevertheless "depended on others for machine work and money—on Peter Harveys and Thurlow Weeds, who spend their lives in it, took most of the abuse, and asked no reward." But inevitably, and "almost without knowing it, the subordinates ousted their employers and created a machine which no one but themselves could run" (*Education*, 764).

The consequences for republican politics were devastating. With the emergence of electoral machines, Adams lamented that "the politics of the United States from 1830 to 1849 offered as melancholy a spectacle as satirists ever held up to derision. Of all the parties that have existed in the United States, the famous Whig party was the most feeble in ideas and the most blundering in management; the Jacksonian Democracy was corrupt in its methods; and both, as well as society itself, were deeply cankered with two desperate sores: the enormous increase of easily acquired wealth, and the terribly rapid growth of slavery and the slave power" (*Gallatin*, 635–36).

The "desperate sores" of easy wealth and slavery demanded the ministrations of statesmen, but none stood out in this period of American history. According to Gallatin, the popular General Jackson was "an honest man and the idol of the worshipers of military glory, but from incapacity, military habits, and habitual disregard of laws and constitutional provisions, altogether unfit for the office"; while his archival John Calhoun was a "smart fellow, one of the first amongst second-rate men, but of lax political principles and a disordinate ambition not over-delicate in the means of satisfying itself" (*Gallatin*, 599).[27] Adams was equally unsparing of Henry Clay and his grandfather, John Quincy Adams. In this he dissented strongly from the opinion of his brother Brooks, who in the introduction to *The Degradation of the Democratic Dogma*, published after Henry's death in 1918, described their grandfather as "an idealistic philosopher who sought with absolute disinterestedness to put the Union upon a plane of civilization which would have averted" the Civil War. Henry had earlier complained to Brooks of John Quincy Adams's support for Jackson's designs on Florida and condemned him for not following Webster in trying to preserve the Union—John Quincy Adams, Henry noted, organized a personal party founded upon sectional antipathies that actually hastened the war.[28]

The absence of genuine statesmen and the prevalence of politicians deprived the republic of genuine leadership in the hour of its greatest need. The representatives of the South, though they were regarded as standards of statesmanship, seemed to Adams "an object-lesson of the way in which excess of power worked when held by inadequate hands" (*Education*, 811). Even before these "traitors" had flown Washington in the spring of 1861, northern "vultures" descended on the city "in swarms that darkened the ground, and tore the carrion of political patronage into fragments and gobbets of fat and lean, on the very steps of the White House. Not a man there knew what his task was to be, or was fitted for it; everyone without exception, northern or southern, was to learn his business at the cost of the public." This applied as much to Lincoln, Seward, and Sumner as it did to lesser lights; all required political instruction, "and their education was to cost a million lives and ten thousand million dollars, more or less, north and south, before the country could recover its balance and movement" (*Education*, 818–19).

For a brief moment after the Civil War, Henry Adams entertained the possibility that republican government might be refounded under the leadership of President Ulysses S. Grant, a man who had "unbounded popular confidence," was "tied to no party" and "under no pledges," and who had "the inestimable advantage of a military training, which, unlike a political training, was calculated to encourage the moral distinction between right and wrong."[29] Perhaps Grant would be able to restore balance to the system and prolong the American experiment with republican government.

Adams's hopes were swiftly dashed, however: "Grant avowed from the start a policy of drift; and a policy of drift attaches only barnacles. . . . Grant had no objects, wanted no help, wished for no champions. The Executive asked only to be let alone. This was his meaning when he said:—'Let us have Peace!'" (*Education*, 964). As if in atonement for his naivete, Henry became a ferocious critic of the administration, Congress, and the American political system more generally. The tenor of his criticism was undoubtedly influenced by his own exclusion from power and position, but the role of Jeremiah also suited a republican historian. Statesmen and citizens alike could be educated by Adams through leading organs of public opinion, and the pedagogical obligation of the historian might thereby be discharged— or so he hoped.

As editor of the *North American Review* from 1871 until 1876, Adams wrote more than twenty "sketches," many of them overtly political, the last of which was "The Independents in the Canvass," coauthored with his brother Charles. The two brothers urged voters to "overcome the tendency of our political system to corruption" by supporting whichever party would dedicate itself to that cause—an act of disloyalty to the Republican Party for which Adams was forced to resign as editor. This desperate plea for independence and a thorough reform of the political system was bound to fail, as Adams came to understand. His anonymously published novel *Democracy* satirized the Washington political scene during the Gilded Age and dramatized the impotence of political reformers.

The central figure in *Democracy* was Madeleine Lightfoot Lee, a widow from New York who had tried and grown weary of both good works and serious books. She wanted a different kind of education and was drawn to Washington by her desire to understand "the great American mystery of democracy and government."[30] The sordid mystery was revealed to Mrs. Lee in her salon, which attracted an amazing cast of political characters, including Senator Ratcliffe, the Prairie Giant from Peonia and prototypical politician of the Gilded Age.[31] Senator Ratcliffe professed to be interested in public service, but he insisted upon the need for a pragmatic, "political" approach to such matters as civil service reform. As he put it: "Public men cannot be dressing themselves to-day in Washington's old clothes. If Washington were President now, he would have to learn our ways or lose his next election. Only fools and theorists imagine that our society can be handled with gloves or long poles. One must make one's self a part of it. If virtue won't answer our purpose, we must use vice, or our opponents will put us out of office, and this was as true in Washington's day as it is now, and always will be" (71).

Ratcliffe never asked how Washington managed to survive as a statesman, if it was true even in his day that the existence of opposition necessitated familiarity with electioneering and a willingness to engage in patronage politics. Indeed, Ratcliffe seemed incapable of distinguishing party politics from affairs of state—a telltale sign of corruption. For him, service to the party was service to the state, and service to the state inevitably redounded to the benefit of political friends. The idea that factions might be inimical to the commonweal was simply lost on Ratcliffe, who used his position as secretary of treasury—the position once occupied by such luminaries as Hamilton and Gallatin—to dispense patronage to the backers of a president he loathed and friends who expected to grow rich at public expense. So long, and so successfully, had Ratcliffe practiced politics this way, that Mrs. Lee was uncertain "that he knew the difference between good and evil, between a lie and the truth; but the more she saw of him, the surer she was that his courage was mere moral paralysis, and that he talked about virtue and vice as a man who is color-blind talks about red and green; he did not see them as she saw them; if left to choose for himself he would have nothing to guide him" (174).

Was it politics that had caused this atrophy of the moral senses by disuse? Mrs. Lee wondered. She herself had been tempted by proximity to power and understood its corrupting effects on the reform-minded. The system of power in need of reform was itself necessary for reform; without power, reformers could not hope to succeed. But the acquisition of power required unsavory compromises that dulled moral judgments. Recognizing the depth of this corruption of politics, Mrs. Lee spurned Ratcliffe, abandoned politics, and left Washington altogether. "'I want to go to Egypt,' said Madeleine, still smiling faintly; 'democracy has shaken my nerves all to pieces'" (182).

No doubt Adams felt the same: he knew better than anyone how important statesmen were to the health of the republic and how far American leadership had fallen into disrepair since the founding. But for a while at least, he remained committed to the democratic-republicanism he associated with the leading statesmen of the early nineteenth century. In *Democracy*, it is Mr. Nathan Gore, like Adams a historian unable to secure a diplomatic appointment, who reluctantly expressed Adams's political creed: "Democracy asserts the fact that the masses are now raised to a higher intelligence than formerly. All our civilization aims at this mark. We want to do what we can to help it. I myself want to see the result. I grant it is an experiment, but it is the only direction society can take that is worth its taking; the only conception of its duty large enough to satisfy its instincts; the only result that is worth an effort or risk. . . . If our age is to be beaten, let us die in the ranks. If it is to be victorious, let us be first to lead the column. Anyway, let us not be skulkers or grumblers" (40–41). On all but the last point, the creator of Mr. Gore no doubt agreed.

IV

Adams's guarded hopes for democratic republicanism shrank as the futility of reform became evident. At the same time, his need to plumb the depths of corruption increased. His own small effort to educate citizens and statesmen had failed; that much was clear. But the reasons for failure had to be exposed before other attempts at republican restoration were made, or the project was abandoned as altogether impossible. Was the failure Adams's? Had he simply not been an effective sentinel of liberty and practitioner of republican historiography? Or was his own irrelevance a harbinger of republican obsolescence? Had modern politics become a struggle, not of men, but of forces that would not yield to moral exhortation, however well-aimed?

Commenting on the 1869–70 session of Congress, Adams outlined the problem. He observed: "The political dilemma was as clear in 1870 as it was likely to be in 1970. The system of 1789 had broken down, and with it the eighteenth century fabric of a priori, or moral, principles. Politicians had tacitly given it up. Grant's administration marked the avowal. Nine-tenths of men's political energies must henceforth be wasted on expedients to piece out,—to patch,—or, in vulgar language, to tinker,—the political machine as often as it broke down. Such a system, or want of system, might last centuries, if tempered by an occasional revolution or civil war; but as a machine, it was, or soon would be, the poorest in the world,—the clumsiest,—the most inefficient" (*Education,* 976).

Adams explained the need to "tinker the political machine" by relating it to the emergence of "a system of quiet but irresistible corruption" embodied in corporations. In his account of the New York Gold Conspiracy, Adams warned that "The corporation is in its nature a threat against the popular institutions spreading so rapidly over the whole world." During the conspiracy, the Erie corporation had demonstrated "its power for mischief, and [had] proved itself able to override and trample on law, custom, decency, and every restraint known to society, without scruple, and as yet without check."[32] And though unsavory capitalists like James Fisk and Jay Gould were eventually forced out, the power of corporate capital over the lives of millions of citizens remained intact.

Regulatory action by the state was of little or no avail; capitalists were quite able to defend themselves in the political arena, as William Graham Sumner, a sometime contributor to the *North American Review,* noted: "Under a democracy . . . the contest between numbers and wealth is nothing but a contest between two sets of lawyers, one drawing Acts in behalf of the state, and the other devising means of defeating those Acts in behalf of their clients. The latter set is far better paid in consideration, in security and money"[33] (*Essays,* 230). Because "the lobby is the army of the plutocracy," there was no easy escape from this predicament.[34] Adams put it more generally: "The national government, in order to deal with the corporations must assume powers refused to it by its fundamental law,—and even then is exposed to the chance of forming an absolute central government which sooner or later is likely to fall into the hands it is struggling to escape, and thus destroy the limits of its power only in order to make corruption omnipotent" ("Gold Conspiracy," 365–66).

In Adams's view, that is precisely what happened when the "gold bugs" defeated the advocates of "free silver."[35] Adams observed with dismay that,

> For a hundred years, between 1793 and 1893, the American people had hesitated, vacillated, swayed forward and back, between two forces, one simply industrial, the other capitalistic, centralizing, and mechanical. In 1893, the issue came on the single gold standard, and the majority at last declared itself, once for all, in favor of the capitalistic system with all its necessary machinery . . . the protective tarriff; the corporations and Trusts; the trades-unions and

socialistic paternalism which necessarily made their complement; the whole mechanical consolidation of force, which ruthlessly stamped out the life of the class into which Adams was born, but created monopolies capable of controlling the new energies that America adored. (*Education*, 1035)

Given the majority's decision, Adams could hardly sustain hope for a return to first principles, the means by which republican politics was traditionally refreshed.[36] Correspondingly, he lost confidence in the power of history-telling to do more than record the passing of the republic. Earlier historians of the republic were unabashedly patriotic, favoring those who extended the glory and life of the republic and excoriating those who failed in this endeavor. These historians felt there was virtue in patriotism: the historian who promoted a public spirit and vigilance among citizens was performing a valuable service by reviving the flagging spirit of a republican citizenry.[37]

Although Adams displayed a similar tendency in his earlier political writings, and even in *Gallatin*, he eventually abandoned the classical project of the republican historian; he noted wearily that he and his friend John Hay between them had "written nearly all the American history there was to write. . . . Both were heartily tired of the subject; and America seemed as tired as they" (*Education*, 1017). Telling the history of the republic no longer served a political function, and this realization colored Adams's assessment of his own voluminous work on statesmanship and the virtues of politics: "He had no notion whether [his volumes] served a useful purpose; he had worked in the dark; but so had most of his friends, even the artists, none of whom held any lofty opinion of their success in raising the standards of society, or felt profound respect for the methods or manners of the time, at home or abroad, but all of whom had tried, in a way, to hold the standard up" (*Education*, 1008).

The futility of upholding the standard suggested that Mr. Gore, the historian in *Democracy*, had been quite wrong to believe "the masses are now raised to a higher intelligence than formerly," that science would elevate them still further, and that enlightened self-government might prove successful. But Adams could hardly blame his fellow citizens for "declaring their preference for the new energies" embodied in corporate capitalism, since he shared much of their admiration for its revolutionary effects on society. Capitalism represented improvement in the material conditions of human life for large numbers of people, and for that reason it was irresistible: once liberals like Sumner uncovered citizens' "bourgeois hungers" and "catered openly to the acquisitive dreams of the American democrat," they assured the eventual hegemony of liberalism in America (Hartz, 205–6).

But Adams was aware of the dark side of capitalist development and the need for human beings to exercise some measure of control over the powerful forces that were carrying the republic toward its destiny, points that were not generally appreciated at the time. In fact, the majority's choice of "the capitalistic system and its methods" rested on the assumption that American life was unquestionably moving forward, that the history of the nation was progressing. If that assumption were questioned, the people might yet prove educable and come to realize the urgency and importance of governance and statecraft in the modern world, as Mr. Gore had hoped.

Toward that end, Adams disseminated a conception of history that flatly contradicted the easy optimism of "progressive" accounts of American development. Adams's 1894 communication to the American Historical Association entitled "The Tendency of History," his 1909 essay "The Rule of Phase Applied to History," and his 1910 "Letter to American Teachers of History," combined with chapters in the *Education* entitled "A Dynamic Theory of History" and "A Law of Acceleration," laid bare the destructive side of modernization.[38] Plainly, "the tendency of history" was toward forms of social and economic organization over which neither statesmen nor citizens had much control—and the role of the historian was to reveal the "lines of force" at work in the evolution of collective life. History was therefore about the vanishing opportunities for statesmanship of the sort described in classical republican historiography, and Adams unflinchingly undertook the necessary reconstruction of American historiography.

Occasionally, Adams's endeavors on this front have been misunderstood as a puzzling and rather clumsy effort to found a genuinely scientific discipline of history, a discipline based on law-like propositions such as those which form the core of the natural sciences. This interpretation has been thoroughly discredited by recent scholars.[39] It is apparent that Adams was not interested in a science of history so much as he sought a history of science, or more broadly, a history of mind. Adams's version of history presumed that "the mind is itself the subtlest of all known forces, and its self-introspection necessarily created a science which had the singular value of lifting" the human species in its quest for power (*Education*, 1155). Through science, human beings acted upon nature, which in turn reacted upon them, "educating" them, often by violent means, and always spurring new efforts to comprehend and harness the forces of nature.

Reflecting on this dynamic process, Adams commented that "[H]e had seen the number of minds, engaged in pursuing force—the truest measure of its attraction—increase from a few scores or hundreds, in 1838, to many thousands in 1905, trained to sharpness never before reached, and armed with instruments amounting to new senses of indefinite power and accuracy, while they chased force into hiding-places where nature herself had never known it to be" (*Education*, 1172). The process of education had accelerated as science progressed, and human beings struggled to comprehend and master the forces put at their disposal by the discoveries of the mind. The crucial question, of course, was whether or not "the social mind" would grasp these forces before they mastered human beings. Would humans employ their new-found powers wisely and justly, or would these forces destroy them in a cataclysmic "accident," e.g., war?

As Herbert Wells put it, the race was between education and catastrophe, and Adams feared the race was nearing its disastrous conclusion. He was desperately searching for an education capable of "running order through chaos, direction through space, discipline through freedom, unity through multiplicity" (*Education*, 731). Such an education would produce a new social mind, representing moral progress equivalent to the advance of scientific reasoning, and necessary for directing its use.[40] Thus far in history the social mind had reacted successfully to this unending challenge, and nothing proved it would fail to react again—"but it would need to jump" (*Education*, 1175). Yet nothing proved that the social mind would make this jump, and in fact Adams worried about the imminent destruction of civilization. The window of opportunity was closing swiftly, and with it, the possibility of republican politics.

V

The jump from the social mind of the eighteenth century to that of the twentieth century eventually defeated Henry Adams. He had turned from history-telling to the philosophy of history once it became necessary to explain the systemic corruption of politics and the disappearance of statesmen, the leading characters in the story of the republic. But the philosophy of history provided no comfort, as it suggested that opportunities for grasping, let alone making history were rapidly vanishing. The sciences could not even agree on the order of things and the place of humans within that order; unified or holistic understandings had been undone by the "multiplicity" of meanings so characteristic of modern life. "Evidently," Adams mused, "the new American would need to think in contradictions, and instead of Kant's famous four antinomies, the new universe would know no law that could not be proved by its anti-law" (*Education*, 1175).

Adams had come face to face with the processes of rationalization identified so well by his contemporary Max Weber.[41] Republican notions of statesmanship, which associated effective leadership with political innovation and the mastery of fortuna, were rendered largely irrelevant in mass industrialized societies.[42] The possibility of innovation had disappeared under the pressure of modernization; no statesman could possibly control a world constantly and violently being transformed by the revolutionary forces of capitalism. Indeed, it seemed as if the very idea of mastering fate was delusionary, for history in the modern world was "simply social development along the lines of weakest resistance, and . . . in most cases the line of weak resistance is found as unconsciously by society as by water" (*Letters*, 2:491).

With this realization, Adams finally leapt—not into the twentieth century with its multiplicity of meanings and new social mind, but backward into the twelfth century and the cosmologically unified world of *Mont-Saint-Michel and Chartres*, where the eighteenth-century imagination of a nineteenth-century man might find what was lacking in his own time and place. *Mont-Saint-Michel and Chartres* portrays a civilization in which the traditional authority of the church and the "charismatic" appeal of the Virgin Mary dominate collective life, in stark contrast to the pervasive rationalization of modern life outlined in the last chapters of the *Education*.

Adams's vision of piety and order or unity in thirteenth-century Christendom is sufficiently romantic as to cause the modern reader to "rub his eyes in astonishment" at the author's characterization of a world every bit as full of tension and discord as Adams's own (Samuels, *Henry Adams*, 358). However, Diggins suggests that Adams was searching less for unity of meaning than for spontaneity of action: the powerful devotion to Mary was for him a heretical challenge to the influence of scholastic theologians, like Aquinas. Precisely because the sentiment of faith was capable of inspiring great and pious actions, such as the construction of the cathedral at

Chartres, it provided an example of resistance to the rationalization of life ("Failure of Light," 181).

Thus, even in retreat, Adams was searching for models that might inspire a heroic reaction from citizens of the republic. What he found, however, was the explanation for their impatience with republican jeremiads of the sort he had regularly offered. The twentieth century from which he recoiled was itself a product of the triumph of Aquinas over Mary, and then of science over religion. The mind's search for order had disenchanted the world, and made faith difficult to sustain. Adams shared Weber's suspicion that when humans begin to reason about their beliefs, they descend from cosmos to chaos, from belief to doubt, and ultimately arrive at the modernist predicament that leaves them "with the ability to question everything, and affirm nothing" ("Failure of Light," 184). Without faith, it was impossible to resist the forces of rationalization that determined the course of history, but faith itself could not withstand these forces.

Thus, once Adams abandoned the search for unity in the present, he effectively relegated republican politics to the past, for republican politics is quintessentially oriented toward "running order through chaos." Republican politics is dedicated to the search for political unity in a community or society of diverse interests, none of which is equivalent to the res publica, and all of which must be taken into account for the commonweal to be the common-weal. To use language that Adams might have employed, republican politics is the achievement of "unity through multiplicity," and the destruction of unity by multiplicity means that republican politics no longer exists, or even more strongly, that it can no longer exist. In Adams's estrangement from history we may read this epitaph for a distinctly republican tradition in American politics.

Notes

Originally published in *ATQ*, Volume 4, No. 3, September 1990. Reprinted by permission of The University of Rhode Island. The authors wish to thank Jeffrey Isaac for providing valuable comments on an earlier draft of this essay.

1. Louis Hartz, *The Liberal Tradition in America* (New York: Harcourt, Brace, 1955), 287. Hereafter cited parenthetically.

2. The leading expositors of this interpretation are Gordon Wood; and J. G. A. Pocock, *The Machiavellian Moment: Florentine Political Thought and the Atlantic Republican Tradition* (Princeton: Princeton University Press, 1975), though they are ably supported by others too numerous to mention here. For arguments against such "republican" revisions of history, see Isaac Kramnick, "Republican Revisionism Revisited," *American Historical Review* 83 (1982): 629–64; Joyce O. Appleby, *Capitalism and a New Social Order* (New York: Cambridge University Press, 1985); and John Patrick Diggins, *The Lost Soul of American Politics: Virtue, Self-Interest, and the Foundations of Liberalism* (New York: Basic Books, 1984). J. G. A. Pocock provides a useful rejoinder against these critics, condemning any "binary reading of the debate, in which the republican thesis is distorted and rigidified so that it may be set in opposition to an equally rigidified liberalism" ("Between Gog and Magog: The Republican Thesis and the *Ideologia Americana*," *Journal of the History of Ideas* 48 [1987]: 344).

3. Gordon Wood, *The Creation of the American Republic, 1776–1787* (Chapel Hill: University of North Carolina Press, 1969), 475. Hereafter cited parenthetically.

4. Lance Banning, "Some Second Thoughts on Virtue and the Course of Revolutionary Thinking," in *Conceptual Change and the Constitution*, ed. J. G. A. Pocock and Terence Ball (Lawrence: University Press of Kansas, 1988).

5. Thomas A. Horne, "Bourgeois Virtue: Property and Moral Philosophy in America, 1750–1800," *History of Political Thought* 4 (1983): 317–40.

6. This interpretation receives support from another quarter: Isaac Kramnick, in "English Middle-Class Radicalism of the Eighteenth Century," *Literature of Liberty* 3 (1980): 5–48, has extensively discussed the language of "commercial republicanism" and "bourgeois virtue." Kramnick also analyzes liberalism's incorporation of republican themes, showing that the language of virtue and the language of rights are both integral components of a historical ideology consistent with the political practices of liberal democracy.

7. We agree with Pocock, *Machiavellian Moment*, that the problematic relation between commerce and virtue is itself constitutive of republican politics. Republican politics is not opposed to commerce, upon which the health of the republic depends. Republicans are preoccupied with the unavoidable consequences of commercial development, i.e., the turn toward self-interest that necessarily accompanies—and "corrupts"—it.

8. See Lance Banning, *The Jeffersonian Persuasion: Evolution of a Party Ideology* (Ithaca, N.Y.: Cornell University Press, 1978).

9. Russell L. Hanson, *The Democratic Imagination in America: Conversations with Our Past* (Princeton: Princeton University Press, 1985), 74–75, 80–83; hereafter cited parenthetically. Perhaps we should note that Wood (*Creation*, 411–13, 501–6, 612) claimed to analyze only the beginning of the end of classical

politics, since he apparently saw Federalists as transitional figures. This impression is confirmed by Wood when he insists that, "despite their acceptance of the reality of interests and commerce, the Federalists had not yet abandoned what has been called the tradition of civic humanism" ("Interests and Disinterestedness in the Making of the Constitution," in *Beyond Confederation: Origins of the Constitution and American National Identity*, ed. Richard Beeman, Stephen Botein, and Edward C. Carter II [Chapel Hill: University of North Carolina Press, 1987], 83). The Federalists remained committed to the idea that at least some individuals might be sufficiently disinterested as to provide the necessary political leadership. Wood concludes that it was the Anti-Federalists who were the political midwives of modernity.

10. Thomas Brown, *Politics and Statesmanship: Essays on the American Whig Party* (New York: Columbia University Press, 1985); Daniel Walker Howe, *The Political Culture of the American Whigs* (Chicago: University of Chicago Press, 1979).

11. Andrew Jackson, *A Compilation of the Messages and Papers of the Presidents, 1789–1902*, comp. James D. Richardson, 10 vols. (Washington, D.C., 1905), 2:1153.

12. Marvin Meyers, *The Jacksonian Persuasion* (New York: Random House, 1957). Hereafter cited parenthetically.

13. See Eric Foner, *Free Soil, Free Labor, Free Men: The Ideology of the Republican Party before the Civil War* (New York: Oxford University Press, 1970).

14. By definition, a party was a part of the republic, and it therefore resembled a faction. The idea of a republican party was consequently an oxymoron.

15. See Hanson, *Democratic Imagination*. Dorothy Ross claims that the republican tradition survived until the Progressive period ("The Liberal Tradition Revisited and the Republican Tradition Addressed," in *New Directions in American Intellectual History*, ed. John Higham and Paul Conkin [Baltimore: Johns Hopkins University Press, 1979]). Interesting residues of republicanism have been sighted in the late twentieth century by Rowland Berthoff ("Independence and Attachment, Virtue and Interest: From Republican Citizen to Fee Enterprise," in *Uprooted Americans: Essays to Honor Oscar Handlin*, ed. Richard Bushman et al., 97–124 [Boston: Little, Brown, 1979]); John Murrin ("The Great Inversion, or Court versus Country: A Comparison of the Revolution Settlements in England [1688–1721] and America [1776–1816]," in *Three British Revolutions*, ed. J. G. A. Pocock [Princeton: Princeton University Press, 1980]); and especially Michael Lienesch (*New Order of the Ages: Time, the Constitution, and the Making of Modern American Political Thought* [Princeton: Princeton University Press, 1987]). These residues furnish contemporary American liberalism with one of its principal modes of self-criticism and doubt, according to Pocock in "Between Gog and Magog."

16. See Henry Steele Commager, "Henry Adams," in *The Marcus W. Jernegan Essays in American Historiography,* ed. William T. Hutchinson, 191–206 (Chicago: University of Chicago Press, 1937).

17. Hartz's work unwittingly demonstrates this point very well: as a member of a liberal culture, Hartz found nothing but liberalism when he examined the history of that culture.

18. While Wood, in *Creation,* and Pocock, in *Machiavellian Moment,* provide the best-known description of republican ideas, Bailyn was among the first to suggest the importance of republicanism in America, and he offered an account of republican thought that remains valuable today. In particular, he emphasizes the conspiratorial orientation that stems from obsessive concerns over corruption and the need to detect and resist it (see Bernard Bailyn, *The Ideological Origins of the American Republic* [Cambridge: Harvard University Press, 1967]).

19. As a species of what George Nadel calls "exemplar history," in "Philosophy of History before Historicism," *History and Theory* 3 (1963): 291–315, republican historiography was predicated on the idea that history is "philosophy learned by example," as Dionysus, paraphrasing Thucydides, noted. Rulers, or men of action, are not instructed by precept; rather, they learn by studying others' experience, especially when that experience is reported in sufficient detail to include the situation, motives, and reasons for the success or failure of past actions. History was the lamp of experience illuminating the ways of—and for—statesmen (see Trevor H. Colborne, *The Lamp of Experience: Whig History and the Intellectual Origins of the American Revolution* [Chapel Hill: University of North Carolina Press, 1965]).

20. Pocock uses the term *vivere civile* in *Machiavellian Moment.*

21. See F. R. D. Goodyear's introduction to *The Annals of Tacitus, Books 1–6* (Cambridge: Cambridge University Press, 1972), 1:27, 34–37; hereafter cited parenthetically; and especially Nadel, "Philosophy of History."

22. Henry Adams, *Henry Adams: Novels, Mont-Saint-Michel, The Education,* ed. Ernest Samuels and Jayne N. Samuels (New York: Library of America, 1983). Hereafter cited parenthetically.

23. Henry Adams, *The Life of Albert Gallatin.* Philadelphia: J. B. Lippincott, 1880. Hereafter cited parenthetically.

24. Aaron Burr and John Randolph were the antitheses of statesmen. Of Randolph, the family nemesis, Adams complained: "He talked quite wildly, and his acts had no relation to his language. This patriot would accept no tawdry honors from a corrupt and corrupting national government! He would not take a seat in the Cabinet, like Clay, to help trample the rights of Virginia! He would not take a foreign mission, to pocket the people's money without equivalent! He owed everything to his constituents, and from them alone he would receive his reward!

This speech was made in February, 1828. In September, 1829, he was offered and accepted a special mission to Russia; he sailed in June, 1830; remained ten days at his post; then passed near a year in England; and returning home in October, 1831, drew $21,407 from the government, with which he paid off his old British debt. This act of Roman virtue, worthy of the satire of Juvenal, still stands as the most flagrant bit of diplomatic jobbery in the annals of the United States government" (Henry Adams, *John Randolph* [New York: Houghton Mifflin, 1898], 293–94).

25. Henry Adams, *The Letters of Henry Adams, 1858–1892*, 3 vols., ed. J. C. Levenson et al. (Cambridge: Harvard University Press, 1982), 2:491. Hereafter cited parenthetically.

26. Henry Brooks Adams, *History of the United States*, 10 vols. (Charles Scribner's Sons, 1889–91), 118. Hereafter cited parenthetically.

27. The words belong to Gallatin, but Adams unquestionably shared these sentiments.

28. See Katherine L. Morrison, "A Reexamination of Brooks and Henry on John Quincy Adams," *New England Quarterly* 54 (1981): 163–79.

29. Henry Brooks Adams, "The Session, 1869–1870," *North American Review* 61 (July 1870): 29–52.

30. Henry Adams, *Democracy: An American Novel,* in *Henry Adams: Novels, Mont-Saint-Michel, The Education*, ed. Ernest Samuels and Jayne N. Samuels (New York: Library of America, 1983), 7. Hereafter cited parenthetically.

31. Ratcliffe was also in part the literary incarnation of James G. Blaine; many other characters were also drawn from real life (see Ernest Samuels, *Henry Adams* [Cambridge: Harvard University Press, 1989]). On two occasions, Blaine had blocked the presidential nomination of Henry Adams's father, bringing to an end the family's success in national politics.

32. Henry Adams, "The New York Gold Conspiracy," in *Historical Essays*, 318–66 (New York: Charles Scribner's Sons, 1891), 365. Hereafter cited parenthetically.

33. William Graham Sumner, *Essays of William Graham Sumner*, ed. Albert C. Keller and Maurice R. Davie, 2 vols. (New Haven: Yale University Press, 1940), 2:230.

34. William Graham Sumner, *What Social Classes Owe Each Other,* 1883. (Caldwell, Idaho: Caxton Printers, 1974), 93.

35. Sumner, on the other hand, proved to be a gold bug. His strident defense of laissez-faire, though presented as a defense of the republic, was in truth profoundly antirepublican: a minimalist state presents only minimal opportunities for statesmanship, citizenship, and the practice of civic virtue.

36. See Sara J. Shumer, "Machiavelli: Republican Politics and Its Corruption," *Political Theory* 7 (1979): 5–34.

37. See Lester H. Cohen, *The Revolutionary Histories: Contemporary Narratives of the American Revolution* (Ithaca, N.Y.: Cornell University Press, 1980).

38. John Patrick Diggins compares Adams's philosophy of history to Weber's analysis of rationalization in modernity in "'Who Bore the Failure of Light': Henry Adams and the Crisis of Authority," *New England Quarterly* 58 (1985), 165–92. Hereafter cited parenthetically.

39. See Ernest Samuels, *Henry Adams;* and Ernest Samuels, *The Biography of Henry Adams,* 3 vols. (Cambridge: Harvard University Press, 1964).

40. See Keith R. Burich for a discussion of the importance of such "phase changes" in Adams's dynamic theory of history. According to Burich, Adams was less concerned with the laws that governed history than with the fateful turning points associated with the emergence of new social minds. The concept of a "social mind" apparently owes much to Auguste Comte, whose work on the three states of understanding—theological, metaphysical, and positive—strongly influenced Adams.

41. See Diggins, "Failure of Light."

42. See Pocock's illuminating discussion of political innovation in Machiavelli, and his treatment of virtue as "that by which we innovate, and so let loose sequences of contingency beyond our prediction or control so that we become prey to fortune. On the other hand, virtue is that internal to ourselves by which we resist fortuna and impose upon her patterns of order, which may even become patterns of moral order" (*Machiavellian Moment,* 167). This tension is resolved by a master innovator—the Prince—who depends as little as possible on circumstances beyond his control.

CHAPTER 2

Democracy: Henry Adams and the Role of Political Leader

B. H. Gilley

SHORTLY AFTER THE CIVIL War, Walt Whitman described with a poignant question how the complexity of industrial society fostered detachment and alienation in Americans and thereby inhibited democratic politics: "Shall a man lose himself in countless masses of adjustments, and be so shaped with reference to this, that and the other, that the simply good and healthy and brave parts of him are reduced and clipp'd away like the bordering of box in a garden?"[1] What Whitman described applied to the political complexity that Henry Adams witnessed in Washington, D.C., after the Civil War and portrayed in *Democracy; An American Novel* (1880). Adams's observations are relevant because they contain biographical overtones, and they foreshadow the complexity in modern political leadership.

In addition to being a major figure in literary and historical writing, Henry Adams, throughout his adult life, observed and analyzed political leaders. And, although he never held office, he was a friend of and mingled with political leaders in the United States government and in the governments of foreign nations. Political leadership was a major theme in many of Adams's books and articles, and much of what he wrote stemmed from an overriding awareness of his father's, grandfather's, and great-grandfather's political leadership roles.

Much has been written about *Democracy*. Ernest Samuels, Adams's definitive biographer, described how contemporary critics in the United States were attracted to the book as a roman à clef, focusing primarily on personalities in the Ulysses S. Grant and Rutherford B. Hayes presidential administrations, especially James G. Blaine. English readers were titillated by the contrast of crude American political mores to those of more polished and sophisticated English and continental leaders.[2] J. C. Levenson emphasized the book's biographical implications—that it was even more than a "document of biography" because Adams demonstrated "variety of situation" and "inventiveness."[3] Like Levenson, Michael Colacurcio, emphasizing Adams's pragmatic tendencies, also alluded to *Democracy's* biographical implications—that its heroine Madeleine Lee was "a curious version of Adams himself," and her problem reflected his own—whether to accept or reject "the Washington morality of power."[4]

Charles Andrew Vandersee concluded that, for Adams, "disinterestedness" was the only "acceptable motive" for political action by individual leaders, and that "disinterestedness" was unappreciated and perhaps impossible in the political complexity of Adams's time as contrasted to that of his father, grandfather, and great-grandfather.[5] Melvin Lyon also adhered to the view that the book revealed Adams's political views, but as reflected through the idealist John Carrington, the former Confederate and southerner. Specifically, Lyon believed that Adams emphasized "the contrast between the moral pretense and the immoral reality" of American democracy. Implicit was the idea that Mrs. Lee (symbolizing the Northeast) might eventually marry Carrington (symbolizing the South), thus reuniting the best elements of American democracy, but being idealistic these entities would be isolated from the political wave of the future—a political democracy dominated by the West, whose leaders were dedicated to pragmatic and realistic politics and to the pursuit of power (self-interest). Senator Silas P. Ratcliffe, the villain–political leader in *Democracy*, epitomized the new breed of Western leader.[6]

In *Democracy* Adams did emphasize how post–Civil War democratic politics undermined the moral tone of its practitioners. Also, the philosopher-historian recorded with remarkable clarity the psychological debilitation of political leaders. The introspection and disillusionment he described also find expression and correlation in his autobiography, *The Education of Henry Adams*, and in some of his political reporting in newspapers and journals.

The political corruption in the presidential administrations of Grant and Hayes formed the backdrop for *Democracy*. In this context, the philosopher-historian denounced the post–Civil War breed of political leaders who, he felt, succumbed to selfish designs. This well-worn observation is valid and merits attention, except as it oversimplifies Adams's portrayal and thereby obscures the extent to which he mirrored how his characters, and himself, reacted to and were influenced by the new political environment.

Disgusted by the Senate's perversion of power during the tenure of President Andrew Johnson, young Adams, recently returned from England, supported Ulysses S. Grant for president. After Grant's election in November 1868, he went to Washington as a journalist to report what he thought would be a reform administration. The young diplomat turned reporter expected to see Grant the Soldier become a magisterial Grant the President and reassert executive leadership. Like many other reformers, he was disappointed. When Adams heard the names of the men Grant had appointed to the Cabinet he was stunned, and "he wondered at the suddenness of the revolution which actually, within five minutes, changed his intended future [journalist-reformer] into an absurdity so laughable as to make him ashamed of it."[7] Many years later, in a letter to his older brother, Charles Francis Adams Jr., he remarked that "Grant wrecked my own life, and the last hope or chance of lifting society back to a reasonably high plane."[8] Adams's statements were indicative; he spent the remainder of his life analyzing—and lamenting—in journalistic writing, in fiction, and in the *Education* what had degraded American political leaders.

In *Democracy*, Senator Silas P. Ratcliffe launched his political career as a well-intentioned Civil War governor of Illinois. But the temptations of political power eroded his will, and social complexity engendered in him a calculating attitude toward politics. Significant to the student of history, Adams portrayed realistically the pressures his political leader experienced. Ratcliffe was unhappy with the character of political life, and he found it detrimental to "honesty and self-respect." Adams amplified his leader's dilemma by depicting his moral decline. Ratcliffe rationalized his political expediency with a detached outlook: "I am a politician because I cannot help myself; it is the trade I am fittest for, and ambition is my resource to make it tolerable."[9] Although Adams did not excuse the senator's selfish rationale, he suggested that the erosion of Ratcliffe's will was a subtle development that, in part, was occasioned by the pressures of impersonal society.

Upon arriving in Washington to pursue journalism, Adams claimed that his sole contact was Attorney-General William M. Evarts. The remark typified Adams's characteristic self-deprecation and understatement. His father, minister to England during the Civil War, was a longtime friend of former Secretary of State William H. Seward, who was still in Washington. Such understatement emphasized Adams's second official contact in the capital, President Andrew Johnson. In short, Adams quickly gained an entrée to Washington politicos. He became acquainted with all of the types, ranging through chief executives, cabinet officers, senators, congressmen, even to Sam Ward, the chief of the lobbyists.[10]

Significant to the focus of this analysis, Adams was appalled by the swarms of lobbyists and persons who sought jobs in the Grant administration. Understandably, he could describe in *Democracy* how, as a post–Civil War senator, Ratcliffe experienced increasingly oppressive demands by such persons. Lobbyists thronged the senator's offices. With them were representatives, fellow senators, and newspapermen—all of whom felt that he had "no other reason for existence" except to work for their selfish interests. Testifying to the lobbyists' impact, Senator Ratcliffe evinced an uninspired attitude. He approached his offices with foreboding; he found it difficult to countenance the favor seekers who awaited him. According to the author, had the senator been free to express his desires, he would have thrown them out.[11] Although he did so partially in irony, Adams portrayed his senator as a man of discretion. Ratcliffe resorted to pretended work in order to evade his supporters' intrusive designs. Contrasted to his demanding petitioners, the senator aspired to noble endeavor and he admired good taste. When the demands of office became unbearable, his better instincts revived, and he experienced a sense of disillusionment with politics.[12]

To humanize his leader further and to set the stage for an ironic thrust, Adams remarked that the faith of Ratcliffe's followers might have been shaken if they had suspected the antipathy that such oppressive political routine generated in their leader. Subjected to selfish demands and dissociated from the electorate, the senator longed for intimate and polite society that would have contrasted strikingly to his repulsive political milieu. In a revealing statement of alienation, Adams described Ratcliffe as "unutterably lonely."[13]

Nine years before he wrote *Democracy*, Adams was less sympathetic, toward senators and cabinet officials. In the *Education,* he recounted how in 1869 a cabinet officer exclaimed to him that "A Congressman is a hog!"—and Adams speculated that the appropriate rejoinder might be, "If a Congressman is a hog, what is a Senator?" Adams concluded that, "This innocent question, put in a candid spirit, petrified any executive officer that ever sat a week in his office."[14] Ten years of introspection and evaluation produced in Adams a more sympathetic appreciation of the pressures to which post–Civil War political leaders were subjected. In that ten years Adams travelled in Europe, taught history at Harvard College, acquired a wife, and established a permanent residence on Lafayette Square in Washington, D.C., where he monitored political life.

In addition to loneliness and disillusionment, Adams portrayed in Ratcliffe how estrangement could divide a leader within himself—indeed, how difficult it was to be one's self. The senator sought power to achieve legitimate political objectives, but the quest for political power obscured his goals and corrupted his relation to the voters. Increasingly, Ratcliffe related to politics only as political activity yielded him personal advantage; means became ends for which he violated his oath of office and frustrated the will of his constituents. The senator sacrificed integrity to expediency; finally he accepted a $100,000 bribe.[15]

Adams was not content merely to condemn his Senator Ratcliffe for betraying the people and for enhancing his personal power. When Madeleine Lee, the heroine of *Democracy*, questioned reformer Nathan Gore about Ratcliffe's conduct, the reformer was evasive. Although he despised Ratcliffe, Gore refused to denounce the senator's easy expediency. Instead, the reformer acknowledged that a heterogeneous relation existed between political means and ends: "Mr. Ratcliffe has a practical piece of work to do. . . . I believe in him myself and am not afraid to say so."[16] Adams's assessment foreshadowed Max Weber's conclusion that modern politics by their complexity undermined the integrity of leaders by compelling them to use unethical means to pursue legitimate ends.[17]

Adams admired George Washington as a leader because Washington refused to acknowledge or to be a part of political factions. This characteristic of the first president the author used to amplify his ambiguous view of post–Civil War political leaders and their changed milieu. In the memorable Mt. Vernon scene in *Democracy* Adams's hero-lawyer John Carrington and Ratcliffe evaluated President Washington in terms that described the changed political climate. After some nostalgic reminiscing, Carrington observed that the first president was the leader of a patrician-dominated society; dedication to principle and to the welfare of the people motivated Washington's public actions. Carrington's remarks were calculated to provoke Ratcliffe. Like Carrington, Ratcliffe realized that the political context of President Washington's time no longer prevailed, but, unlike Carrington, the senator was neither nostalgic nor moralistic. The first president, Ratcliffe remarked, would have had difficulty succeeding in contemporary political life; Washington had been able to refrain from partisan politics, but, in order to be reelected in the present, he would have had to change his political philosophy.[18]

Albert Gallatin was another older leader by whom Adams measured post–Civil War political leaders. In his biography of Jefferson's secretary of the treasury, the young historian defined the leader's relation to his party. Unlike Washington, Gallatin had to deal with a political party. However, Adams noted that in Gallatin's time a leader could maintain his ideals while participating in party activity. As Charles Vandersee emphasizes, party loyalty in Gallatin's time did not "demand assent to a party action, though it might conflict with judgment, conscience, and conviction."[19] Clearly, Adams believed that party principles were corrupted by the Jacksonian revolution—or by universal white male suffrage. Politics came under the influence of leaders who acquiesced to party caucuses.

Irony permeated Adams's assessment of Ratcliffe. His characterization of the senator was inspired by James G. Blaine, who from 1869 to 1875 was Speaker of the House of Representatives. Adams disliked Blaine because in 1872 he had helped deny to Adams's father, Charles Francis, the Republican presidential nomination. Rejection of the elder Adams was an especially bitter blow to Henry Adams because he felt that his father epitomized the mentality of the ideal party leader: "Charles Francis Adams possessed the only perfectly balanced mind that ever existed in the [Adams] name."[20] Despite his bias toward Blaine, Adams, in *Democracy*, never denied Ratcliffe's ability or energy. This assessment accords with an evaluation of Blaine by a historian who has analyzed in depth the political mentality, as well as the political activity, of the period and who concluded that, although Blaine was expedient, he was nevertheless pragmatic and versatile.[21]

In later years, Adams probably was intrigued by the complexity of character he created in Ratcliffe. In the "Critical Notes" of his *Symbol and Idea in Henry Adams*, Melvin Lyon evaluated scholars' interpretation of Ratcliffe and noted that most see him as a villain—and, unquestionably, this is what Adams intended him to be. But, as Lyon stresses, Ratcliffe was that and more.[22] Perhaps Irving Howe was most accurate when he observed that Ratcliffe ended up as a more powerful character than Adams intended him to be—a consummate and talented, albeit corrupt, politician: "What Ratcliffe possesses so abundantly, and far more so than any of his opponents, is experience—the experience of a man for whom nothing has been prepared or easy, a man who has had to make his own life."[23]

Adams amplified the impact of political complexity on individuals by viewing it from a contrasting perspective. If an experienced political leader succumbed to disorientation, what could be expected of a sophisticated lay member of the political community? Mrs. (Madeleine) Lightfoot Lee, Adams's heroine in *Democracy*, was bored with foreign travel and dilettantish pursuits. In biographical terms she embodied the views of both Adams and his wife, Marian ("Clover").

One can detect in Madeleine's reactions to Washington's political leaders some hint as to why Adams took time away from writing history to produce *Democracy*, a novel. Following his disillusioning experience observing the Grant administration at Washington, Adams taught history at Harvard College, where he became intrigued with psychology. According to William Jordy, this circumstance, combined with his wife's incisive social observations and the urbane atmosphere of Washington, D.C., especially the society of their close circle of friends, the John Hays and Clarence King, provided Adams the inspiration to produce the novel.[24] Another factor that may have influenced Adams to write the book was his growing pessimism about democracy and history. Man and the universe appeared to be products of determinism. In a January 1883 letter to Samuel J. Tilden, the Democratic presidential candidate in 1876, Adams asserted that "history is simply social development along the line of weakest resistance."[25]

Madeleine, an attractive widow, proposed to solve "the great American mystery of democracy and government."[26] Like Adams, she went to Washington confident that she was equipped to explore and to understand the complexities of political leaders and political power. What Adams proposed to demonstrate was that Madeleine Lee was ill-equipped to evaluate political leaders. Charles Vandersee emphasized that Adams learned the realities of political interaction by bitter experience and in so doing became an astute political observer and commentator. To emphasize this point and the complexity of politics, Adams portrayed Madeleine as a novice.[27] Although sophisticated and well intentioned, she misjudged political complexity; she misjudged herself.

Adams's description of Madeleine Lee was a candid self-appraisal reminiscent of an admission in the *Education* about his evaluation of Ulysses S. Grant when he supported Grant for the presidency and witnessed his early months in office: "Adams was young and easily deceived, in spite of his diplomatic adventures, but even at twice his age he could not see that this reliance on Grant was unreasonable."[28] Adams's point was that, like many political novices, Madeleine Lee, and perhaps himself in 1868–69, confused government with the power and prestige of directing governmental affairs. "Perhaps," said Adams, "the force of the engine was a little confused in her mind with that of the engineer, the power with the men who wielded it." Adams was specific; it was the human interest of politics—the fascination with power and with leaders who sought power—that appealed to Mrs. Lee.[29]

Madeleine resolved to pursue political enlightenment by studying Senator Ratcliffe. Recently this "high-priest" of American politics had narrowly missed his party's presidential nomination. By virtue of her charm and social eminence, Madeleine made Ratcliffe her devoted admirer. She was amused and confident—amused at the ease with which she captured Ratcliffe's attention, confident that she could win him as a suitor. The senator's romantic capitulation Adams humorously likened to a "two-hundred-pound salmon" that was landed with scarcely a struggle.[30]

The "salmon" analogy was as ironic as it was humorous. The widow, he observed, had in the senator "fully her match";[31] she, too, was a "salmon" in danger of being "landed." Madeleine identified with the senator's drive for power, so much so that she was tempted to marry him. The prospect startled her because such a marriage would unite her with a man whose moral and political philosophy she abhorred. Mrs. Lee questioned her own stability. Was she about to be corrupted by the political society of which she found herself a part? Was Ratcliffe merely pragmatic because he accepted "the good and the bad" together, and conformed to the prevailing moral and political norm?[32]

In later years, Madeleine's questions must have aroused in Adams memories of the two great tragedies in his life: his failure to fulfill the Adams legacy of leadership in high federal office and, in 1885, following a period of depression and intellectual frustration, the suicide of his sensitive wife, Marian ("Clover").

Much has been written about Adams's omission in the *Education* of any reference to Clover Adams. For such a private person as Adams, reference to the most intimate and tragic facet of his life would have been inadmissable. It is sufficiently revealing that in *Democracy* he chose a woman, modeled on his wife, to express his political views and to be the "responding intelligence."[33] The choice also testified to the significant role that Clover played in the formulation of his political views. As Clover Adams's biographer, Eugenia Kaledin, indicated, *Democracy* illustrated Adams's personal frustration that both he and his contemporaries had failed to provide a proper role for intellectually talented women like his wife.[34]

Madeleine's doubts about Ratcliffe subsided quickly, and, despite warnings from her sister and Carrington, she announced her intention to marry the senator. Only documentary evidence of his blatant acceptance of the $100,000 bribe, supplied by Carrington, convinced Madeleine to reject Ratcliffe.

Adams's analysis was perceptive. Craving political power for its own sake appealed to even the most sophisticated and well-meaning person. Madeleine Lee, as had Adams, learned that political life in post–Civil War America was more complex than she realized. Michael Colacurcio specifically ascribed this deduction to Adams. If in *Democracy* Madeleine Lee's rejection of Ratcliffe's suit was the "ultimate fact," even more striking was "the strength of her attraction to him in the first place."[35] In his early years, Adams yearned to participate in politics and perhaps even to be a leader. But the moral level of political leaders and the depersonalization that he witnessed in them during and after the Grant era depressed and repelled him. However, in spite of these circumstances, political leaders and politics remained for him an abiding interest.

The terms "force," "engines," "energy," and "mechanization" for many years had conjured up images that appealed to Adams's interest in a scientific approach to history—and specifically to his conclusion that mass compulsion and scientific forces were stronger than individual men. In February 1863, he wrote to Charles Francis Adams Jr. that "the engines he [man] will have invented will be beyond his strength to control."[36] In his pessimism, Adams likened the depersonalization and subordination of men in politics to the way industrial workers were depersonalized and subordinated to machine technology. The philosopher-historian even addressed the dilemma in the *Education*: "Modern politics," he said, "is . . . a struggle not of men but of forces." Men became "creatures of force, massed about central powerhouses" until the battle was no longer between men but between "the motors that drive the men." Inevitably, men "succumb to their own motive forces"; increasingly they served the political combinations and became predictable pawns in the struggle for power.[37]

Adams portrayed this same depersonalization and mechanization in *Democracy*. Mrs. Lee aspired to "touch" the "massive machinery of society"—only to recoil when she was almost devoured by it. Because of their awkward and contrived actions at the White House reception, she described the president and his wife as "mechanical figures," which might be "wood or wax."[38] Commenting on the passage, J. C. Levenson asserted that in *Democracy* "mechanization has taken command and human reality has departed from politics."[39]

Adams also amplified depersonalization and subordination in a December 1884 letter to the historian Francis Parkman. Describing democracy as the only subject for history, he declared that "I am satisfied that the purely mechanical development of the human mind in society must appear in a great democracy so clearly . . . that in another generation psychology, physiology, and history will join in proving man to have as fixed and necessary development as that of a tree; and almost as unconscious."[40]

Mrs. Lee's description of depersonalization and mechanization in *Democracy* implied the weakness and naivete of the chief executive. At the outset of his administration, the president vowed not to allow the senatorial clique of Ratcliffe and two associates who headed the party to dictate policy. The president's pretensions to independence and vigorous executive leadership angered Ratcliffe. Just as he had employed calculated managerial technique and manipulation through the party organization to secure the president's election, he now orchestrated his own appointment to the office of secretary of the treasury and imposed upon the new president the party's choices for other cabinet positions and other important offices.[41]

Such weakness in the chief executive was indicative. Adams had complained about Grant's failure to assert the power of a chief executive to rouse the House and the electorate to force the Senate to relinquish its power over the Executive secured through the Tenure of Office Act;[42] and it was just such leaders as Ratcliffe and his associates who had secured Hayes's elevation to the presidency in the disputed election of 1876.

The description of the president in *Democracy* probably was provoked by some of Adams's strongest antipathies. For him the most oppressive political entities that inhibited political leaders were the caucus and the political machine. In 1869 in his critique of the congressional session, the young journalist-reformer wrote that

> the condition of parties precludes the chance of reform. The "rings" which control legislation—those iron or whiskey, or Pacific Railway, or other interests, which have their Congressional representatives, who vote themselves the public money—do not obtain their power for nothing. Congressmen themselves, as a class, are not venal, it is true. . . . But though Congress itself has still a sense of honor, party organizations have no decency and no shame.[43]

It is significant that Ratcliffe, failing to secure the presidency, seized upon he office of secretary of the treasury. For Adams, as for many students of early national politics, economic dilemmas were the major problems of the young nation, and secretaries of the treasury had been the significant custodians of power and policy. This view was evident in Washington's appointment of Alexander Hamilton to the office, and it was Adams's thesis in his biography of Albert Gallatin.[44] When President Grant appointed the inept and partisan George S. Boutwell to the office, Adams was understandably appalled, and his doubts were confirmed by subsequent scandal and economic chaos.

Charles Vandersee made a provocative and no doubt valid point when he asserted that the idea of Ratcliffe probably originated when Adams was writing the biography of Gallatin, and that in *Democracy* he was contrasting Gallatin as the example of dedication and integrity in political leadership to Ratcliffe as the epitome of expediency in public office.[45] "The Treasury," according to Adams, was "the natural point of control to be occupied by any statesman who aims at organization or reform, and conversely no organization or reform is likely to succeed that does not begin with and is not guided by the Treasury."[46] Also, for Adams, making Ratcliffe secretary of the treasury emphasized Blaine's questionable financial dealings as exemplified in the "Mulligan Letters" scandal.

With reference to financial reform, Adams, in 1869, like his fictional reformer Nathan Gore, attempted, without success, to advise President Grant and the new Congress. In "American Finance, 1865–1869," published in April 1869 in the *Edinburgh Review*, Adams described how the previous Congress had failed to implement the secretary of the treasury's recommendation to resume specie payment. Instead, the Congress had surrendered to the protectionist persuasions of business leaders.[47] In a *North American Review* article that followed shortly, he was more specific: "But with a large surplus revenue, a rapid diminution of taxes, a reduction of interest on the debt and a decrease in its value, sooner or later the time must come when return to specie payments will be unavoidable."[48]

Adams was shocked at the apathy of Americans. In his youthful enthusiasm and reform zeal, he had expected a great relation to his exposé of lobbyists in the *Edinburgh Review*. But, as he noted later, his revelation alarmed no one in the United States, and only one English publication, a Yorkshire newspaper, took note of it.[49] From his early years Adams had been imbued with the idea that government was a moral agent to help men achieve virtue and that the Constitution embodied the moral law. Very quickly he came to realize that in the struggle between right and wrong in government, reform could fail, and that the "moral purport" of the Constitution might be in danger of being lost.[50] In his *North American Review* article that followed that in the *Edinburgh Review*, he described the nature and power of lobbyists and the difficulty of legislating reform: "the effort required to accomplish necessary legislation becomes more and more serious; the machine groans and labors under the burden, and its action becomes spasmodic and inefficient."[51]

In *Democracy*, Ratcliffe's blatant rationalization and manipulation of the president reflected the degree to which his personal detachment and his exploitation of party power contradicted human values and the representative process. In an effort to convince Madeleine Lee of his integrity, the senator emphasized that he had yielded his personal opinion to the will of the party. Adams probably was alluding to the compromises that party leaders supposedly made in the famous smoke-filled room at the Wormley Hotel that helped to resolve the disputed election of 1876. Madeleine Lee was intrigued. Had the senator never refused to vote with his party? Ratcliffe's negative reply evoked from her still another query: Did he put "party allegiance" ahead of everything else?[52]

In summary, Adams concluded that many well-meaning officeholders, like Ratcliffe, intended to serve the people but lost their grip on right and justice. Although corrupt, Ratcliffe prevailed. Adams, like his fictional Mrs. Lee and Carrington, retreated from the field of direct political endeavor. By virtue of the senator's strength both as a character and in terms of political reality, Adams grudgingly conceded that political leaders of his day became pragmatic and expedient.

Herein lies the crux of Adams's political critique. As George Hochfield stated, Henry Adams, like his grandfather, John Quincy Adams, believed that "government was a moral agent designed to aid man in the achievement of 'virtue.'"[53] Also, like his grandfather, the philosopher-historian evaluated all government in terms of the moral or immoral actions of individuals. He could not conceive of life as having meaning "apart from a goal that is outside of and larger than the individual."[54] Young Adams was profoundly shocked when President Grant did not measure up to this expectation: Grant did not confront the United States Senate and he did not name strong cabinet members.

One reason Adams was so disillusioned by Secretary of the Treasury Boutwell was his conviction that government should avoid debt and resist borrowing. As a reformer-journalist, Adams expounded pointedly on debt and borrowing in his *North American Review* and *Edinburgh Review* articles. Hochfield emphasized that debt and taxation especially hurt the small farmers and small businessmen, the very groups Adams's hero Gallatin had defended with his financial policies.[55] Boutwell, Adams wrote, encouraged questionable financial practices by failing "to wield the power of his office, and instead of stamping upon the President [Grant] and his administration the impress of a strong controlling mind, he drew himself back into a narrow corner of his own, and encouraged and set the example of isolation at a time when the most concentrated action was essential to the rescue of the Executive."[56]

The failure to hold high government office was a tragedy in Henry Adams's life, not only because his great-grandfather, grandfathers, and father had been able to do so while rising above party turpitude, but because party turpitude blocked Adams's aspirations for a similar career. Adams was drawn to Washington because the capital symbolized ultimate political power. Subconsciously, he craved political power just as Madeleine Lee came to covet political power. But, while Madeleine Lee fled in disgust when she witnessed the corrupting influence of political power, Adams orbited at the periphery of politics the remainder of his life, and despite his disillusionment, he cherished his early investigative-reportorial years in Washington.

Much to his chagrin, Adams's closest personal friends were involved with the very politics and politicians he so bitterly criticized. John Hay, his next-door neighbor and ambassador to England in the 1890s and secretary of state under William McKinley and Theodore Roosevelt, not only supported Blaine for the presidency, but developed an affection for him. Also, the notorious Pennsylvania politician and financial magnate, Senator James Donald Cameron, was a frequent guest in his Washington home, and, after Marian Adams's death, Cameron's second wife, Elizabeth, became Adams's closest female confidante and correspondent.[57] Henry Cabot Lodge, the highly partisan foe of Woodrow Wilson, was one of Adams's students at Harvard and his assistant editor on the *North American Review*.

The rise of partisan politics, the emphasis on party loyalty and the pressures of impersonal society convinced Henry Adams that the individual political leadership of Washington's and Jefferson's time was no longer viable. American democracy, which had never been perfect, would continue to be flawed because leaders were human and susceptible to the increased pressures defined by mechanization and depersonalization. Modern Americans would have to practice democratic politics in a broader and more subtle context; partisan party loyalty and pursuit of personal goals to the exclusion of social considerations would have to be corrected by education in more humanistic and socially oriented political values.

In his despair, Henry Adams, through his gentlemanly and cultivated reformer Nathan Gore, at least testified to this long-range educative hope implicit in democracy—that it raised the masses "to a higher intelligence than formerly." Government and public agencies should strive to sophisticate political comprehension: "I am glad," said Gore, "to see society grapple with issues in which no one can afford to be neutral." And if, in the final analysis, democracy was only an experiment, it was, nevertheless, "the only direction society can take that is worth its taking."[58]

Notes

Originally published in *Biography: An Interdisciplinary Quarterly*© (Volume 14, No. 4, 1991) by the Biographical Research Center.

1. Walt Whitman, *Specimen Days, Democratic Vistas, and Other Prose*, ed. Louise Pound (Garden City, 1935), 296.

2. Ernest Samuels, *Henry Adams, The Middle Years* (Cambridge, Mass., 1958), 69–97, esp. 69, 78, 81, 87–89.

3. J. C. Levenson, *The Mind and Art of Henry Adams* (Boston, 1957), 86.

4. Michael Colacurcio, "*Democracy and Esther*: Henry Adams' Flirtation with Pragmatism," *American Quarterly* 19 (Spring 1967): 55.

5. Charles Andrew Vandersee, "The Political Attitudes of Henry Adams," Ph.D. diss., University of California, Los Angeles, 1964, 148.

6. Melvin Lyon, *Symbol and Idea in Henry Adams* (Lincoln, 1970), 34.

7. Henry Adams, *The Education of Henry Adams* (Boston, 1919), 262.

8. Worthington Chauncy Ford, ed., *Letters of Henry Adams, 1892–1918* (Boston, 1938), 575.

9. Adams, *Democracy: An American Novel* (New York, 1880), 309. Adams began *Democracy* in 1878, and it appeared in March 1880. His authorship remained anonymous until 1921.

10. Adams, *Education*, 244–53.

11. Adams, *Democracy*, 146–47. One is reminded of a modern-day assessment of how a political leader is pressured by his adherents: "His plight resembles that of Red Cross girls on duty at a jungle island wartime base because the congestion of petitioners tends to keep all but the most ruthless and aggressive from reaching his presence. Attracting unattractive attention from unattractive persons tends to make him either a dogmatic misanthrope or a pushover, to turn him too far away from people and too close to principle, or to corrupt him" (Stimson Bullitt, *To Be a Politician* [Garden City, 1959], 75).

12. Adams, *Democracy*, 150.

13. Ibid., 152. Hamlin Garland attributed a similar feeling to Brennan, the king of the lobby. Brennan "felt a touch of weariness with his unscrupulous work," especially when he associated with respectable people. He confessed his inability to deal with political pressure: "The trouble is a man can't always say what he won't do." People who thought they "knew him best," said the author, were impressed by his "sincerity of passion" (Garland, *A Member of the Third House* [1892; rpt., New York, 1897], 29, 31).

14. Adams, *Education*, 261.

15. Adams, *Democracy*, 331. Adams concluded that many well-meaning officeholders intended to serve the people but lost their grip on right and justice. Similarly, Hamlin Garland's politician Davis understood his own plight better than the well-intentioned reformer Wilson Tuttle, who believed Davis to be innocent of lobby influence. Davis confessed that he had referred to Tuttle as a "scholar in politics" but admired his "grit and honesty." But then he explained, defensively, that Tuttle did not understand the pressure that Davis experienced (Garland, 29, 3).

16. Adams, *Democracy*, 75–76.

17. H. H. Gerth and C. Wright Mills, eds., *From Max Weber: Essays in Sociology* (New York, 1958), 125–26.

18. Adams, *Democracy,* 140–141. For an analysis of the President Washington imagery in *Democracy,* see C. Vann Woodward, *The Burden of Southern History* (Baton Rouge, 1960), 121–22; Lyon, 28–32; Levenson, *Henry Adams,* 94–95.

19. Vandersee, 117.

20. Adams, *Education,* 26–27.

21. H. Wayne Morgan, *From Hayes to McKinley: National Party Politics, 1877–1896* (Syracuse, 1969), 67–69.

22. Lyon, 249–50.

23. Irving Howe, *Politics and the Novel* (New York, 1957), 179–80.

24. William H. Jordy, *Henry Adams: Scientific Historian* (New Haven, 1952), 65.

25. Harold Dean Cater, ed., *Henry Adams and His Friends; A Collection of His Unpublished Letters, Compiled, With a Biographical Introduction by Harold Dean Cater* (Boston, 1947), 126.

26. Adams, *Democracy,* 10. For an analysis of Adams's political ideas, see Vandersee.

27. Vandersee, 142.

28. Adams, *Education,* 260.

29. Adams, *Democracy,* 12.

30. Ibid., 35.

31. Ibid., 37.

32. Ibid., 144.

33. Henry Adams, Henry James, and Francis Marion Crawford placed high value on the sensitivity and judgment of women and used women's "responding intelligence" in their novels. "Women," for Adams, "had instinct and emotion and could move from the promptings of the one to the actualities of the other without becoming lost or distraught in the midway bog of logic and fact" (R. P. Blackmur, *The Expense of Greatness* [New York, 1940], 267). James and Crawford exemplified their views in *The Portrait of a Lady* (New York, 1882 [1881]) and *An American Politician* (New York, 1906 [1884]), respectively.

34. Eugenia Kaledin, *The Education of Mrs. Henry Adams* (Philadelphia, 1981), 10–11. Immediately after *Democracy* appeared, there was wide speculation as to its authorship. One rumor that must have amused Adams was that his wife had written the book. In a letter to John Hay, January 7, 1883, he remarked that his sister-in-law Ellen Gurney heard "that Hon. J. G. Blaine at a dinner party in New York said that Mrs. H. A. 'acknowledges' to have written *Democracy.* You know how I have always admired Mr. Blaine's powers of invention!" (Ford, *The Letters of Henry Adams* [1858–1891] [Boston and New York, 1930], 345). When she

noted in *Democracy* the similarity of remarks about civil service reform to those in Adams's *North American Review* article (1869), Mrs. Humphrey Ward speculated that Henry Adams might have written *Democracy*. See Mary A. Ward, *Fortnightly Review* 32, n.s. (July 1, 1882): 78–93, as cited in J. C. Levenson, Ernest Samuels, Charles Vandersee, and Viola Hopkins Winner, eds., *The Letters of Henry Adams* (Cambridge, Mass., and London, England, 1982), 2:468 n.2.

35. Colacurcio, 55.

36. Levenson et al., 1:290.

37. Adams, *Education*, 421–22. Van Wyck Brooks recorded that "The tragic testimony of Henry Adams, looking back a century and a quarter later, was that this machinery [of society], instead of subsiding into its place as the servant of human beings, had become the soulless master, and that man had lost forever his grip on the rudder of his own destiny" (Van Wyck Brooks, *Sketches in Criticism* [New York, 1932], 198). In a letter to Edward Everett Hale, Feb. 8, 1902, Adams remarked that "Our century is gone, and if I can judge from the new one that I watch here, it has only a decorative use for us, and for our ideals, whether Washingtonian, Hamiltonian or Jeffersonian. We have created and established a new religion of Energy with a very big E, and of man with a very small m" (Levenson et al., *The Letters* [Cambridge, Mass., and London, England, 1988], 5:336).

38. Adams, *Democracy*, 86.

39. Levenson *Mind and Art of Henry Adams*, 87–88. Adams used the symbolism of mechanization when Madeleine Lee became convinced of Ratcliffe's duplicity and how she had been tempted by the lure of political power. She was "chilled . . . with mortal terror" that "she had barely escaped being dragged under the wheels of the machine, and so coming to an untimely end" (Adams, *Democracy*, 341).

40. Levenson et al., *The Letters*, 2:563.

41. Adams, *Democracy*, 80–82, 184–90.

42. Adams, "The Session," *North American Review* 108 (1869): 614–15.

43. Ibid., 617. "Party organizations in America have obtained a wonderful development and a dictatorial power. Resting as they must upon the most numerous and therefore the poorest classes of society, they undertake to account for the political opinions of every citizen. They are marvelously effective, but they are excessively costly, and they can be held together by two influences, money and patronage" ("American Finance, 1865–1869," *Edinburgh Review* 129 [April 1869]: 525).

44. Adams, "The Session," *North American Review* 111 (July 1870): 35.

45. Vandersee, 119, 141.

46. Adams, *The Life of Albert Gallatin* (Philadelphia, 1879), 267.

47. Adams, "American Finance," 504, 507–8.

48. Adams, "The Session," 622.

49. Levenson et al., eds., *The Letters*, 2:32, 37; Samuels, *The Young Henry Adams* (Cambridge, 1948), 180.

50. George Hochfield, *Henry Adams: An Introduction and Interpretation* (New York, 1962), 7.

51. Adams, "The Session," 611.

52. Adams, *Democracy*, 81–82.

53. Hochfield, 5.

54. Ibid., 32.

55. Ibid., 17.

56. Adams, "The Session," *North American Review* 111 (July 1870): 39.

57. Levenson et al., *The Letters*, 2:501; *The Letters* (Cambridge, Mass. and London, England, 1982), 3:285, 557.

58. Adams, *Democracy*, 77.

CHAPTER 3

Democracy and *Esther*: Henry Adams's Flirtation with Pragmatism

Michael Colacurcio

NO DOUBT PRAGMATISM IS, as William James insisted, a new name for some very old ways of thinking. Certainly few teachers of American literature can reserve the word specifically for the intellectual milieu of Peirce and James. The result is probably a lessening of the world's supply of clear and distinct ideas, but it seems somehow unavoidable when there are so many temptations. When Benjamin Franklin abandons the mechanical deism of his pamphlet *On Liberty and Necessity* because this doctrine, "though it might be true, was not very useful," most of us, I suspect, think "pragmatist." There is also Huck Finn's famous experience with the relationship between prayer and fishhooks. And more cogently there is Emerson; even if one shuns the Yankee-Plato view as too popular to be accurate, it is hard to overlook the famous pragmatic dictum in *Nature* that "the advantage of the ideal theory over the popular faith is that it presents the world in precisely that view which is most desirable to the mind." Evidently workability and human satisfactoriness are important to America's highbrows and lowbrows alike.

But one may recognize this evidence of a sort of pragmatism deeply rooted in the American character and still hesitate in the case of Henry Adams. Here it seems one ought to draw a line in order to keep the categories clear: no American, one could argue, ever searched more tirelessly for a single principle which, quite apart from human needs and wishes, would explain the ultimate Truth of the universe. Adams's final reading of all history in terms of the super-abstraction of "force" adequately suggests, even to those who read it metaphorically, the lengths to which he was driven in search of a totally objective principle of unified understanding. Indeed, one can scarcely read William James's defenses of "plural" explanations of the universe without almost imagining that his adversary is Henry Adams and not the idealist purveyors of the Hegelian Absolute.[1] Nor is it ultimately my purpose to overturn the well-established view of Henry Adams as an absolutist. Indeed, I shall end by supporting it—but, I hope, with important qualifications. For there was, as it seems to me, a very strong drive toward the practical, toward operation, toward power in Henry Adams; and more important, a very keen understanding of what would eventually become the philosophical position of William James.

Several critics have already noted in passing certain pragmatic tendencies in Adams's thought, chiefly in connection with *Mont-Saint-Michel and Chartres;* one even points to a direct connection between him and the members of the Harvard Metaphysical Club of the early 1870s where pragmatism as a coherent system was formulated.[2] The directness of this connection seems an open question, and in any case the clearest examples of Adams's pragmatist leanings are his two underrated novels. *Democracy* (1880) deals with pragmatism of a rather popular sort, a kind James would later single out as a gross misunderstanding of his doctrine. But *Esther* (1884), written fourteen years before James's official announcement (in "Philosophical Conceptions and Practical Results") of the name of his doctrine, and twelve years before the crucial "Will to Believe," seems to anticipate, sympathize with, but ultimately judge in advance the cardinal tenet of James's religious philosophy—that one may without dishonor, indeed everyone actually and necessarily does, give the assent of faith to propositions not susceptible of rational proof.[3] Thus even though Henry Adams must not finally be regarded as an adherent of Jamesean pragmatism, any more than of Franklin's shopkeeper morality or Huck Finn's fishhook theology, one important dimension of his interest for us must be his curious ambivalence toward the various American pragmatisms.

The kind of pragmatism that is central to *Democracy* is certainly not that espoused by James or by any of his followers. Senator Ratcliffe's harangues on the need to stuff ballot boxes in order to preserve the Union are far different in tone and intention from Professor James's lectures on the right to adopt beliefs that "help us to get into satisfactory relations with the other parts of our experience." Despite the persistent charge of hostile critics that

James made the *end* of favorable relations justify the *means* of adopting any belief whatsoever, his doctrine is in no sense reducible to a mere instrumental ethic.[4] But it is just this sort of worthy-end-justifies-base-means instrumentalism that seems to attract Adams in *Democracy.* The ultimate fact about the novel may be Madeleine Lee's categorical rejection of Ratcliffe, but surely the more striking one is the strength of her attraction to him in the first place.

Even if one resists the temptation to read the novel as scarcely veiled autobiography, one cannot avoid the conclusion that Madeleine Lee is a curious version of Adams himself.[5] Her essential problem—to accept or reject the Washington morality of power—had recently been Adams's own problem. Thus it must have taken considerable honesty and insight to create in Mrs. Lee the queer combination of idealism and ennui, reforming zeal and death wish, that brought her in touch with the temptation of political pragmatism. She can sound like Thoreau in expressing her desire to "get all that American life had to offer, good or bad, and drink it down to the dregs," but that is not her only tone. Like a passenger on a steamship who will not rest easily "until he has been in the engine room and talked with the engineer," she wanted "to see with her own eyes the action of the primary forces."[6] And she may have been, as the narrator suggests, "eating her heart out because she could find no worthy object of sacrifice" (4), but at bottom "what she wanted, was POWER" (12).

Clearly a confused woman at the opening of the novel, Mrs. Lee grows more so before she finally sees herself plain. She comes to imagine that absolute primeval power is not incompatible with a worthy object of sacrifice. With Ratcliffe presumably she can have it both ways: she can control the mysterious sources of the great American political and governmental processes and reform them too. And with her naive ideas about America's society of nature's noblemen, she is in an extremely dangerous position for one about to engage in "something very like a flirtation" with the incarnation of American "political genius." For, as it turns out, Ratcliffe and his expressed doctrine are extremely seductive: "there was a certain bigness about the man; a keen practical sagacity; a bold freedom of self-assertion; a broad way of dealing with what he knew" (60). He publicly crucifies the would-be wit Mr. French on the question of civil service reform; to his hard-headed realism it is only "a clock with a showy case and a sham works" (12). Under cross-examination by Mrs. Lee, who continues to hope that

"respectable government" is not "impossible in a democracy," Ratcliffe unflinchingly answers that "no representative government can long be much
better or much worse than the society it represents. Purify society and you
purify government. But try to purify government artificially and you only
aggravate the failure" (71).

This is bold indeed. It calls to mind a whole tradition of touch-minded
opposition to the idea of instant reform—Emerson, who distrusted the
Brook Farm experiment because it did not aim to leaven "the whole lump
of society"; Thoreau, who steadfastly defined that it was possible to "do a
man good"; and even Hawthorne, who carefully detailed the futility of reform that did not begin with "that inward sphere." Somewhat less favorably,
though still perhaps respectably, one may think of those social theorists of
Adams's own day who, stressing the deterministic development of society,
scorned "the absurd effort to make the world over." Actually Ratcliffe holds
none of these positions; he has, in fact, no position at all. But Madeleine
is kept ignorant of this fact. Adams himself was well aware of the authority such conservative positions might draw from the social implications of
Darwinism,[7] and for the sake of the novel's conclusion Madeleine is allowed
to be properly impressed.

Other characters offer her alternatives to Ratcliffe's view, but not
strongly, and she can only wonder, "Who and what is to be believed?" While
thus trying to discover "whether America is right or wrong" (a question
almost as simplistic as Esther's "Is religion true?"), she defends Ratcliffe's
operational compromises by denying that a consummately effective politician need also be a crusader. Her mind, perilously balanced between power
and sacrifice, is conspicuously tipping toward power. Mr. Gore senses the
drift of her thinking and, though embarrassed by the need to verbalize it,
offers her the "fixed star" of his own political creed: "I believe in democracy.
I accept it. I will faithfully serve and defend it. I believe in it because it
appears me to the inevitable result of what has gone before it. . . . I grant it
is an experiment, but it is the only direction society can take that is worth
taking; the only conception of its duty large enough to satisfy its instincts;
the only result worth an effort and a risk" (77). But this tentative, qualified,
evolutionary, trial-and-error doctrine is not the kind of absolute Mrs. Lee
requires. It is in its own way rather pragmatic.

Nor does the study of history offer Madeleine Lee any saving doctrine. More appealing than the present, perhaps, which is typified by a

mechanical nightmare of presidential handshaking, the mind of the past is nevertheless characterized by a hopeless fogging of political issues with "elaborate show-structures" of philosophy. Alongside these delusions Ratcliffe's position again seems seductively real: "He had very little sympathy for thin moralizing, and a statesmanlike contempt for philosophical politics. He loved power, and he wanted to be president. That was enough" (85). At an important crisis in Madeleine's judgment of him, Ratcliffe very ingenuously (as it seems) reveals his part in rigging a presidential election. The government, he argues, *had* to be kept out of the hands of the rebels; the Union *had* to be saved. "I am not proud of the transaction, but I would do it again, and far worse if I thought it would save the country from disunion" (107). This is strong stuff—the only dogmas concern undeniably good ends; the means are totally open. And its effect is not lost on Madeleine Lee.

Not even comparison with George Washington, the touchstone of unequivocal honesty in public life, can weaken Ratcliffe's appeal. Washington shows up lesser men who aspire to the ideal of political purity, but Ratcliffe lives in a different world. Pragmatism can judge virtue, but not the other way around. "If Washington were President now," Ratcliffe affirms, "he would have to learn our ways or lose the next election. Only fools and theorists imagine that our society can be handled with kid gloves or long poles. One must make one's self a part of it. If virtue won't answer our purpose, we must use vice, or our opponents will put us out of office" (141). Surely this doctrine is mature, adult, undeceived. Deep down, perhaps, Madeleine cannot fully accept Ratcliffe's doctrine of "accepting the good with the bad together," feeling that it is somehow "better to be a child and cry for the moon and stars"; but there is no doubt that she is being "tainted."

Adams is, of course, scoring satirical points at Ratcliffe's expensive throughout, and Madeleine herself is far from ignorant of the boorishness of his private nature. She herself puts him in his place a number of times. But she never sees him at his worst—as the petty, intriguing, political manipulator whose real motivation is not "the Union," nor even party loyalty, but only the crassest sort of unenlightened self-interest. Consequently she continues to deceive herself and believe the best of him. When Ratcliffe comes to her seeking "advice" on whether to accept a cabinet post, he has already decided how to trick the honest but naive new president into appointing him secretary of the treasury, despite the irreducible political and personal opposition between them. (He has also all but convinced Madeleine that politics has nothing to do with morality.) Thus when in his "simple, straight-forward, earnest" manner he asks for her opinion, she answers, baffled, that he should do "whatever is most for the public good." What *is* most for the public good Madeleine cannot decide; such questions are nearly always more tangled than those of "private right," and Madeleine's confession that "life is more complicated than I thought" is in effect a surrender to Ratcliffe's point of view.

From this point until her final reversal, Madeleine is much less hypothetical in her endorsement of Ratcliffe: "She reconciled herself to the Ratcliffian morals, for she could see no choice." She is never completely comfortable with a double standard of morality, but basically Ratcliffe seems to her to be "doing good with as pure means as he had at hand" (196). She is partly joking when she suggests to Mr. Gore that she has already taken the "first step in politics" by having "got so far as to lose the distinction between right and wrong" (199), but her judgment of herself is truer than she knows.

And thus, significantly, her latent sexual attraction to Ratcliffe now becomes more and more important; only after her evident fall from grace does she really become capable of marrying a man with whom, by education and native sensibility, she has nothing in common. Nothing, that is, except the love of power. Once she has denied the absolute primacy of the private moral imperative, she becomes capable of using Ratcliffe to satisfy her power-sacrifice-reform lust much as Ratcliffe uses everyone else. Evidently power morality corrupts absolutely. Madeleine continues to deny to her friends that she is in any danger of marrying Ratcliffe. She regards Carrington's hints about the senator's character as the moral fussiness of an incorrigible innocent. But to those strongly disposed to power, Washington is a dangerous moral climate indeed. Even as Ratcliffe proposes marriage to Mrs. Lee he makes a strong plea for his "position" that in politics it is utterly impossible to keep one's hands clean: "To act with entire honesty and self-respect, one should always live in a pure atmosphere, and the atmosphere of politics is impure" (309). Playing masterfully on Madeleine's mixture of motives, he asks her to be the domestic purity in his otherwise sordid life and, per contra, to take her rightful place in public influence. Nothing can now save Mrs. Lee from marrying a shabby political opportunist except Carrington's revelation of the blackest episode of Ratcliffe's career.

The knowledge that Ratcliffe once took a bribe for approving a bill he opposed "on principle" clearly shows Mrs. Lee that had she married the Prairie Giant her life would have been "an endless succession of moral somersaults." At first she is enraged, chiefly with herself—that she could almost agree to marry a "man who could take money to betray public trust." She guesses almost immediately that Ratcliffe will defend his action, but she also remembers his constant avowals that "if virtue did not answer his purpose he used vice" (335). The realization of the extent of her own involvement by "tacit assent," of her radically mixed motives, and of her "weakness and self-deception" results in a "helpless rage and despair," a wish that "the universe were annihilated" (337).

But Adams is not yet ready for an apocalypse, and by the time Ratcliffe pays his last call, Madeleine has recovered herself considerably. Carrington's letter had tried to demonstrate Ratcliffe's perfect unscrupulousness, his lack of morality of any kind; but Madeleine, idealistically, continues to grant him the integrity of his announced position—she tries not to judge what he had done "as a politician . . . according to his own moral code." She claims only the right to "protect herself." She tells Ratcliffe she has reverted to her "old decision," that there is too great a philosophical difference between them: "You and I take very different views of life. I cannot accept yours, and you cannot practice on mine" (347). On his side, Ratcliffe has ready a more or less convincing pragmatic justification of his action, the principle this time being "party loyalty"; his story is, of course, pure fabrication and would have brought out a "smile of professional pride" from his colleagues, had they been present. Madeleine, guileless, accepts the story at face value. She is never fully undeceived about Ratcliffe, and this is certainly a key fact in estimating Adams's exact attitude toward the crass sort of pragmatism he represents.

In a sense, the novel goes out of its way to have Mrs. Lee reject Senator Ratcliffe not as the self-interested blackguard he is but as a fairly consistent exponent of the whatever-*must*-be-done theory of politics. He repeats all his old generalities: constituents, party, people, Union. He takes his stand once again on the premise of complexity: "there are conflicting duties in all the transactions of life, except the simplest. However we may act, do what we may, we must violate some moral obligation" (356). He is so cogent, in fact, that Mrs. Lee loses her self-possession and retreats to the weaker ground that she is "not fitted for politics," she would be a "drag" on him. She grants his sincerity and urges only her wish to get away from politics. Her ideas, she admits, were naive; her standards of purity would, no doubt, mean the end of democratic government. Nevertheless, she insists, "we must at all events . . . use our judgment according to our own consciences" (362). Earlier, with Sybil, Madeleine had decided that Ratcliffe "talked about virtue and vice as a man who is color blind talks about red and green" (353), but this is not her final word. Now, granting him his position, and denying only its adequacy *for her*, she breaks with him only when he tries most blatantly to bribe her with the power of his eventual presidency.

That the book should come out in favor of private conscience over public good is not surprising. Even Madeleine's wish to "live in the Great Pyramid and look out at the Polar Star" (370) is predictable enough. The search for a stable reality and a fixed moral star is a characteristic Adams pursuit, and here the shifting, relative, equivocal morality of Ratcliffe calls forth, by reaction, the steady, the absolute, the univocal. But surely it is significant that Adams refuses to let the battle between Ratcliffe and Mrs. Lee ever be fairly joined on theoretical grounds. On the one hand, her rejection of him as a pragmatist and not simply as a villain tends to strengthen our sense of Adams's own rejection; but on the other, the failure to answer the pragmatic arguments themselves seems to suggest that in Adams's view they might be practiced without dishonor *by somebody*. Two things are clear: first that pragmatic political principles may often serve to make simple amorality seem respectable; and second, even if this is not always so, they will not long satisfy persons of the most refined moral sensibility. Beyond this, however, Adams is ambiguous. Perhaps successful government does depend on the rather free use of power by men more honest than Ratcliffe but less scrupulous than Adams.

Biographically considered, one might urge, *Democracy* dramatizes Adams's flirtation with the morality of Reconstruction politics; Mrs. Lee's experience seems to be Adams's recognition that, *for him*, private integrity and public power were incompatible. The conclusion was especially difficult to reach, and Adams hesitates to state it in general terms, because the history of the Adams family seemed to prove the opposite lesson. Nevertheless, in *Democracy* one can see Henry Adams consciously disciplining himself, trying to deal with what he considered the unruly drives in his nature. Power attracts, deranges the moral sensibility, as a strong man attracts an unstable woman. Evidently the best way to deal with such seductive temptations is to put them out of the mind entirely. Thus Adams's solution and

Madeleine Lee's were the same—flight from Washington. For although the conclusion suggests that Madeleine may come back to marry Carrington, the novel clearly *ends* with her departure. Nor would Adams ever return to Washington in a purely political capacity. Adams's conclusion in favor of absolute private integrity (even when it cannot explain itself) would be the same whenever he took up the question of morality and power—notably in the *Education*. But it would be no less difficult to reach, and it would be marked by the same ambiguities. The argument from expediency was not an easy one for Adams to overcome.

In *Esther*, the problem of expediency is raised in a specifically religious context. Although in one sense the novel is, as Ernest Samuels carefully shows, a tour de force on the relation of religion and science in the nineteenth century,[8] it is also, and perhaps more centrally, a study of the absolutist and the pragmatist attitudes toward religion. Hazard and Strong agree, after all, that there is no essential conflict between religion and science, and certainly neither feels such a conflict. For Hazard, everything is religious: all thought and all being rise up to and are included in the universal I AM. For Strong, everything is just as simply secular: religious experience is completely foreign to his nature. More important, the novel is about the conflict within Esther—and she knows and cares nothing about science. Her problem is not whether to believe in Hazard's theology or in Strong's archeology (and both clearly involve major acts of faith), but whether she may freely adopt faith at all, and if so, how to go about it. Esther's problem, in short, concerns the "will to believe."[9]

At stake, in terms proper to the late nineteenth century but susceptible of translation into more traditional ones, is the nature of faith. Is faith a completely mysterious, quasi-divine "free gift" which one, as if by election, either has or has not? Or is it in any sense acquirable by voluntary human action, either intellectual or devotional? Strong at first urges Esther to accept the mysteries of religion in the same way he accepts those of science: they lead on to more conclusions and to a generally satisfactory life-experience; and, by living them, one can make them true. Even the traditionalistic Hazard, faced with the prospect of losing the scrupulously honest Esther, urges a less than absolute acceptance of his church's dogmatic creed. And Esther herself tries, to the limit of her will, to will religious faith. Nothing happens. Once again the feminine character, symbol of Adams's deepest moral sense, rejects all halfway measures.[10]

Esther's rejection of the fashionable high churchmanship in Hazard's religion is, of course, very easy to predict; her inheritance of old William Dudley's "Puritan" force of character and simplicity of ethical vision takes care of that. But her waterfall worship is likely to seem a sport unless one sees that this ultimate antipragmatic action is also a vindication of her basic nature, which is as much pagan as Puritan. Adams works very carefully to describe the Esther who is about to face the serious temptation of pragmatism. Instinctively moral, and deadly serious about such matters as getting married or joining the church, she is often as spontaneous and uninhibited as a natural phenomenon. Hazard's opening sermon on the cosmological and historical omnipresence of the I AM does not touch her being: "I thought it very entertaining," she informs her aunt. "I felt like a butterfly in a tulip bed. Mr. Hazard's eyes are wonderful."[11] From the first her response is to Hazard and not to his church, and it is decidedly "natural." Wharton notices Esther's paganism almost immediately; to him she belongs "to the next world which artists want to see, when paganism will come again and we give a divinity to every waterfall" (29). This anticipation of Esther's final, spontaneous religion of nature is part of a pattern. Her charity—she visits the sick, a corporal work of mercy—is completely innocent of supernatural motive: "Esther got more pleasure out of it than the children" (52). She does not enjoy any aspect of Hazard's worship service, his preaching least of all; but the empty church building itself she finds a delightful place of "retreat and self-absorption, the dignity of silence which respects itself; the presence which was not to be touched or seen" (74).

The church is, for Esther, chiefly the scene of her "ecclesiastical idyl," a summer world of innocent art and love. Despite Hazard's "deep instruction on the inferences to be drawn from the contents of crypts and catacombs," she continues to care very little for "what the early Christians believed, either in religion or art" (93). And despite Wharton's stern lectures on art, religion, and life as struggle rather than joy, she continues to paint Catherine Brooke her own way—as the sanctity of naif and spontaneous joyfulness. In the end, everyone admits that her picture is totally out of keeping with Wharton's impressive medieval vision of the church but that it is nevertheless exactly right and perfectly true for Esther. Her idyl also includes translating Petrarch's sonnets (her version of Strong's heaven of reading novels in church), and falling in love with Hazard. But she grows no closer to the spirit of his Christianity. He may argue that the Christian

God embraces and includes all secular life, but Esther merely annexes His symbolic church into her own private world of innocent paganism.

The idyl ends abruptly with the intrusion of Wharton's degenerate wife and the death of Esther's father. One expects a certain transformation in Esther, but for all the obvious similarities and direct allusions to Hawthorne, this is not *The Marble Faun* revisited; Esther does not follow the prescribed course from innocent natural joy, to deadening spiritual gloom, to renewed Christian faith and hope on the other side of despair. That myth, indeed "as familiar as Hawthorne," might by its very familiarity have sufficed to shape the outcome of Esther's experience, but Adams is telling a different story—the inability of some souls to generate faith, even under the most favorable "Hawthornean" conditions, and even with a number of excellent pragmatic reasons.

Although Esther does not apply to Hazard for the conventional "religious help and consolation," she does, out of her vein of natural, feminine mysticism, talk with him about "the purity of the soul, the victory of spirit over matter, and the peace of infinite love" (160). But it soon becomes evident that, though they are in love, they are not talking the same language, and that Hazard's commitment to a religious creed stands between them. Again at his church, she finds the music sympathetic, but "parts of the service jarred on her ear," and she "began to take bitter pleasure in thinking she had nothing, not even religious ideas, in common with the people who came between her and her lover. . . . By the time the creed was read, she could not honestly feel that she believed a word of it, or could force herself to say that she ever could believe it" (171–72).

And yet this is precisely what she tries to do—generate a belief where none spontaneously exists. Her first confidante and adviser in this matter is Catherine Brooke. This charming and ingenuous "sage hen" from the pragmatic American prairie has very little sympathy with the niceties of Esther's ethical discriminations. The argument that Hazard's congregation constitutes a rival is easily disposed of: on the basis of her personal experience with the Calvinistic Presbyterianism of the American West, Catherine advises Esther to thank God she lives in a "place where your friends let your soul alone." Esther's scruple that she can never believe what Hazard preaches Catherine declares beside the point: "You never heard your aunt troubling her head about what Mr. Murray says when he goes into court." And yet cogent as Adams makes this seem, Esther rejects it for herself.

She continues to feel that if she is to marry Hazard she must believe in dogmatic Christianity. She does indeed want to marry him; and so in one sense, certainly, she wants to believe. Thus, despite Hazard's warning that her love will eventually settle the question of her faith, Esther sets out to learn theology. Catherine continues to advise the direct approach—"How many people at his church could tell you what they believe?"—but the matter is too serious for that, and Esther is led on in her study with a sort of fatal fascination that does not serve to increase her credulity.

The matter is also too serious to be answered by Strong's "droll" approach. Esther presses her cousin on the subject of religion as relentlessly as Madeleine Lee pressed Gore on democracy. "Will you answer me a question? Say yes or no! . . . Is religion true?" (198). This is precisely the question William James was refusing to answer either *yes* or *no*, to the consternation of his critics—this and the lesser questions that comprise it. Does God exist personally? Is the universe one or many? Is the will free or determined? Is the soul immortal? To answer absolutely James felt was impossible; to answer pragmatically—that is, in terms of the human meaningfulness of the various answers—he held to be not only legitimate but necessary. And Strong's first answer to Esther is cogently Jamesean.

Concerning the "truth" of religion he is not competent to answer directly, but science, he says is *not* true in the simplistic sense of her question. He personally does not "believe in it"; he "belongs to it" because he wants to "help make it truer." Religion seems to him an analogous case: "There is no science which does not begin by requiring you to believe the incredible. . . . I tell you the solemn truth that the doctrine of the Trinity is not so difficult to accept as any one of the axioms of physics" (199). Repeating the position of Catherine Brooke, he reminds Esther that the wife of his mathematical colleague never thinks to ask herself whether she believes a point has neither length, breadth, nor thickness. But Esther cannot square this pragmatic doctrine with Strong's habitual skepticism. She cannot believe he is serious, and to her this is a "matter of life and death."

Strong has not, however, been dishonest. His drollery is not irresponsible. He gives the impression of saying what, at one level of his mind, he really believes. But struck by Esther's extreme earnestness, he goes on to answer her from another level: "The trouble with you is that you start wrong. . . . You need what is called faith and you are trying to get it by reason. It can't be done. Faith is a state of mind, like love or jealousy. You can never reason yourself into it" (281). This, it hardly need be said, is precisely the doctrine of *Mont-Saint-Michel and Chartres*. There too Adams would flirt with the attractions of dogmatic religion as a life-philosophy: it must be true, look at the cathedrals it built. But his rejection would also be the same: the springs of faith lie deeper in the psychological makeup of man than either intellect or conscious will. However conclusively James might prove our *right* to adopt a rewarding belief, the problem of our *ability* remained and was by far the more important problem.

But before the ineffable absolute of Esther's private moral nature is finally vindicated, she must submit to a third pragmatic temptation, this time from Hazard himself. In their final interview, at Niagara Falls, she pleads her constitutional inability to accept dogmatic Christianity: "Some people are made with faith. I am made without it." But Hazard scoffs at this trifle of "common, daily, matter-of-course fears and doubts." It is, in his view, "a simple matter of will." Pressed to the limit of his apologetical skill, he offers her the example of his own deepest faith, based, as it turns out, on a version of Pascal's wager: "What do you gain by getting rid of one incomprehensible only to put another in its place, and throw away your only hope besides? The atheists offer no sort of bargain for one's soul. Their scheme is all loss and no gain. At last both they and I come back to a confession of ignorance; the only difference is that my ignorance is joined with both faith and hope" (241). As Ernest Samuels has pointed out, this is the way James's "Will to Believe" opens, and is, within the framework of his own highly original set of philosophical distinctions, the substance of his modern voluntaristic defense of faith.[12] A retreat of this kind, to the skeptical fideism of Pascal, represents quite a setback of Hazard. The sermon with which he opens the novel is as blatantly rationalistic as any page in Descartes and is full of Cartesian language. Pascal and Descartes, like St. Francis and St. Thomas, represented for Adams the polar opposites of Christian experience—the total distrust of human intelligence and consequent refuge in the absolute of faith on the one hand, and the confident assertion of reason's sure ability to establish the essential truths of religion on the other.[13] Thus Hazard's shift from the language of Descartes to that of Pascal represents a complete about-face, at least tactically, and brings the argument for religion into plainly pragmatic terms: grant that God and not-God are, in our ignorance, equiprobables; choose the more rewarding alternative.

But Hazard's pragmatism becomes even more ironic. Throughout the novel we are assured that Hazard's "orthodoxy was his strong point," and that "like most vigorous-minded men, seeing that there was no stopping place between dogma and negation, he preferred to accept dogma. Of all weaknesses he most disliked timid and half-hearted faith" (208). Esther herself has clearly seen these alternatives and has already rejected the "timid and half-hearted" alternative proposed by Catherine Brooke and George Strong. Now, shockingly enough, Hazard himself proposes it.

> "But I suppose you believe at last in something, do you not?" asked Hazard. "Somewhere there must be common ground for us to stand on; and our church makes large—I think too large, allowances for difference. . . . There are scores of clergymen today in our pulpits who are in my eyes little better than open skeptics, yet I am not allowed to refuse communion with them. Why should you refuse it with me? You must at last trust in some mysterious and humanly incomprehensible form of words. Even Strong has to do this. Why may you not take mine?" (291–92)

Here one expects the discussion to fly apart. Esther has already had her mysterical insight into "the next world [as] a sort of great reservoir of truth" into which "whatever is true in us just pours . . . like rain drops" (273). But she restrains herself until Hazard finally reveals the degree of restraint to which his partly selfish passion will subject her. Esther sees that, even were she capable of it, her pragmatic acceptance of faith would in this case mean a complete loss of freedom.

In a sense Esther falls back on a pragmatism of her own, deeper and more fundamental than Hazard's. She insists on the right to a belief and a style of life more congenial to her nature than what Hazard proposes. Thus in the quarrel that flashes up concerning the "fleshliness" of Hazard's Christianity, the question is not one of true or false doctrine. A *personal* God, the resurrection of the body, the real presence in communion—all these are simply distasteful to Esther, who finds the idea of self loathsome. As strategy, then, Hazard's final appeal to Esther's female instincts ("Can you . . . think of a future existence where you will not meet once more father and mother, husband and children?") is exactly wrong. Esther's unfleshly paganism has already found concretion in the impersonal force of Niagara Falls. Hazard's pragmatism seems to permit her to choose only absorption into the human and personal, say what he will about the infinite I AM. But

Esther's nature demands an absolute. From one point of view, her religion pays as much attention to human psychic need as his; but her highest psychic need is ultimate selflessness. Given this need, her final rejection of Hazard is as complete as Madeleine Lee's rejection of the infinitely more reprehensible Ratcliffe.

One is tempted to say that Adams, as did Esther, rejects one pragmatic doctrine and accepts another—without challenging the basic pragmatic assumption of the relation between human truth and human need. Certainly Catherine Brooke, George Strong, and (until the very end) Hazard are all sympathetic characters and make a strong statement of their case. Their advice to Esther is not, as I read the novel, irresponsible. The severe critics of Jamesean pragmatism, men like Huxley and Clifford, argued that belief in excess of evidence constitutes bad faith. This is certainly not Adams's position.[14] He actually goes far beyond James in asserting the degree to which even the "skeptical" scientist is forced to accept and endorse belief beyond the range of proof. And, as I have suggested, Esther's final position itself looks a little pragmatic.

But there is another way to state the case. Esther's acceptance of a paganism congenial to her nature is not so free as Hazard says his own acceptance of Christianity has been, or as the reader guesses it has been. One suspects that Hazard's arguments, whether out of Descartes of Pascal, are really quite after the fact. Hazard's orthodoxy and Esther's paganism seem equally, at bottom, biases of nature. It is probably safe to say that, were it possible for Esther to accept Christianity, it would also be moral. But the primary fact seems to be that it is impossible.

Esther finds that her will is as powerless as her intellect: one can will faith as little as one can reason it. Granted Esther *may* choose religion if she wishes; the problem is whether she really *does* wish. In fact, she both does and does not. She does insofar as she wishes to marry Hazard—a strong pragmatic motive indeed; but even stronger is another complex of wishes that do not entirely depend on her conscious will. Her puritan-paganism seems to put conventional Christianity beyond her range of real choices. For Esther Christianity is, in James's phrase, not a "live option." James admitted there might be persons for whom this would be so; and such persons were, of course, free to disbelieve. But James's exception becomes Adams's rule; James assumed the task of justifying belief, Adams tried to explain unbelief. For him, faith was investigated more profitably as an ability than as a right.

It is, perhaps, not much of a solution to say with Esther that some people are made with faith and some without, but on the whole this statement of the case seemed to Adams more honest, and more sound psychologically and theologically, than any other. For Adams, it appears, had already gone beyond James in the direction of anti-intellectualism. James stopped with the will; Adams went on to identify the locus of faith with the biological sources of consciousness. At this extreme faith turned out to be, as the church had always taught, a free gift.

If the evidence of *Esther* is biographically trustworthy, Adams felt the lure of Jamesean logic quite keenly. *If* the matter could really be seen as open to argument, then the arguments James was coming to use were valid. But more deeply he seems to have felt that the problem of faith was not an open question, and that James's prolonged effort to convince both scientists and clergymen that freely invested belief was honorable constituted misplaced ingenuity. One of his letters to James suggests as much.[15] Of course one could believe if one so willed, and of course the role of the intellect would be ancillary at best, but the determinant in belief and nonbelief could not be merely the will. If the will ceased to depend on the intellect for its motives, it would have to depend on, indeed be identified with, instinct. All this is merely to say that for Adams the problem of faith had ceased to be a moral problem and had become a psychological one. The ultimate explanation of Esther's rejection of religion is to be found as deep in the unfathomable recesses of subconsciousness as Madeleine's rejection of political opportunism. Neither can answer pragmatic arguments, and both have a strong desire to bend experience to their wills; but behind them both stands Henry Adams's commitment to the moral integrity of the individual's private nature.[16]

The pragmatism of *Democracy* is, of course, very different from that of *Esther*. They are alike only in their antidogmatism, their flexibility, their concern for the needs of practice as against those of pure speculation. But it is under this aspect that both had a certain appeal to Adams. The need to operate effectively in politics made some sort of operational compromise seem *almost* a necessity; and the constitutional need to view the world as a unity made the church an attractive option. Adams's characteristic anti-intellectualism—his doubt that reason had ever "got hold of one fact worth knowing," his frequently expressed trust in the superiority of instinct—made pragmatism, anti-intellectual in all its varieties, a tempting solution to a number of dilemmas.[17] But these anti-intellectual strains in Adams ultimately found a nonpragmatic expression.

Philosophical pragmatism, in its emphasis on truth as something partly created by the total living human personality rather than as something fixed, final, "out there," to be discovered merely, is obviously a forerunner of modern existentialism.[18] Both doctrines oppose the "block universes" of nineteenth-century ideology; both seek to destroy the idealistic notion of a Truth that exists in formulations prior to all experience and the notion of a Reason that alleges to discover such a Truth; both urge, against the tyrannical claims of speculative intellect, that truth must be a function of man as a unified subject of experience. One may argue that the reaction against ideology begins with the American pragmatists because of the unique effects of American experience: Americans seem always to have known that truths are forged in experience and that, in a sense, man makes himself. Culturally considered, American pragmatism, even of the Jamesean variety, may be as much an outgrowth of Franklin as a rejection of Hegel. However one assigns priorities, the complex of influence affected Adams and James in common.

But the late-nineteenth-century anti-intellectual reaction, fostered by the American experience, and given respectability by a Darwinian "logic of life," could take more than one direction. It could lead to a simple "dynamic" morality of primeval power, the appeal of which Adams examines in *Democracy.* Or, coupled with a lingering belief in free will and responsibility, it could become a defense of the purely voluntary religious option in a world where, more and more, intellectuality meant science, skepticism, and a purely secular response to the world; *Esther* seems to resolve Adams's ambivalence on this alternative. Or finally, and paradoxically, it might produce a determinist who was also a rigid moralist—in Herbert Schneider's famous phrase, a "desperate naturalist"; in such a case one would have to rest on the moral sufficiency of instinct pretty much unexplained and undefended.

Hence none of the pragmatic arguments of either *Democracy* or *Esther* is ever answered; they are allowed to stand as if possessing a certain abstract validity *as arguments*, and in novels of ideas this is certainly significant. But the reader is to feel these arguments as unavailable to the characters Adams most approves. Perhaps the logic of power is the only politically workable one—evidently certain things *had* to be done; but Madeleine Lee cannot accept it. Perhaps faith is the only salvation—the church alone, as Adams would demonstrate to himself in *Mont-Saint-Michel,* stands for unity; but Esther cannot accept it. Nor, in either case, could Adams. He could never accept either the determinist or the voluntary logic by itself. He could not feel that even the Jamesean pragmatism was completely faithful, as it claimed to be, to both objective scientific and subjective religious logic. And because Henry Adams could not stop pursuing either one, his novels flirt with, but do not espouse, any form of pragmatic doctrine.

Notes

Colacurcio, Michael, "*Democracy* and *Esther*: Henry Adams' Flirtation with Pragmatism," *American Quarterly* 19:1 (1967): 53–70. © The American Studies Association, Reprinted with permission of The Johns Hopkins University Press.

1. Lecture Four of *Pragmatism,* "The One and the Many," asserts that to the radical empiricist the world "is neither a universe pure and simple nor a multiverse pure and simple" but that "its various manners of being One suggest, for their accurate attainment, so many distinct programs of scientific work"; this surely, if indirectly, comments on Adams's attempt to find a single, scientific explanation of history.

2. Robert Hume has argued that, for Adams, "illusions carefully erected may well be honored for their convenience though not for their assured objective truth" (*Runaway Star* [Ithaca, 1951], 190); more cogently, perhaps, J. C. Levenson has observed that "with his pragmatic method, [Adams] 'proved' religion by its power to get things done" (*The Mind and Art of Henry Adams* [Boston, 1957], 271). Levenson also suggests that "Adams had more than a casual acquaintance with the founders of pragmatism" (130), but it is easy to overstate this connection. Peirce makes no mention of Adams in his report on the makeup of the Metaphysical Club (See Ralph Barto Perry, *The Thought and Character of William James* [Boston, 1935], 1:534–35); and although Adams was at Harvard during the height of the club's activity and was a member, with James, of an almost equally distinguished dining club, it is unlikely that he took part in the discussions that hammered out the early versions of pragmatism. His most significant connection with that philosophy, also mentioned by Levenson, may well have been his publication (in the *North American Review* for October 1871) of Peirce's seminal article on Berkeley.

3. In asserting the primary of the ethical and the religious in James's philosophy, I am attending primarily to *motive.* Though an epistemology probably lies at the technical center of his system, that system is obviously less rigidly a logical doctrine than Peirce's (see Perry, *Thought and Character,* 538–42); and James's intention, as expressed in "The Present Dilemma in Philosophy" and

"What Pragmatism Means," is clearly to find a way to be religious without ceasing to be scientific.

4. One might begin the study of James's efforts to make himself absolutely clear to his critics in the "Author's Preface" to *The Meaning of Truth* (1909). This had been preceded by A. O. Lovejoy's "The Thirteen Pragmatisms," which may have suggested to James that in the long run intelligent opposition to his system would stress not its "immorality" but its ambiguity (see *The Journal of Philosophy* 5 [1908]: 5–12, 29–39). James had steadfastly refused to dissociate himself from the average philosophical man; with characteristic honesty and good humor, he adverted to the popular elements in his thought by repeatedly talking about the "cash value" of ideas and about his pragmatism as a "practicalism." In doing so, unfortunately, he seems to have encouraged a less sophisticated understanding of his doctrine than it requires; even Peirce objected to his loose formulations and renamed his own doctrine "pragmaticism."

5. For a full reading of *Democracy* as roman à clef, with a convincing discussion of its biological implications, see Ernest Samuels, *Henry Adams: The Middle Years* (Cambridge, 1958), 68–97.

6. Henry Adams *Democracy* (New York, 1933), 10. Hereafter cited parenthetically.

7. The key work on the implications of Darwin in American social theory is, of course, Richard Hofstadter's *Social Darwinism in American Thought* (Boston, 1955). A useful briefer discussion of Darwin's influence on Adams and on the other philosophical minds of the period is Perry Miller's introduction to *American Thought: Civil War to World War I* (New York, 1954).

8. *Middle Years*, 218–58. Samuels is especially helpful in his identification of the personality and doctrine that lie behind Stephen Hazard and his insightful comparison of *Esther* with Hawthorne's *Marble Faun*. This connection is far more significant than the vexing one of what Adams meant by choosing his heroine's name from Hawthorne's "Old Esther Dudley."

9. "The Will to Believe," delivered as a lecture to the Philosophy Club of Yale and Brown universities in 1896, is, in my view, the clearest statement of the religious import of James's philosophy; accordingly that essay forms the basis of my comparison between Adams and James. Also central, of course, is "Pragmatism and Religion," the last essay in *Pragmatism* (1907).

10. For a discussion of Adams's view of the superiority of women and their instinctual natures, see E. N. Saveth, "The Heroines of Henry Adams," *American Quarterly* 8 (Summer 1956): 234–42.

11. Henry Adams, *Esther*, Scholars' Facsimiles and Reprints (New York, 1938), 11. Hereafter cited parenthetically.

12. *Middle Years*, 255–56. In "The Will to Believe," James carefully explains

that the "logic" of Pascal works only if the particular faith in question represents a "genuine option"—being "live" (really attractive), "forced" (based on a complete disjunction), and "momentous" (making noticeable life-differences).

13. I have discussed Adams's attitudes toward the intellectualist and the fideist strains of Christianity in an article based on the last three chapters of *Mont-Saint-Michel and Chartres*: "The Dynamo and the Angelic Doctor," *American Quarterly* 17 (Winter 1965): 696–712.

14. James quotes both men in "The Will to Believe." According to his self-defense there, the Huxley-Clifford position amounts to an unexamined acceptance of the axiom that it is "better [to] risk loss of truth than chance of error"; there is, he argues, no more *reason* to accept this than its opposite.

15. A possible source for *Esther* is to be found in Adams's letter to James of July 27, 1882 (see Harold Dean Cater, *Henry Adams and his Friends* [Boston, 1947], 121–22). Commenting on James's "Rationality, Activity, and Faith," Adams writes: "As I understand your faith, your X, your reaction of the individual on the cosmos, it is the old question of free will over again. You *choose* to assume your will is free. Good! Reason proves that the will cannot be free. Equally good! Free or not, the mere fact that a doubt can exist, proves that X must be a very microscopic quantity." As Ernest Samuels suggests, the tone of Adams's letter indicates an argument with self as much as with James (*Middle Years*, 233). Similarly, Adams's markings in his copy of James's *Principles of Psychology* reveal the objections of one who would, but could not, be convinced (see Max I. Baym, "William James and Henry Adams," *New England Quarterly* 10 [1937]: 717–42).

16. This unexplained absoluteness in Esther's decision is the center of an article by Millicent Bell ("Adams' *Esther*: The Morality of Taste," *New England Quarterly* 35 [1962: 147–61), who complains that, for a novel of ideas, *Esther* is uncommonly private. Referring to Yvor Winters's famous essay on Adams (see *In Defense of Reason* [Denver, 1947]), she associates Esther's "ethical instinct more refined than that of the church" with "the Protestant conscience severed from its support in theology and forced to operate by the rule of faith alone" (153).

17. As Ernest Samuels has noted, Strong's disparagement of man's intellectual history echoes Adams's own slur on James's respect for great men: "Not one of them has ever got so far as to tell us a single fact worth knowing" (Cater, 122; quoted in *Middle Years*, 232). Although Adams's boundless energy for investigation always makes him seem an enthusiastic and even idealistic intellectual, his failures and frustrations led him more and more to express philosophical ideas that are, as Yvor Winters has shown, profoundly anti-intellectual.

18. A helpful introduction to the various reactions against nineteenth-century ideology is Morton White's "The Decline and Fall of the Absolute," introductory to *The Age of Analysis* (New York, 1955).

CHAPTER 4

Henry Adams's *Democracy*: Novel Sources of Democratic Virtues

Denise Dutton

PUBLISHED ANONYMOUSLY IN 1880, Henry Adams's *Democracy: An American Novel* was an "instant bestseller."[1] In *Democracy*, Adams chronicles the quest of wealthy New York widow Mrs. Madeleine Lightfoot Lee to get "to the heart of the great American mystery of democracy and government."[2] Bored with her stultifying life in aristocratic circles, she wishes to see "the tremendous forces of government and the machinery of society at work" (14). And so she moves to Washington, D.C., establishes a fashionable and lively salon, and takes particular interest in "the high-priest of American politics," Senator Silas P. Ratcliffe (26). While serving partly as her tutor and partly as the subject of her study, Senator Ratcliffe exposes Mrs. Lee to the more unseemly side of politics: he confesses to having helped rig an election; he rationalizes the buying and selling of public office; he exaggerates the meanness of politics in his accounts to Mrs. Lee in order to throw "his own [vulgar] qualities into relief" and to "rouse her sympathy" (92). He unashamedly declares his own personal ambition for power and admits to being willing to use vice, when virtue won't do, to accomplish his purpose.

Well-versed in the practices of power politics, Ratcliffe successfully teaches Mrs. Lee that, amidst the personal ambitions, incompetence, and corruption at play in American politics, the public interest is seldom identified, let alone served. But he fails to persuade her of morality's irrelevance to politics. As the subject of her study, Ratcliffe disconcerts her with his Machiavellianism. She resists his rationalization of vice and presses him for an adequate explanation as to why moral statesmanship is neither possible nor desirable. She momentarily considers accepting his marriage proposal, in part because it might allow her to reform his moral judgment, and through him, the political process itself. But the novel climaxes with Mrs. Lee's realization of Ratcliffe's "moral luna[cy]": when she learns that the senator has sunk so low as to demand bribes in exchange for votes for certain legislation, she abandons her vain ambition to reform either him or the politics of the day (180). What Mrs. Lee learns from Ratcliffe and what she witnesses in Washington lead her to conclude that democracy is "nothing more than government of any other kind" (175). She quits her political education, bitterly lamenting that "nine out of ten of her countrymen would say [she] had made a mistake" in her decision to preserve her virtue rather than pursue the power and prestige of a marriage to Ratcliffe (190).

This lament, literally getting the last word in the novel, privileges Mrs. Lee's concluding disillusionment and encourages readers to interpret *Democracy* as a condemnation of the political practices animating American democracy and as a disparagement of the poor judgment of the voters who elect the politicians who betray the people so reliably. Indeed, much of the novel advances an explicit and serious critique of democracy. Political corruption propels the plot forward; party patronage reduces the notion of public good to greedy self-interest and political intrigue. Elections are rigged in the name of preserving the Union; the halls of Washington "reek with the thick atmosphere of bargain and sale" and "wealth, office and power are at auction" (63). Positions of public importance are distributed perversely to those "who hate with the most venom" and "who intrigue with the most skill" (63). The people, who supposedly elect their representatives, are either willfully ignorant of, or irresponsibly apathetic about, these political practices that pursue everything except the public good. Ninety percent of them, Mrs. Lee estimates, either are incapable of recognizing virtue as its own reward, or prefer the temptation of power.

The similarities between Adams and his heroine further support this interpretation of *Democracy* as a scathing critique of the failure of America's novel experiment in self-government. Like Mrs. Lee, Adams engaged in politics only at a distance: he, too, declined to partake in the pomp and circumstance of White House dinners; and he also preferred the intimate company of his salon to the public debates in Congress. As we know from *The Education of Henry Adams*, he incessantly searched to find adequate guides for right action, and this search, much like Mrs. Lee's search for a moral code in politics, yielded something akin to her disillusionment with the good intentions of reform efforts and her realization that she "could do nothing sillier" than undertake such reform (184). Adams seems to vindicate his own principled refusal to enter into politics on the terms by which it was practiced when he has his heroine resolve to "quit the masquerade" of democratic politics in order to preserve her moral senses (175). Through Mrs. Lee's disillusionment with democracy, Adams seems to both express and justify his own political pessimism.[3]

Without denying that Adams criticizes much about American democracy, I wish to resist this temptation to assume that Adams endorses Mrs. Lee's resignation from democracy and that he shares her disparaging judgment of it. By too closely associating Adams with Mrs. Lee, we risk missing his critique of her refined high-mindedness. Despite his empathy with her longing to purify politics, Adams depicts Mrs. Lee as guilty of moral posturing. She misrepresents her personal ambition to power as self-sacrificing devotion to duty. And Adams exposes how her moral rationalizations used to justify the pursuit of political power are as corrosive to the integrity of democracy as Ratcliffe's disregard for moral principle altogether. Teasing out how Adams characterizes Mrs. Lee as a less than heroic heroine and Senator Ratcliffe as a less than villainous villain, I labor in the first section of this essay to distill the constructive recommendations Adams offers in the course of satirizing both its corrupt practices and feeble efforts at reform.

Below, I argue that by critically exposing the similar shortcomings of the wealthy and righteous Mrs. Lee and the powerful and self-interested Ratcliffe, Adams warns the reader against insisting, as Mrs. Lee does, on an answer to the question of "whether America is right or wrong" (45).[4] It is partly right and partly wrong, and the inability of these two main characters to recognize and respond to America's ambivalence leads them both to prematurely foreclose on the distinctive moral promise of democracy. Adams urges his readers to resist their unwarranted conclusions, and in so doing, he affirms the responsibility, as well as the capability, of the common American citizen to help determine the success and legitimacy of our experiment in self-government.

When *Democracy* was first published, this affirmation was more readily apparent. Not knowing Henry Adams to be the author, an acquaintance of the Adamses wrote that the novel struck him as a profound and ardent assertion that "America made the only solution worth having to the problem of government."[5] Through the opposing temperaments of Ratcliffe and Mrs. Lee and their shared tendency to exhaust the moral promise of democracy, Adams depicts the precarious nature of this solution. But at the same time, Adams enlists a whole host of secondary characters who testify to, and evince, the promise of America's solution. In lieu of abstract moral reasoning and practical political calculation, these supporting characters turn to their personal attachments, professional aspirations, and concrete duties in order to successfully navigate the often-conflicting demands of moral principles and political action. Their personal ties to others draw them outside of themselves. In contrast to the solitary nature and proud independence of both the wealthy Mrs. Lee and the powerful Ratcliffe, these secondary characters work in concert with one another to accomplish their aim. Despite the fact that none of them holds any formal positions of power, they succeed, and they do so without having to sacrifice their moral integrity. With their ability to cooperate across generational, professional, and temperamental differences and to rightfully discharge competing obligations, these secondary characters affirm the moral promise of democracy. Their example helps us to imagine how it yet may be that "social morality, rather than reason or science, provide[s] the hope of the world."[6]

In the second part of this essay, I focus on two of these secondary characters: Sybil, who is Mrs. Lee's younger sister, and Carrington, who, as an old family friend, introduces the ladies to Washington society.[7] Though Adams doesn't present them as the novel's heroes, the naive but sincere Sybil and the dignified but self-effacing Carrington end up serving that role. Despite Sybil's disinterest in politics, despite Carrington's lack of wealth and influence, and despite their differences in age, temperament, experience, and interests, Sybil and Carrington successfully cooperate, against all odds, to secure the triumph of virtue (Mrs. Lee's integrity) over vice (her own ambition for power and Ratcliffe's manipulation of it to his own advantage).

Sybil's and Carrington's concern for Mrs. Lee and their respect for one another are fueled by a compassion that contrasts sharply to the lonely ambition that drives both Mrs. Lee and Ratcliffe and to the calculating interests that shape their relationships. In her conversations with Carrington, Sybil reveals a depth of insight and strength of character that we don't expect from such a giddy socialite; in return, Sybil's company elicits from Carrington an expression of heartfelt emotion and youthful spontaneity foreign to his usual stiff dignity. The way in which they interact, along with their simple determination to protect Mrs. Lee, provides the most persuasive example for why democracy "is the only direction society can take that is worth its taking" (46). In Sybil and Carrington, I hope to show, Adams offers us models for how ordinary men and women might redeem democracy from its corruption at the hands of wealthy interests, ambitious politicians, and pretentious dogmatizers.

Democracy, Adams suggests, is distinct because it is that polity where the individual person, rather than power or wealth or status, ultimately exercises influence.[8] If each person matters, then Mrs. Lee is indeed mistaken in her resignation from democratic life and her unwillingness to engage it in all its complexity. Despite the many reasons to disparage democratic politics, Adams affirms that American democracy may yet be right, if only we can distinguish the claims of duty from the pursuit of self-interest, and the personal from the selfish. Something greater than self-interest and more personal than abstract principle is needed. And that something is found neither in Ratcliffe's resignation to the politics of the day, nor in Mrs. Lee's retreat to her "true democracy of life," which remains only an abstraction (175). Instead, it is found in the supporting characters' varied, sincere, and ever precarious efforts to discern and discharge their duty to one another.

Adams's political satire, as I read it here, engages less in a critique of democratic politics than in a recasting of the distinctive nature and moral character of democratic society. Instead of looking, as Mrs. Lee does, to the halls of government, where all is "wasted effort and clumsy intrigue," to see if America is right or wrong, Adams directs his readers' attention to alternative democratic spheres—namely the salon at Mrs. Lee's house and the hallowed ground of Washington's Mount Vernon (105). In these social settings, sincere intellectual inquiry and genuine personal attachments lead ordinary men and women to conceive of, and discharge, their duties toward one another in ways far more admirable than our normal conception of democratic politics allows us to imagine. Through Sybil and Carrington in particular, Adams inventories the common talents and ordinary virtues that are all too easily overlooked and underestimated when democratic practice is reduced to the pursuit of individual self-interest. When he invests Sybil and Carrington with the awesome responsibility of averting the tragedy anticipated by the novel, Adams seems to propose that the fate of democracy ultimately turns, not on political reform, but rather upon our willingness to recognize our duties to one another as free and equal citizens.

Heroine and Villain: A Warning against the Insufficiency of Individual Judgment

Mrs. Lee is the first character we meet, and we are immediately entrusted with her most intimate confession: she is "tortured by *ennui*" (9).[9] Since the death of her husband and child, "she had become serious," unable to find amusement in New York society and unfulfilled by the philanthropies and charities whose effect struck her as inconsequential (9). Being brought into such a confidence, the reader quickly sympathizes with Mrs. Lee. And by attributing to her a determination to find an "object worth a sacrifice," Adams renders her just as readily admirable (10). There is something noble to her deep yearning to rediscover a purpose to her life, to seek out how she might best be of service to her fellow man. Even as this yearning gives voice to the universal question that haunts all self-conscious beings, there is something distinctly heroic about her restlessness to adequately respond to it. She resists the easy comfort of convention and any mind-numbing retreat into routine. In contrast to her shallow acquaintances, who are insensible to her longing and who deem her interest in the political world "ridiculous," Mrs. Lee appears all the more praiseworthy: she trusts her own independent judgment rather than slavishly seeking the approval of others (9).

As the main protagonist, Mrs. Lee is certainly likeable and capable, and she displays heroic qualities. On more than one occasion, her social grace and generous hospitality solve a political conundrum or help avert a diplomatic crisis. Her critical objections to democracy's shortcomings labor to call America to its best formulation by offering constructive corrections. Struck dumb by the "strange and solemn spectacle" of the president and his wife receiving guests, "their faces stripped of every sign of intelligence," Mrs. Lee chastises her home country for "its droll aping of monarchical forms" (50–51). She worries that "this was to be the end of American society; its realization and dream at once," critically warning Adams's reader against the social pretenses, personal vanities, and trivial concerns colluding in democratic politics to degrade men to nothing more than "toy dolls" and to render individuals but a shadow of themselves (50–51).[10] And yet, even as she advances such a pressing internal critique, she also ardently (and literally) defends the talents and promise of American society against the condescending judgment of English nobility and the mean estimation of party politics advanced by Ratcliffe (69).[11] In the end, we can't help but applaud her climactic refusal of Ratcliffe's marriage proposal, a proposal that would, in all likelihood, secure for them both their ambition to live in the White House. Her own refusal to be seduced by the promise of power testifies to the capacity of democratic government to distinguish itself from "government of any other kind" with its refusal to allow material might to determine principled right (175).

But however talented and praiseworthy Adams renders Mrs. Lee, he also attributes to her some of those same self-serving vices more promi-nently associated with the villain Ratcliffe. Like the power-hungry senator, Mrs. Lee is ambitious for herself. "What she wanted was *power*," Adams writes, "however strongly she might deny it" (14). And her "first great politi-cal discovery in Washington," Adams reveals, is the pleasure to be found in exercising power (49). "To tie a prominent statesman to her train and to lead him around like a tame bear" provides "amusement" to Mrs. Lee (49). Weighed against Ratcliffe's frank admission "that the pleasure of politics lay in the possession of power" and that "he loved power, and he meant to be President," Mrs. Lee's calculated efforts to secure influence over the great statesman seem more Machiavellian than any of Ratcliffe's intrigues (50). Under the pretense of seeking to be useful herself, Mrs. Lee seeks to make use of Ratcliffe; "flatter[ing] him to the extent necessary for *her* purpose," she wanted "to bring up from its oozy bed that pearl of which *she* was in search" (26; emphasis added). She cleverly schemes to subject Ratcliffe to her own ends. She "willfully allow[s] the Senator to draw conclusions very different from any she actually held," and she easily quiets the doubts raised by her conscience with reference to the nobility of her cause and the integrity of her character (26). She is, in short, not only ambitious but also duplicitous.

The general public quickly attributes these vices to her. They gossip that she is "cold-blooded" and "heartless" and "ought to be ashamed of herself" for so indecently and eagerly pursuing "the first candidate for the Presidency" (54–55). While Adams partly defends Mrs. Lee against such vicious gossip, he confirms their suspicions as true. He softens the harsh-ness of the accusation by attributing it to the idle gossip of envious wives of rival politicians. Yet, as the novel progresses, Mrs. Lee becomes less pleased with herself for the exact reasons that public opinion says she should be ashamed. However ungenerous the public is toward her, Adams reveals the public to be prescient in its gossip about her ambitiousness. Similarly, the initial impression of Mrs. Lee as courageously independent recedes. Where once "she vowed that she would pursue her own path . . . without regard to all the malignity and vulgarity in the wide United States," she increasingly presents herself as a victim of forces beyond her control (55). She bemoans that her immersion in politics has only led her to lose the "distinction between right and wrong" (105). But this complaint, of course, isn't entirely true. At the very beginning of her study of politics she is already adept at blurring, if not dissolving, this distinction, as she reveals by cleverly manipulating Ratcliffe. She avoids an open and honest self-assessment of her driving motives and particular actions by emphasizing her general longing to see right principles rule and her disappointment in learning "no straight road was to be found [in politics], but only the tortuous and aimless tracks of beasts and things that crawl" (92). She judges others harshly, condemning politicians as snakes for lacking "a principle to guide" (92). Yet, she declines any responsibility herself of determining right action in a complex world.[12] She can neither identify the public good nor advise Ratcliffe how best to act on its behalf; at the same time, she proudly refuses to adjust her longing to see right principles rule to the limitations of the political context in which she wants them to govern (94).[13]

Just as Adams taints his heroine with the villain's vices, so too does he redeem Senator Ratcliffe with some respectable virtues. In contrast to Mrs. Lee's calculated flattery of the senator in order to establish her influence over him, Senator Ratcliffe displays genuine and deep feelings for Mrs. Lee. In a moment of reflection, feeling "out of sympathy" with "political life," Ratcliffe longs to escape his position: "he would have given his Senatorship for a civilized house like Mrs. Lee's with a woman like Mrs. Lee at its head. . . . He felt that Mrs. Lee was more necessary to him than the Presidency itself; he could not go on without her; he needed human companionship. . . . He felt unutterably lonely" (81–82). In this moment, Adams humanizes Ratcliffe, who feels rather than schemes, his cold political calculation giving way to pure and simple sentiment. And, falling for Mrs. Lee because of the virtues he attributes to her, Ratcliffe loves that which is good simply because it is good. His affection for her as the very model of virtue renders his desire for her assistance and advice in political affairs more genuine and less self-serving than his later schemes suggest. We even sympathize with him in his loneliness. His yearning resonates with the same sort of loneliness that made Mrs. Lee serious and drove her to move to Washington in the first place.[14]

Though he later manipulates Mrs. Lee's weaknesses (for example, her need to be useful and her unacknowledged ambition for power herself), in this moment Ratcliffe recognizes and admires Mrs. Lee as a woman of principle. That he is willing to sacrifice his personal pursuit of power for a private life with her companionship moderates the extent to which we celebrate his romantic defeat. For when Mrs. Lee rejects his marriage proposal, he is not just the ambitious politician thwarted; he is also the lover spurned.

In addition to this sincerity that sharply contrasts with Mrs. Lee's manipulative flattery, Adams attributes to Ratcliffe a frankness that contrasts with Mrs. Lee's duplicity. Of course, his frankness isn't the virtue of honesty. He, too, is guilty of duplicity. He intentionally deceives and manipulates the newly elected president in order to secure his party's interest; he purposefully plays on Mrs. Lee's devotion to duty in order to manipulate her to his own advantage; and he instinctively lies to himself about the extent of his secret intrigues and deceptions. Like Mrs. Lee, he avoids a full accounting of his self-serving motives. "Like most men," the narrator explains, "he did not stop to cast up both columns of his account with the party, nor to ask himself the question that lay at the heart of his grievance: How far had he served his party and how far himself?" (81).

But unlike Mrs. Lee, Ratcliffe takes responsibility for his expectations of politics. He admits to being guided by party loyalty; he defends his allegiance to party (and the patronage it requires him to practice) on the grounds that it provides him with the best guidance for calculating "what is most for the public good" and serving his nation (48). He openly admits to "loving power," and to wanting to exercise more of it by becoming president (50). He doesn't pretend to be unique in his ability to use power well; he is satisfied that his desire for power justifies his pursuit of such high office. However distasteful we may find his understanding of politics, he at least avoids engaging in political hypocrisy and pompous self-importance.

In this light, Ratcliffe's consistent and public impatience with "thin moralizing" strikes the reader as a reasonable and responsible response to the hypocrisy and presumption that Adams exposes as animating Mrs. Lee's search for first principles (50). Ratcliffe confesses to her, long before she feigns shock at the revelation that he took a bribe, that he is willing to engage in immoral actions for the sake of power. Since, in his formulation, power is necessary to further principles, Ratcliffe reasons that "if virtue won't answer our purpose, we must use vice, or our opponents will put us out of office" (76). Indeed, in one of his first conversations in Mrs. Lee's parlor, Ratcliffe admits to stuffing ballot boxes in order to ensure the election of President Lincoln. He genuinely and persuasively reasons that the good of preserving the Union justified such electoral fraud (61). With this example, Adams forces his reader to recognize a justification for Ratcliffe's practical politics and the merit of its accomplishments. However many intrigues he may be behind, it is no secret the sort of political game he plays; and at least one of these intrigues shows the positive consequences of playing politics by his rules.

Of course, Adams doesn't go so far as to recommend Ratcliffe's approach to politics. He intones Ratcliffe's defense of it with great sarcasm, ironically labeling Ratcliffe a statesman because he avoids "the foolishness" of President Washington's model. Adams exposes Ratcliffe as the fool instead, inviting the reader to scoff at Ratcliffe for mistaking Washington's virtuous attention to duty for the vice of "think[ing] much of trifles" and "fuss[ing] over small matters" (75). Still, in another passage, Adams subtly but significantly concedes that Ratcliffe, however objectionable in his character, may actually deserve our sincere praise. He asserts "Ratcliffe was a great statesman," citing "the smoothness of his manipulation [which] was marvelous. No other man . . . in politics in this country, could—his admirers said—have brought together so many hostile interests and made so fantastic a combination" (85–86). The language in this passage is cautious; Adams clearly resists directly praising Ratcliffe's success at building coalitions by "fantastically" promising everyone everything. The impossibility of fulfilling such unrealistic promises reveals Ratcliffe's intention to renege on his promises. Still, Adams acknowledges that the building of coalitions is a political good, indeed, a necessity in democracy. Adams even goes so far as to concede that Ratcliffe's success in securing these necessary coalitions depends upon the very vice that renders him so objectionable: "the skill with which he evaded questions of principle" (86).

Adams, of course, doesn't encourage us to perfect this skill. He clearly intends for us to be relieved when Ratcliffe's corruption is exposed and his designs on Mrs. Lee are thwarted. At the same time, I believe Adams intends to praise Ratcliffe as skillful, not just crafty, so as to blur the distinction between the moral zeal exercised by Mrs. Lee and the unprincipled power politics practiced by Ratcliffe. The plot suggests as much, reaching its climax when it exposes the hypocrisy of Mrs. Lee's high-mindedness.

The plot turns less on the fact that one of Ratcliffe's political intrigues is exposed—since no one but Mrs. Lee is surprised by this revelation—and more on Mrs. Lee becoming fully aware that "in the depths of her soul very different motives had been at work: ambition, thirst for power, restless eagerness to meddle in what did not concern her, blind longing to escape from the torture of watching other women with full lives and satisfied instincts, while her own life was hungry and sad" (171).

To be sure, this revelation does much to restore the reader's esteem of Mrs. Lee. Once she realizes her error in judgment, she displays the grace to be "more angry with herself" than with Ratcliffe. She finally takes responsibility for her own "self-deception," courageously standing up to Ratcliffe and resisting the temptation of power that his proposal promises (170–71). And yet, this revelation also vindicates Ratcliffe's impatience with thin moralizing in politics. Responding to her abhorrence at his willingness to take bribes and rig elections, Ratcliffe argues that "however we may act, do what we may, we must violate some moral obligation" (182). Mrs. Lee assumes from this line of argument that his moral senses have atrophied from disuse. But in light of his initial conversation with her, during which he justified his rigging of an election as an act of patriotism, her outrage at his stance is unpersuasive. Ratcliffe accuses her principled resignation from politics of being morally irrelevant and irresponsible. He insists that "if all true men and women were to take the tone you have taken, our government would soon perish" (184). To this charge, Mrs. Lee gives no adequate reply.[15] And in her silence Adams reveals the inadequacy of *both* Ratcliffe's disregard for principled conduct and Mrs. Lee's insensibility to the consequences of inaction. Neither main character deserves the reader's emulation, and in their shared shortcomings Adams offers instructive caution.

In their final exchange, both characters suffer from too narrow a sense of their own duties. The moral compass Mrs. Lee so self-consciously employs relies too heavily on abstract principle, just as Ratcliffe's disdain for moralizing relies too heavily on rationalizing what is expedient as public virtue. Though clearly guided by disparate moral orientations, both invoke the sovereignty of their own judgment.[16] Both insist that "all that can be asked of us is that we should guide ourselves by what we think the highest" (182). But both are misguided in their application of this principle to their daily decisions. Both err in their discernment of their duties because neither thinks anything is much higher than themselves.[17] Each, in their own way, is too self-absorbed, too dogmatic: Mrs. Lee in her quest for right, and Ratcliff in his quest for power.

Adams intimates that their solitary nature accounts for much of their mistaken exercise of individual judgment.[18] Both Mrs. Lee and Ratcliffe are regularly described throughout the novel as disconnected, self-absorbed, willfully distanced, if not disconnected, from their colleagues and friends. Ratcliffe is "preoccupied with his own interest," hiding behind the "pretense of work" to draw a curtain "between himself and the world" (64, 80). Mrs. Lee is introduced as "pure steel" insensitive to the outcome of events, and Adams reminds us regularly that she has "long since hardened herself" against personal attachments (13, 136). Fearing the vulnerable position of losing those closest to us, she keeps even her sister at a distance. Mrs. Lee's "hardness of heart" and Ratcliffe's "cold head" and "strong will" impoverish their understandings of duty (63, 57). Eschewing the affection of family and friends, they both rationalize their ambition for power or their desire to control events as the only way to live purposefully. In their obsession with their own personal quests, both Mrs. Lee and Senator Ratcliffe embody a warning against not just crude ambition, but more emphatically against the ancient vice of hubris. In Mrs. Lee's disillusionment, as well as in Ratcliffe's downfall, Adams admonishes the sort of individual judgment that is so certain of itself, and wholly wrapped up in itself, that it presumes either to exempt itself from, or impose itself upon, the collective judgment of society.

Undeniably, Adams casts Mrs. Lee in a more favorable light. He allows her to recognize her own self-deception, to check her own craven ambitions, and to abhor the ease with which such ambitions lurked behind her sincerely pursued good intentions. But, when she bitterly laments that the public judges her unfairly and foolishly, Mrs. Lee reveals that her own judgment remains partial and self-serving: she simply can't see beyond herself. The general public judged more correctly than she did, both her own motives and Ratcliffe's character. There seems no reason for her to disparage their judgment, except insofar as it allows Adams to reaffirm Ratcliffe as fairly accurate in his judgment of Mrs. Lee as a "hard critic," unreasonable in her expectations and irresponsible in her refusal to give advice (93).

Indeed, there really is no reason for Mrs. Lee to be bitter at all. Every member of her salon, save Ratcliffe, supports her and celebrates her rejection of his marriage proposal. She is rich with friends who all had a hand in helping her arrive at this decision. "The real moral" of *Democracy*, according to an intimate friend of the Adamses who knew Henry Adams to be the author, "is that in a democracy, ALL good, bad, indifferent are thrown together in the circling eddy of political society, and the person within the whole field of view who has the least perception, who most sadly flaunts her inability to judge of people without the labels of old society" was Madeleine Lee.[19] Her unwarranted despair and unpersuasive indictment of democracy are not conclusions for the reader to adopt, but well-intended mistakes the reader is meant to learn from so as to be able to avoid.

Mrs. Lee begins well enough. Against the backdrop of her shallow existence and mindless routine in New York's high society, Mrs. Lee's courage to follow her conscience in search of living more deliberately and significantly illustrates the distinctive dignity available only through democratic government. As a free and equal citizen, she possesses the opportunity to think and act for herself, to judge for herself how best she may serve her society and her state.

But her instinct for self-sacrifice wastes the opportunity democracy presents. Instead of seeking to be self-authorizing and civically responsible, her interest in politics misleads her into the foolish quest to gain "mastery over her surroundings" (15, 136). She strives to impose order on democratic society without deigning to be a part of it. Her search for mastery and her dissociation from her friends and fellow citizens pervert her sovereign individual judgment with too much self-certainty and too little reciprocity. As the novel ends with her pretension to judge her fellow citizens as poor judges themselves of right action, Adams cautions against mindless condemnations of democracy. Such judgments are neither correct nor helpful. Ratcliffe exposes the errors in Mrs. Lee's final critique: he forces her to admit "life is more complicated than [she] thought," and her silence in reply to his final challenge reveals that she lacks the courage to live and act amidst such complexity (94). Adams calls us, as his readers and fellow democratic citizens, to face such complexity with greater resolve. Such uncertainty and ambiguity not only render our own individual judgment necessary, but also enlist such independently free and morally responsible democratic citizens in the project of providing their own remedies to the shortcomings of democratic politics. Far from expressing contempt for the people through Mrs. Lee's disdain for democracy, Adams uses her character to admonish the pretense to mastery that degrades the democratic principle just as much as Ratcliffe's moral paralysis and complacency with the status quo thwarts the realization of democracy's distinctiveness.

The Secondary Characters: A Lesson in the Merits of Common Sense and Sympathy

Luckily, Mrs. Lee's righteous idealism and Ratcliffe's practical politics are not the only models Adams provides his readers. With democratic élan, Adams employs a host of secondary characters whose moral judgment, discernment of duty, and political effectiveness far surpass Mrs. Lee's and Ratcliffe's. The two secondary characters who best model alternative ways of acting both rightly and effectively in democracy are Miss Sybil Ross, who is Madeleine Lee's sister, and Mr. John Carrington, who, having been "a distant connection of her [late] husband, called himself a cousin" (18). They are the true heroes of the novel, successfully conspiring to rescue Mrs. Lee from her disastrous pursuit of power. Their conspiracy is really nothing more than a simple alliance between friends. Unlike the complex political intrigue Ratcliffe conducts to tie the hands of the incoming president, Sybil and Carrington unite openly and intimately, not for their own gain but out of a common concern for the well-being of Mrs. Lee.

They first attempt to rescue Mrs. Lee by having Carrington steal her away from Ratcliffe. Carrington genuinely adores Mrs. Lee, so there is no deception here. While their scheme initially appears to advance Carrington's own self-interest, because Carrington knows Mrs. Lee so well, he rightly anticipates her unwillingness and inability to accept his affection, let alone reciprocate it. "Feel[ing] acutely the harm he was doing to his own interests," Carrington proceeds to warn Mrs. Lee against Ratcliffe (138). So certain that his counsel is biased by his unrequited love of her, she pays no heed to his warning. All the same, Ratcliffe recognizes Carrington, whose trustworthy character Mrs. Lee rightly respects, as an obstacle to his designs on Mrs. Lee. When Ratcliffe succeeds in securing a government post out West for Carrington, Sybil is left with the lonely and weighty responsibility for executing their Plan B (142). Should Ratcliffe propose to Mrs. Lee, Sybil is simply to reason, entreat, and then beg her sister to reject him. Should that fail, Carrington entrusts Sybil with a highly confidential letter, the contents of which will hopefully dissuade Mrs. Lee from uniting with Ratcliffe. This secondary plan succeeds. When Sybil rightly suspects Ratcliffe to be proposing, she intrudes on the conversation and prudently whisks Mrs. Lee away. Mrs. Lee recognizes that her sister has rescued her from an uncomfortable conversation. But Mrs. Lee, still so certain she knows what is best, dismisses Sybil's objections to the proposed union as nothing more than a spoiled child throwing a tantrum. Fantastically linking one wrong and self-aggrandizing assumption to another, Mrs. Lee rationalizes that it is her duty as a sister to marry Ratcliffe: once married, she's unavailable; seeing she's unavailable, Carrington will fall in love with Sybil; and Sybil, Mrs. Lee incorrectly surmises from her recent melancholy, pines for Carrington's affections.

Sybil, rightly perceiving Mrs. Lee to be impervious to right reason, delivers Carrington's letter. In it, Carrington betrays a professional confidence. He tells Mrs. Lee of an instance when Ratcliffe hijacked a bill in committee and held it for ransom. He exposes Ratcliffe's willingness to betray the public trust for money. And this description of the vulgar and greedy side of Ratcliffe's practical politics finally persuades Mrs. Lee to dissociate herself from him. She is moved, in the end, neither by Carrington's noble affections nor by the loving concern of her sister. Where their admirable actions and sincere acts of friendship leave her unmoved, moral outrage and disappointment with the meanness of the world convince her both of the dangers of a union with Ratcliffe and of the darker ambitions that drove her to pursue him in the first place (138, 167).

In this turn of events, we encounter again the dangers of Mrs. Lee's abstracted reasoning: in her need to keep others at arm's length and in her effort to remain independent, she presumes the right and the power to control events. But with Sybil and Carrington, Adams shifts tone, balancing his cautionary warning against Mrs. Lee's tragic hubris and insensitivity with a hopeful recommendation of the simple resolve and compassionate determination that fuel the alliance between Sybil and Carrington. Adams tells us that Mrs. Lee learns from Sybil and Carrington what she would have known had she possessed more common sense and had she retained the capacity to feel.[20] Contrasting Sybil's common sense with Mrs. Lee's quest for "first principles" and "extravagant notion about self-sacrifice and duty," Adams subtly casts doubt on the merit of a too rigorously intellectual idealism (117). Sybil "never troubled herself about the impossible or the unthinkable. She had feelings . . . she was equally quick in getting over them and she expected other people to do likewise" (113). While we might mistake this ability to resist deep and sustained reflection as a flaw in individuals charged with the awesome exercise of political sovereignty, Adams reminds us of its merits here. Sybil's natural sympathy with the world around her renders her thoughtful of others in ways that are easy to overlook. It fuels a spontaneous gaiety that may all too easily be misread as frivolousness, and it expresses a trust in the world that may all too easily be mistaken for shallowness and naivete. But such natural sympathy yields a deep recognition of, and instinctive respect for, the fact that each individual possesses their own experiences of, and disappointments with, this world. And this recognition prevents Sybil from presuming, as Mrs. Lee does, the power to control those experiences or the responsibility to alter them. Similarly, Sybil's common sense disciplines her independent judgment with a focus on concrete facts and particular situations. Trusting appearances and contented with her situation, Sybil has no desire to decipher the "great American mystery of democracy," but she acts in it more effectively and democratically than Mrs. Lee, whose habit of self-introspection distorts, rather than deepens, her understanding (13, 113).

Sybil's capacity to feel and to see grounds her judgment and lends it an admirable flexibility. Though Mrs. Lee thinks it her duty to take care of her younger sister, Sybil, who recognizes that she is one of her sister's projects, turns out to be simultaneously capable of acting as Mrs. Lee's guardian. While admittedly uninterested in and naive about politics, Sybil's sincere engagement with, and response to, life's circumstances make her not only a better judge of character than Mrs. Lee, but also better able to influence events than her sister, who seeks to master them. Adams notes, "Sybil, without being a metaphysician, willed anything which she willed at all with more energy than her sister did, who was worn out with the effort of life" (178). Without describing Sybil as heroic, Adams esteems the practical power of her common sense and sincere sympathies. The fact that such ordinary and simple talents enable Sybil to play the indispensable role in rescuing Mrs. Lee suggests that, contrary to Mrs. Lee's condescending conclusion, the politically naive but personally sincere many who comprise the public possess the capacity to judge rightly, and to act effectively, to preserve democracy's honor.

Of course, Sybil's actions effectively influence the plot of the novel only after she enters into an alliance with Carrington, who is as thoughtful as she is spontaneous. By revealing Sybil's depth of character and powerful influence within the context of this alliance, Adams reminds us of the wisdom possessed by common sense, without going so far as to denigrate the merits of intellectual curiosity and sustained inquiry about first principles. Through Carrington, Adams offers an example of how the moral senses, informed by feeling and common sense, need not atrophy with the accumulation of political experience, be silenced by rational reflection, or be abdicated with the loss of innocence. In contrast to Sybil's character, Adams invests Carrington with a temperament similar to Mrs. Lee. He, like Mrs. Lee, has suffered serious hardships in his life. As a former rebel soldier, Carrington can be said to have lost a way of life with the defeat of the Old South. A Virginian whose sympathies lay with the Union cause but who fought for the Confederacy all the same, Carrington knows all too well what it means to feel torn by conflicting duties and to be called to sacrifice one's self for a worthy cause. But unlike Mrs. Lee, Carrington neither deceives himself about his own ambitions nor mistakes his duties to others with his own need to be useful. There is nothing duplicitous or self-serving in his devotion to his duty. So, for example, though he "feel[s] acutely the harm he was doing to his own interest," he still directly warns Mrs. Lee against Ratcliffe (138). But when she asks him if he "know[s] anything against him [Ratcliffe] that the world does not," Carrington resists the temptation to divulge what he knows, even though such a divulgence would probably advance his own personal desires (136–37). He resists confiding to Mrs. Lee his private reasons for why he "thinks so ill of Mr. Ratcliffe," until sharing such confidential knowledge is the only option left (137).[21] Carrington agrees with Mrs. Lee that "we must at all events . . . use our judgments according to our own consciences," but he exercises his conscience far more responsibly than Mrs. Lee (185). And I think he is able to do so in part because he, like Sybil, retains the capacity for sympathy.

This capacity for sympathy is one of the few characteristics Sybil and Carrington share. At its most general, it seems to be a sympathy for the human condition; both Sybil and Carrington accept the world as it is without becoming fatalistically resigned to it or bitterly resentful toward it. More specifically, their courage to act responsibly in this world and to invest themselves in it, given its complexities, uncertainties, joys, and disappointments, displays a willingness to engage another person's perspective and to feel for them. The distinctiveness of this virtue is perhaps best discerned in contrast to Mrs. Lee. Carrington's commitment to right action in his personal and political life is instructively free from the hardening of heart that provokes Mrs. Lee's curiosity about politics. He loves Mrs. Lee in a selfless way, in contrast to Mrs. Lee's selfish need to be of use to some worthy cause. He knows the aches entailed by the loss of things loved, and yet he pledges to love Mrs. Lee, "whether [she] cares for him or not" (135). In the course of his making such a pledge, Mrs. Lee recognizes him as "her superior" (136). Though less wealthy than Mrs. Lee and rejected by her, Carrington is a "true man" because he carries "his burden calmly, quietly, without complaint, ready to face the next shock of life with the same endurance he had shown against the rest" (136). Mrs. Lee seems to praise Carrington precisely for his capacity for sympathy with this all-too-human life. And such praise amplifies Adams's warning against the dangerous insufficiency of unmoored individual judgment. As we have seen, Mrs. Lee's judgment fails when her moral reasoning resists the pull of personal affections and disdains particular contexts. Mrs. Lee confesses to feeling herself a fraud in comparison to Carrington. Where he humbly endures life's trials, she strives to limit her vulnerability to them. She wants power, but when she realizes how she has abused that power, she quits democracy altogether. In contrast, Carrington shows no interest in either grabbing power or abdicating influence. His dignity as a "true man" arises from his steady resolve to accept the "constant responsibility and deferred hope" presumed by, and necessary to, democratic life (136, 19). Such resolve seems to be the heroic feat yielded by a capacity for sympathy.

In this spirit of moderated expectations and tempered disappointments, Carrington accepts a government post that he doesn't wish to take. He suspects, and rightly so, that Ratcliffe arranged the appointment to dispose of Carrington's influence over Mrs. Lee. But since he is unable to confirm his suspicion, Carrington dutifully accepts the position because of the higher salary it affords. At first glance, such a claim—that one's duty may be to accept a higher salary—sounds disingenuous. Adams, I think, intends it to give us pause. We expect to have to choose between what is right and what is expedient, between our duty toward others and the pursuit of our own self-interests, between whether we'll accept virtue as its own reward or not. The main characters dogmatically insist that we take sides. Through Carrington, Adams complicates our expectation and their insistence. For Carrington, on most, if not all, occasions, does what he ought to do, and is rewarded for it in some significant way, even as the duty demands a sacrifice from him. In this particular instance, Carrington's dutiful acceptance of a higher salary really does demand a sacrifice. If we didn't know him so well—and we wouldn't know him so well if it weren't for his alliance with Sybil that invites his confidence—we might suspect he indulges here in Mrs. Lee's habit of rationalizing one's desires as self-sacrificing duties. But we do know him. And sympathizing with the financial hardships and familial tragedies that have befallen his mother and sisters since the war, we rightly esteem him for resisting the temptation to use his obligation to defend Mrs. Lee's virtue as an excuse to decline the post and stay in Washington in order to pursue his romantic yearnings.

Carrington's calculation of duty here critically contrasts with Mrs. Lee's "saint[ly] capacity for self-torment" (146). In contrast to her abstract reasoning that rationalizes as right that which advances her ambitions, Carrington's cautious weighing of his options effectively distinguishes his duty from his desires and reveals a straightforward path by which to fulfill his duties without failing Mrs. Lee. Through Carrington, Adams demonstrates that reasoning about right action needn't conflict with the responsibility to secure good consequences. Through Carrington's alliance with Sybil, Adams presents an alternative to Ratcliffe's depiction of politics as a zero-sum game. And with these examples, he whispers to his reader that democratic life offers its citizens something more than the opportunity to coldly calculate and pursue one's self-interest.

Adams invites the reader to imagine what this something more is, especially when his characters take a day trip to Mount Vernon and entertain the merits of President Washington's statesmanship and its relevance to contemporary democracy. By likening Carrington to President Washington, Adams privileges Carrington's voice and uses him to distill what democracy, as a morally dignified and dignifying ideal, requires of us and secures for us. When Mrs. Lee first meets Carrington in Washington, she "trusted in him by instinct. He is [her] idea of George Washington at thirty" because he "never talked or seemed to think of himself" (19). Mrs. Lee's natural instincts here are spot on: he proves himself to be both self-effacing and selfless. Other characters also recognize him as the model of Washington.[22] They turn to him in search of an explanation of Washington's universal appeal. Why he is revered by not only his fellow Virginians but also by "New Englanders who never were country gentleman at all, [who] never had any liking for Virginia," and who even wondered, "What did Washington ever do for us?" (73).[23]

The answer Adams has Carrington give serves to instruct both the characters in the novel and the reader of the novel in what right action specifically looks like in American democracy. Washington, Carrington suggests, embodies the abstract virtues of "Morality, Justice, Duty and Truth" because of his careful attention to concrete details. Washington dissects his particular duty to each individual he encounters (73). He is frugal in money matters, Carrington explains, taking pains neither to be overcharged nor to underpay. In contrast to using money to buy elections, Washington weighs and reweighs his purchases; he purchases only what he can afford; he insists on providing the change due rather than extending a credit and becoming indebted to another; and he insists on paying the fair value of the goods he consumes, even when this fair value is more than he is charged (74–75). He is worthy of our reverence, in short, because "he carried his rules of virtue down to a pin's point" (75). Such consistent application of general principles to each particular interaction one freely enters into is the epitome of integrity. While it requires much care and attention, it doesn't demand self-sacrifice. Quite to the contrary, Carrington intimates that had all Virginians followed Washington's model of fairness and frugality, the Old South would have been able to sustain its way of life.

Carrington's description of Washington serves two purposes: Carrington hopes to "lay a little trap" for Ratcliffe that will expose his moral paralysis to Mrs. Lee, and Adams hopes to provide a portrait of Washington's principled relations that his readers may undertake to emulate (74). Ratcliffe, as we've already seen, fails to see any virtue in Washington's devotion to detail. He dismisses the anecdotes as examples of fussiness rather than virtue; he refuses to believe that any Virginian "did not die insolvent"; and he brags that the unsettled West from which he hails "is a poor school for reverence" (74). Ratcliffe's inability to appreciate Washington's distinctive virtue exposes, if not to Mrs. Lee then at least to the reader, the limits of his political realism. First, such practical politics inhibits Ratcliffe's imagination. Because he traffics in the vices of human nature, constantly searching for, and preying on, others' weaknesses, the fairer side of human nature and our capacity for virtue sound fantastic to Ratcliffe. But even if conceivably possible, Washington's model remains wholly foreign to him. For Ratcliffe, democratic politics was contained by that "clash of interests"

Mrs. Lee travels to Washington to observe (14). He lives in the age of the political machine where power and influence are bought and sold precisely to gain an advantage over others. If Washington really was as virtuous as history tells us, then Ratcliffe reasons "he was no politician" and must have "stood outside of politics" (76). But Washington's model reminds us that democratic aspirations aim not merely at advancing one's self-interests, but more profoundly at securing and safeguarding liberty. Washington accepted the responsibility that falls to all individuals in democratic society: to act freely on equal terms with one's fellow free citizens. Washington's concern with what Ratcliffe mistakenly calls mere "trifles" served to protect his independence and to resist imposing on another's independence or mistreating another as a means through which to gain his own advantage (75).

Carrington's plan to expose Ratcliffe's corrupted notion of politics succeeds only in part. Ratcliffe's inability to appreciate Washington's virtue, his skepticism about the effectiveness of Washington's virtue, and his insistence that such virtue would fail in the party politics of his day, all disconcert Mrs. Lee. In fact, his inability to be moved at all by Washington's statesmanship is what seems to provoke Mrs. Lee to worry about the status of her own moral integrity. At the same time, Adams suggests that Mrs. Lee is in part convinced that Ratcliffe is "right in accepting the good and bad together" (78). She is genuinely conflicted between her moral intuition that statesmen *ought* to follow Washington's principled model and her political observation that personal ambitions and party intrigues *actually* determine the course of democracy. By emphasizing Mrs. Lee's discomfort with Ratcliffe's disregard for virtues in politics, Adams intimates to the reader that, however compelling, and even unavoidable, Ratcliffe's practical politics may be, it remains incomplete.

It remains incomplete because a man like Washington exists in Carrington. His presence in the novel, his diligence in dutifully looking out for his mother, sisters, and late friend's wife (Mrs. Lee) and her sister, prove that "we might produce men [like Washington] still if we had the same field for them" (71). Though such men may be only rarely elected to power, and though Carrington lacks a position of influence, his personal influence testifies that democracy still depends on such men (and women) of integrity. In addition, Carrington and Sybil's ultimate success in the novel affirms that such principled devotion to duty can indeed triumph over the schemes of those willing to make recourse to vice when virtue won't do.[24]

Admittedly, the fact that their simple right action triumphs over Ratcliffe's complex intrigues does not assure us that virtue will always triumph over vice. After all, Ratcliffe's political intrigues successfully advance his position and power. But the success of their alliance does affirm that their trust in right action is neither a foolish guide destined to be trumped, nor a mindless retreat from our responsibilities in this complex world.

Adams insists on the incompleteness of Ratcliffe's position by reminding the reader of the limits of politics. Ratcliffe concedes this point when he offers a justification for his impatience with political reformers. There he reasons that "no representative government can long be much better or much worse than the society it represents. Purify society and you purify the government" (43). But where Ratcliffe justifies his base political practices as suited to the society they govern, Carrington and Sybil demonstrate that democratic society deserves better politicians and warrants more respectable political practices. They wield only the power of compassionate devotion to a friend, and their success in saving Mrs. Lee confirms the priority given to the social over the political in a liberal democracy. To amplify the importance of social relations and the influence of personal duty, Adams depicts Washington's model statesmanship as being wholly focused, not on the political duties of democratic office, but rather on the reciprocal duties of free and equal individuals in democratic society.

The unexpected partnership between Sybil and Carrington testifies to the creative power unleashed by trusting in our capacity to discharge these duties. Their alliance confounds expectations, and pleasantly surprises us.[25] Only in a democratic society where individuals understand themselves to be free and equal can a partnership between such disparate personalities arise. When first introduced, "Sybil averred that he was certainly dull," and Carrington found Sybil "not very profound" (19, 115). Before united by their common concern for the well-being of Mrs. Lee, they are, at best, acquaintances. Given the gaiety of her disposition, the charmed quality of her life, and her impatience with the intellectual discussions that amuse her sister so, it is not surprising that Sybil found very little reason to get to know Carrington in any real depth. The only reason the two discover their mutual concern for Mrs. Lee is because each exercises common decency. They practice good manners, not to reify their differences of age, wealth, and social standing, but rather to practice that democratic respect of difference that recognizes the other as an individual in his or her own right.

Their friendship begins as mere politeness. Carrington recognizes Sybil's fondness for equitation, and so he offers to take her on a ride through Arlington. He hesitates to make good on his promise, Arlington being a place fraught with such strong memories for him. But Sybil holds him to his word, and once there, she is observant of, and inquires about, the stories that make the Lees' old homestead, and the many graves that replaced it, such a haunted place for Carrington. The common decency with which each recognizes their shared humanity and their distinctive personalities allows them to transcend their differences. In contrast to Mrs. Lee's "patronizing air" and condescending dismissal of Sybil's sound judgment, Carrington recognizes and appreciates Sybil's sympathy and is touched by her "little oration" where she so insightfully recognizes Mrs. Lee's dangerous predicament (117–19). Carrington is able to perceive in Sybil a depth and profundity that is all too easily overlooked by those who, like Ratcliffe and Mrs. Lee, "treat [her] like a child," reduce her to her frivolous flirtations and her love of evening gowns (172). In return, what Sybil learns of Carrington's past travails deepens her estimation of him. She "never again called him dull"; indeed, she even declines a handsome young gentleman caller to keep a date with her newly found ally, Carrington (119).

Just as unexpectedly as this new alliance arises, so too does it confound our expectations of both Carrington and Sybil. They so sincerely and genuinely engage one another that they come to know each other much more clearly and precisely than Mrs. Lee is able to know either of them. They collaborate as equals, despite Carrington's moral seriousness and greater political experience. Sybil teaches Carrington how best to profess his love for her sister, and Carrington provides both the plan, and the damning information, that Sybil uses to thwart Ratcliffe. The respect they extend to the other's individual talents and the trust they share contrast sharply with the dissemblance and manipulation that characterizes the courtship between Ratcliffe and Mrs. Lee. Where the latter leads to downfall and disillusionment, their personal alliance enjoys practical success and personal affirmation. In this contrast, Adams hints that the realization of democracy's morally distinctive promise depends upon our willingness to believe in its promise: by respecting one another as free and equals and genuinely engaging each other on such terms, we advance the reality of our actually being free and equal. Certainly, to act on such a belief is no easy undertaking. Ratcliffe is deaf to it, and Mrs. Lee lacks the courage for it. But as the resolution of the plot turns on Carrington and Sybil's ability to act on it, so too, Adams suggests, does the fate of democracy rest on our decision to subject our practices to this demanding faith in the moral agency of others.

Adams highlights the distinctiveness of this accomplishment by ironically framing their admirable alliance in terms of the old adage that "whenever a man reaches the top of the political ladder, his enemies unite to pull him down" (112). Though usually an indictment of democracy's tendency toward mediocrity and hostility toward greatness, Adams turns this political truism on its head. In the example of Carrington and Sybil, friends, not enemies, unite, and they unite not for base or envious motives, but for the noble purpose of defending their friend. In the process of pursuing another's advantage, at the expense of their own immediate self-interest, both Carrington and Sybil are enriched. Their friendship cultivates what is best in each, as well as reveals hidden talents and capacities in each.

Adams presents their friendship as a powerful corrective to the corrosive effect of calculated self-interest. First, it is a compelling desire. Even Ratcliffe experiences it: "he needed human companionship; . . . some avenue of communication with that social world, which made his present surroundings look cold and foul" (82). However invested Ratcliffe is in his pursuit of power and narrow self-interest, that pursuit fails to satiate this longing. Second, the universal longing for companionship is self-regulating. As successful as Ratcliffe may be in scheming to his advantage, he can neither buy nor otherwise bribe the companionship he desires. The sort of company found in his cold and foul world—office seekers, party toadies, and newspaper gossips—doesn't connect and affirm; it simply uses and exhausts. In such instrumental relationships, man is reduced to another man's measure. Finally, the recognition of this universal longing for companionship is edifying. When articulated, this longing exposes a narrow pursuit of self-interest as self-defeating, and it simultaneously suggests the personal rewards of practicing a concern for others. The pull of this desire suggests to self-regarding creatures that devotion to duty may actually advance their self-interest, properly understood. As an alternative to the mean impulse to make use of others or otherwise master them, this longing for companionship endorses the prudence of acting in accord with the principle of equality.

The equality and respect with which Sybil and Carrington treat one another dignifies their relationship with Mrs. Lee as well. In contrast to Ratcliffe, who manipulates her weaknesses to his own advantage, Carrington and Sybil openly and honestly seek to bolster Mrs. Lee's strengths. Compassionate rather than calculating, they forgive her her weaknesses, and address themselves to her better tendencies. Though they both seek to secure her well-being, they carefully avoid righteously imposing their judgment on her. They address her respectfully rather than condescendingly. Carrington directly acknowledges to Mrs. Lee that Ratcliffe "can put forward a strong claim to your sympathy and help, if not to your love. He can offer you a great field of usefulness which you want" (136–37). He warns her simply to "be on her guard" and to "keep out of his influence until [her] mind is fairly made up" (137). When she tries to turn this straightforward warning into an expression of paternalistic condescension, Carrington checks her unfair insinuation. Reaffirming that he would never presume to impose his judgment on her, and generously refraining from disparaging her motives and pretensions, Carrington offers a democratic resolution to their disagreement: they "are wide apart in our estimates of Mr. Ratcliffe" because they have experienced different sides of him (137).

Adams clearly prefers Carrington's ability to maintain the courage of his convictions without imposing his judgment on Mrs. Lee. But it is a bit difficult to discern how Carrington's equanimity offers a corrective to Mrs. Lee's harsh criticism and her intolerance for uncertainty and ambiguity. Indeed, I do not believe Adams offers us one. Mrs. Lee quits democracy. She describes her firsthand political education as a "horrid story" and continues to lament how most of her countrymen unfairly judge her (190). But what makes the story so horrid and her lament so disappointing is not that democracy failed her, but rather that it asked too much of her. She has neither the temperament for it nor faith in it. Adams suggests as much by attributing to her the inverse virtues modeled by Washington. In contrast to Washington's economic frugality, Mrs. Lee is liberal. She always happily "paid the bills" for luxuries ranging from her sister's evening gowns to hosting her salon's endless stream of visitors (17). Her social position in Washington, Adams insinuates, arises in part from this wealth. At the same time, she is as frugal with her esteem of others as Washington is said to have been generous. Where Washington consistently engaged others as equals, neither seeking to use them to advance his self-interest nor to be sacrificed to advancing theirs, Mrs. Lee can neither risk the constant responsibility of sorting through the complexities of life to discern her particular duty nor suffer the disappointments integral to the deferred hopes of democratic life. She prefers a settled order to democracy's capacity to surprise. Having become "pure steel" in her response to the tragedies that have befallen her, she has not the heart to accept the risks, or relish the rewards, of democratic life.[26]

The Moral of the Story

The plot of Adams's novel is rather simple. It is the complexity of the characters that renders the story compelling. Adams's ability to invest each character with such depth and vitality suggests the merits of conducting a symposium on democracy through a novel. The novel, after all, allows Adams to democratically consider the various estimations of democracy. In contrast to a philosophical treatise where consistency and order are esteemed, the novel allows Adams to address the predictable tendencies of human nature without ignoring the fact that one human tendency is to act unpredictably. His characters are in flux, and by allowing them to learn, grow, change, and reveal themselves, Adams illuminates the partial truths about democracy possessed by critics and defenders alike. By highlighting the vices of Mrs. Lee's principled idealism, the virtues of Ratcliffe's practical politics, and the perceptive insights of Sybil's and Carrington's common sense and the effective power of their sympathy and compassion, Adams calls our attention to false dichotomies and moves us to transcend them. By exploring these tragic and redeeming aspects of democracy in novel form, Adams pays tribute to the creative nature of democracy. Carrington and Sybil illustrate the self-correcting capacity of democratic society, and remind us that the capacity for reform exists in surprisingly commonplace actions and ordinary talents.

Finally, the novel form encourages the reader to judge the various characters and the concerns they represent, independently and provisionally. Adams's novel—especially with its misleading information, partial perspectives, hidden talents, dark ambitions, noble aspirations, good intentions, intimate confessions and purposeful deceit—engages the reader in the complex sort of judgments that the novel recommends as integral to democratic citizenship. And in synthesizing the various bits of information that the plot reveals to us about each character, the reader practices the sort of common sense, generous sympathy, and humility Adams depicts as democratic duties owed free and equal citizens. We are forced to adapt to

new facts, to revise our estimations of characters in light of how they act in
different situations, and to tolerate uncertainty about the sincerity of their
motives and integrity of each character. The reader must, in the end, discern the implication of Mrs. Lee's rejection of Ratcliffe, the prospects of her
correspondence with Carrington, and the fairness of her disparagement of
nine out of ten of her fellow countrymen. In observing how Adams employs
his reader in perceiving and judging these characters, I do not mean to
attribute to Adams a mindless relativism about democracy or a complacent
disregard for it. I simply wish to highlight how he uses the novel to situate
the reader. He invites the reader to practice, not just study, the constant
responsibility and deferred hope democratic life entails.

His narrative persistently refers to democracy as an inevitability of
our times. We cannot escape democracy, indeed we cannot disregard it,
however much we may be appalled by it.[27] "There may be some mistake
about a doctrine which makes the wicked," Adams warns, "when a majority,
the mouthpiece of God against the virtuous, but the hopes of mankind are
staked on it" (96). From this argument that we must hold faith in democracy because of the absence of any alternative, Adams continues to ground
that faith by observing its advantages: "If the weak in faith sometimes quail
when they see humanity floating in a shoreless ocean on this plank, which
experience and religion long since condemned as rotten, mistake or not,
men have thus far floated better by its aid than the popes ever did with their
prettier principle; so that it will be a long time yet before society repents"
(96). Of course, Adams's defense of democracy here concedes that it may be
a mistake, and one for which penance will be paid. However, in the absence
of certain knowledge about abstract ideals (religion's prettier principles or
Mrs. Lee's righteous idealism) and in defiance of our all-too-human nature
(experience's condemnation and Ratcliffe's rationalization of the necessity
of vice), Adams invites his reader to accept the weight of the responsibility
to act—in particular situations and in particular relations with others—
without pretending to possess the whole of the truth and without presuming
the power to control. As I reread the concluding lines of Adams's novel,
though Mrs. Lee's postscript gets literally the last word, Sybil's "privately
inserted" note powerfully counters Mrs. Lee's lesson of bitter resignation
with a resolve to sustain hope (190). "If I were in your place," Sybil em-
pathetically writes to her friend Carrington, "I would try again after she
comes home" (190).

Notes

I would like to thank Natalie Taylor, David Alvis, Patrick Deneen, Susan McWilliams, Greg Renoff, Alfred Cuzan, and an anonymous reader for their thoughtful comments about *Democracy* and their insightful suggestions on previous drafts of this essay.

1. Its popularity grew in part from the "national guessing game" it fueled regarding the identity of its author (Patricia O'Toole, *The Five of Hearts: An Intimate Portrait of Henry Adams and His Friends 1880–1918* [New York: Simon and Schuster, 1990], 73). Insofar as the novel is a roman à clef, its popularity probably also benefited from the public's interest in political scandals of the day. For an extended explanation of the historical figures inspiring the novel's characters, see Ernest Samuels, *Henry Adams: The Middle Years* (New York: Bookspan, 2003), 89–96.

2. Henry Adams, *Democracy: An American Novel* (Clinton, Mass.: Colonial Press, 1968), 13. Hereafter cited parenthetically.

3. "Like his heroine, [Adams] saw much, and what he saw shook his nerves to pieces also. . . . Adams seems to say with her, 'No, no! No responsibility. You ask more than I can give'" (James P. Young, *Henry Adams: The Historian as Political Theorist* [Lawrence: University Press of Kansas, 2001], 113). Mrs. Lee's "mind and temperament was that of Henry Adams and to a degree that of his wife Marian" (Samuels, 95).

4. With Young, I want to argue that "underneath the apparent surface moral simplicity of Adams' novel there is a much more complex argument" (Young, 113). But where he reads Mrs. Lee and Nathan Gore as expressions of Adams's disappointed idealism, I read Sybil and Carrington, and the contrasting model they provide to Mrs. Lee and Ratcliffe, as expressions of Adams's hopes for, and disappointments with, democracy.

5. Young, 274 n.10.

6. Patrick Wolfe, "The Revealing Fiction of Henry Adams," *New England Quarterly* 49, no. 3 (September 1976): 425. Adams advocates such a hope in his 1858 Class Day Oration.

7. Of course, Sybil and Carrington are not the only alternatives Adams offers to Ratcliffe's practical degradation of democratic aspirations to power politics and Mrs. Lee's principled resignation from democracy and its demanding responsibilities. The Baron Jacobi, "a witty, cynical, broken-down Parisian roué," exclaims that American "cities are all corrupt" (27, 44). But unlike Ratcliffe, who uses the observation of others' vices to rationalize his own political intrigues, Jacobi employs his own unseemliness to expose, and ultimately thwart, Ratcliffe. Indeed, Adams allows this old retired diplomat to literally beat Ratcliffe with his walking stick

at the end of the novel. Jacobi's critique of American democracy is balanced by Nathan Gore, a literary man and an aspiring diplomat, who confesses: "I believe in democracy. I accept it" (46). Through this character Adams gives voice to its fairer aspirations without forgetting its shortcomings and challenges or being defeated by their presence, as Mrs. Lee ultimately is (46).

8. Young asserts that *Democracy* is undemocratic because "it longs to see power placed in the hands of its best men and it simultaneously resigns to the ruling principle that insists one man is as good as the next" (114). I argue instead that the novel affirms democracy through its secondary characters' modest talents, sincere virtue, and effective collaboration.

9. "It was only to her closest intimates that she honestly acknowledged herself to be tortured by *ennui*" (9).

10. "We shall grow to be wax images, and our talk will be like the squeaking of toy dolls. . . . No one will have any object in this world, and there will be no other. It is worse than anything in the 'Inferno.' What an awful vision of eternity!" (51).

11. "'America had still her story to tell; she was waiting for her Burns and Scott, her Wordsworth and Byron. . . . You want peaches in spring,' said she. 'Give us our thousand years of summer and then complain, if you please, that our peach is not as mellow as yours.'" (69).

12. It is worth noting that Adams attributes to Mrs. Lee a cleverness that makes her adept at such manipulation. She chooses not to attend church, but she does not want to risk telling her sister that she has lost faith. So to avoid having to explain herself to Sybil, Mrs. Lee employs a "little maneuver" and suggests that because she cannot sing in the choir with Sybil, Mrs. Lee could not possibly accompany her to church. "This outrageous fallacy seemed perfectly to answer its purpose, and Sybil accepted it, in good faith, as a fair working principle which explained itself" (17).

13. In response to Ratcliffe's plea for her to advise him "where virtue lies" if she expects him to act rightly in accord with principle, she cries "No, no! no responsibility. You ask more than I can give" (94).

14. We ought to sympathize with Ratcliffe even more, if we take seriously his confession that he does not enjoy politics. If this is true, he enters politics simply because it is what he is good at, whereas Mrs. Lee chooses to enter politics for her own amusement.

15. For a related discussion on Ratcliffe's compellingness, see Young, 112–14. I agree with Young, except insofar as he assumes Adams to stand wholly with Mrs. Lee. Instead, I read the similarity of these two main characters as critiques of the sort of political beings Adams sought most urgently to warn us against.

16. To be sure, both characters take into account others' opinions, interests, and aspirations, but both do so poorly, self-servingly.

17. This isn't quite true. Mrs. Lee feels ashamed in being called perfect by Carrington, a man whose moral superiority she immediately recognizes. Likewise, Ratcliffe recognizes Mrs. Lee's superior refinement. Despite these recognitions, though, Mrs. Lee and Ratcliffe remain wholly suspicious of all but their own ways of evaluating present situations and assessing potential alternatives.

18. In a letter to a discouraged young teacher, Adams writes: "there is, in our modern society, a singular want of solidarity—a lack of purpose and direction—which you and I are not responsible for, and cannot counteract. We are not the only victims" (Herbert Edwards, "The Prophetic Mind of Henry Adams," *College English* 3, no. 8 [May 1942]: 719).

19. O'Toole, 126.

20. "She might have known it by her own common sense, but now that experience had proved it, she was glad to quit the masquerade" (175). "She had long since hardened her heart" to defend against the sufferings of lost love; she "had no heart to give" (135–36).

21. Carrington worries about betraying the confidence of Mrs. Baker, observing both his moral obligation to discretion and the practical consequences that could harm both his and her reputation. He avoids any immoral action by trusting Mrs. Lee not to abuse his confidence. She proves worthy of his trust, burning the letter as soon as it had served its purpose (167–69).

22. Wondering whether "Carrington or Lord Dunbeg would best suit her in the rôle of the General," Miss Dare declares: "Mr. Carrington is exemplary. But oh what a joy to be Martha Washington and a Countess too!" (78).

23. Adams, *Democracy*, 73. See also *The Education of Henry Adams*, in particular the chapter on Washington.

24. Ratcliffe "knew [Carrington] well enough to feel sure that in any event he would act a perfectly straightforward part." But even with that knowledge, Ratcliffe's attempt to manipulate the virtuous Carrington fails (123).

25. Adams contrasts the liberating virtue of Sybil and Carrington's capacity to surprise us with the stultifying reminder of the human tendency to be disappointed, captured so well in Mrs. Lee's insensitivity and Ratcliffe's suspicion.

26. Perhaps Mrs. Lee lacks both heart and soul. Sybil discloses that, in response to the tragic death of her child, Mrs. Lee "rave[d] about religion and resignation and god" and "has never been what she was before" (131).

27. As Edwards reads *Democracy*, "no one had a deeper faith in the democratic form of government than Adams" (715).

CHAPTER 5

The Flowers of Freedom or the New Tyranny: Science, Art, and Religion in Henry Adams's *Esther*

Natalie Fuehrer Taylor

IN THE MIDST OF founding a new democratic nation, John Adams regrets he cannot indulge his interest in paintings and sculptures: "I must study politics and war that my sons may have the liberty to study mathematics and philosophy. My sons ought to study mathematics and philosophy . . . in order to give their children the right to study painting, poetry, music, architecture, statuary, tapestry, and porcelain." Biographer Richard Brookhiser explains John Adams's hope for democratic life: "He presented the sciences and the arts as flowers of freedom and peace, which he would not enjoy, an intellectual promised land that, like Moses, he could never enter."[1] This democratic prophecy seems to have been fulfilled by John Adams's great-grandson Henry Adams. Despite his ancestors' commitment to public life and his own flirtation with public service, Henry Adams claims that, for him, "literature offers higher prizes" than politics. Published in 1884, Adams's second novel, *Esther,* is the tale of a young, independent-minded woman choosing between a minister and a scientist for her husband. It would appear that John Adams's commitment to the study of politics and war had left his great-grandson free to follow the comparatively trivial concerns of private life.

Although Henry Adams preferred literary pursuits to public office, it is not clear that Adams has forsaken the study of politics and a commitment to American democracy. Indeed, Adams's literary pursuits and the Adams family commitment to American democracy are quite compatible. Graduating from Harvard College in 1858, Henry Adams reveals his future plans: "My wishes are for a quiet and literary life, as I believe that to be

the happiest and in this country not the least useful."[2] Like generations
of Adamses before him, Henry Adams works in the service of the American regime. In his novel *Esther*, Adams questions the extent to which the
American people are free from tyranny. To be sure, the American people
are no longer threatened by the British king, nor must they fear the instability of popular rule, which menaced the early republic. Yet, new forces have
emerged to threaten American self-governance. Ironically, it is the very
"flowers of freedom" that have great potential for tyranny. In Adams's seemingly domestic tale, the artist and the preacher are "princes . . . as tyrannical
as any in the Almanach de Gotha, and those who submitted to them would
suffer slavery."[3] The scientist, who challenges the teaching of the church,
would seem to be an alternative to the tyranny of the minister. However, he
is to some extent the accomplice of these princes. In the end, Esther, with
the help of her fellow Americans, escapes at least for the moment the new
tyrants. Adams demonstrates to his readers the capacity of the American
people to overcome the corruption of his day, in the hope that his literary
life will be "in this country not the least useful."

Adams Family Values

Curious to find out whether or not his book would find a sympathetic audience, Adams instructed his publisher to publish the novel under a pseudonym and without the benefit of any promotion. The sales were slow, and
Esther received little recognition during Henry Adams's lifetime. Although
students of Henry Adams have returned to his little-known second novel,
it remains generally unknown to American readers. Earl N. Harbert explains: "*Esther* must be regarded as both a flawed novel and a dated novel.
It survives chiefly as a repository for Adams' thoughts" (83). In contrast to
his first novel, *Democracy*, which had been a political tale, Harbert considers Adams's second novel nonpolitical and an unfortunate departure from
the Adams concern for American democracy, which had survived for generations. Harbert considers the novel simply as a series of abstract debates
between science and religion: "By eliminating the political values . . . the
novelist had sacrificed much of his strength, based on those political themes
about which he knew most. In consequence this nonpolitical novel appears
to us clumsy and uncertain in its arguments and inconclusive over all" (84).
    Although the reading public and Henry Adams's commentators have

found little value in *Esther*, the author placed great value on the novel. Adams writes to a friend, "I care more for one chapter, or any dozen pages of *Esther* than for the whole history [*The History of the United States of America during the Administrations of Jefferson and Madison*], including maps and indexes."[4] The import of the novel to Adams is often explained by personal or biographical details.[5] Esther shares many of the qualities of Adams's wife, "Clover" Adams. Clover committed suicide shortly after the novel's publication, and so Adams's attachment to it seems to some scholars to be sentimental. Political scientist James P. Young notes the personal reasons for Adams's preference for his novel. However, he also suggests that the novel paves the way for his later, lengthier works, namely *Mont-Saint-Michel and Chartres* and *The Education of Henry Adams.*[6] Like the novel, these two works are concerned with the place of religion and science in the modern age. Written several years after the novel, *The Education of Henry Adams* is marked by disillusionment and biting irony. This impression has come to characterize Henry Adams and has distorted our understanding of his earlier writings. However, Adams's interest in science was ambivalent. He could not but recognize its profound influence, yet wondered if it would be able to provide the moral purpose religion had.

Young is correct to see *Esther* as part of an inquiry that will occupy (at least the latter half of) Henry Adams's lifetime. However, the novel should not be read simply as early mutterings of Adams's later, more familiar, discontented grumblings. Rather, we should heed the advice of William Merrill Decker: "we must not let Adams the ironist keep us from duly recognizing the major if always tentative project of his early middle years: to create a symbology by which the 'national mind' might receive the impress and accept a vision of cultural possibilities that could be applied to the task of high national culture."[7] *Esther*, according to this interpretation, is an "attempt to publish . . . the text of a redeemable America" (Decker, 207).

It is also a mistake to regard *Esther* as a nonpolitical novel, written by an author concerned only with an abstract discussion on religion and science, as Harbert claims. In his second novel, Adams explores the particular influence of science and religion on the American character. Adams allows his readers to witness the reign of religion give way to the reign of science. Furthermore, he considers how these flowers of freedom have bloomed by the late nineteenth century. Religion has been corrupted and threatens American self-governance. As science emerges as the new creed, it is unclear whether it will also become tyrannical or whether it can serve the American regime. Adams has not abandoned "the traditional Adams family values," as Harbert has suggested, but remains committed to preserving American democracy like generations of Adamses before him.

One of the Most Marked American Types

By way of introduction to the character for which Adams's novel is named, his readers are told that Esther Dudley is "as familiar as Hawthorne" (*Esther*, 14). Adams's commentators have not overlooked his introduction to the title character of his novel. Rather than Hawthorne's short story "Old Esther Dudley," Adams's commentators draw comparisons between Esther and Hester Prynne, the better-known character of Hawthorne's well-known novel *The Scarlet Letter.*[8] Passing over Hawthorne's short story in favor of the novel may seem to be the more fruitful comparison. At first glance, the young, lively, and independent woman in Adams's novel seems to have little in common with the old, ghostlike character of Hawthorne's short story. Mistress Dudley is the last loyal occupant of the Province House, home to British royal governors before the Revolutionary War. Hawthorne's tale begins as the royal governor abandons Province House, leaving it in the care of Mistress Dudley, "who had dwelt almost immemorial years in this mansion."[9] Hawthorne's readers watch Mistress Dudley's pathetic attempt to maintain the royal splendor of Province House, for she is certain that the British governor will return in triumph. By the time that John Hancock, the governor of the new state of Massachusetts, arrives to take possession of the mansion, Mistress Dudley has been "unable to regulate her mind by a proper reference to present things" and "appears to have grown partially crazed" (231). Hawthorne's tale ends with Mistress Dudley's death: "[T]he ancient woman sank down beside one of the pillars of the portal. The key of the Province-House fell from her grasp, and clanked against the stone. 'I have been faithful unto death,' murmured she. 'God save the king!'" (234). Despite the obvious differences between Mistress Dudley and Esther Dudley, a comparison and a contrast between Hawthorne's short story and Adams's novel proves instructive.[10]

Like her namesake, Henry Adams's Esther Dudley bears witness to a change in the reign of "princes" in the American regime. Esther Dudley also has great difficulty "regulating her mind by a proper reference to present things" (Hawthorne, 231). Yet, in contrast to her namesake, Esther does not die a pathetic death at the novel's end. As a particularly interesting American type, Esther Dudley resists the corruption of the flowers of freedom, which are represented by the minister, the scientist, and the artist, encouraging Adams's readers to consider how American self-governance will be preserved as the reign of science replaces the reign of religion.

Both Hawthorne's short story and Adams's novel begin as a change in rule takes place. "Old Esther Dudley" begins at the moment that Sir William Howe, the British commander during the Revolutionary War, is to flee Province House: "With an ominous perception that, as his departing footsteps echoed down the staircase, the sway of Britain was passing forever from New England, he smote his clenched hand on his brow, and cursed the destiny that had flung the shame of a dismembered empire upon him" (Hawthorne, 226). Adams's tale also begins at the moment that one prince, the minister, is to make his last stand in old New York. As we shall see, by the novel's end, religion is seemingly defeated by science. The disappearance of religion in the United States nags Henry Adams for years to come and will be a compelling mystery to him as he writes *The Education of Henry Adams*: "Of all the conditions of his youth which afterwards puzzled the grown-up man, this disappearance of religion puzzled him most."[11] Though the grown-up man attempts to recover the "religious instinct" and is tempted to consider his inability to recapture it as a "personal defect," he recognizes that the disappearance of religion is common to his generation and has profound consequences for American intellectual and moral life: "[T]hat the most intelligent society, led by the most intelligent clergy, in the most moral conditions he ever knew, should have solved all the problems of the universe so thoroughly as to have quite ceased making itself anxious about the past or future, and should have persuaded itself that all the problems which had convulsed human thought from the earliest recorded time, were not worth discussing, seemed to him the most curious social phenomenon he had to account for in a long life" (*Education*, 34). The disappearance of the "religious instinct" represents the loss of a certain seriousness in human beings.

In Adams's novel, however, religion plays an ambivalent role in American democracy. No longer occupying the place that it had in the past, religion is nevertheless portrayed in *Esther* as having the potential to influence American life—a potential that Adams seems to think it has lost by the time he pens the *Education* decades later. At the start of the novel, we can already see that religion has faded from the hearts and minds of Americans. Indeed, the worship of God seems to be corrupted. The novel opens with the very first service at St. John's, the newly built and yet partially decorated church on Fifth Avenue: "As a display of austerity the show was a failure, but if cheerful content and innocent adornment please the Author of the lilies and roses, there was reason to hope that this first service at St. John's found favor in his sight, even though it showed no victory over the world or the flesh in this part of the United States" (3). Still, one is obliged to recognize that "there was in this new temple to-day a perceptible interest in religion. One might *almost* have said that religion seemed a matter of concern" (3–4; emphasis added). The novel's young heroine is particularly interested in the questions that religion promises to answer. This suggests that Americans might recapture their seriousness of purpose, which seems to so poignantly elude Adams. And if religion no longer excites an interest in "all the problems which had convulsed human thought from the earliest recorded time," perhaps science will.

Both Mistress Dudley and Esther represent, to greater and to lesser extents, the threatened regimes—colonial rule and American self-governance. Mistress Dudley is "so perfect a representative of the decaying past—of an age gone by, with its manners, opinions, faith, and feelings, all fallen into oblivion or scorn—of what had once been a reality, but was now merely a vision of faded magnificence" (Hawthorne, 228) that we need not say much about this distinctive character. Esther is also a very distinctive "American type." In *The Mind and Art of Henry Adams*, J. C. Levenson notes the early and enduring influence of Tocqueville on Henry Adams: "To him, the Frenchman was a model as well as a teacher. Like the historian he was one day to become, he responded most deeply when concrete example and theoretical exposition could be contemplated at once."[12] In the spirit of Tocqueville, Adams ponders the loss of the ideal hero to democracies as he simultaneously writes the *History* and *Esther*. The "type" took the place of the hero. John Ernest explains how Adams had come to understand types while writing the *History*: "To consider oneself a 'type' is to place oneself within the matrix of historical forces, to understand one's character as a microcosm of history, the 'product of influences.'"[13] Despite the apparent loss of importance of the individual in a democracy, Adams continued to appreciate the importance of an individual as a type: "American types were especially worthy of study if they were to represent the greater democratic evolution the world could know. Readers might judge for themselves what share the individual possessed in creating or shaping the nation; but whether it was small or great, the nation could be understood only by studying the individual" (Adams quoted by Ernest, 32). In this instance, it is by studying Esther that we shall see the potential for the individual to shape the nation as science challenges religion.

We meet Esther on the first pages of the novel. Esther attends the first service at St. John's with her cousin George Strong, a scientist. From the start, she is an observer at the church rather than a faithful member of it. Typical of her generation, Esther seems to have lost the "religious instinct." But like the grown man Henry Adams, Esther also seems sensitive to the loss. She comments upon leaving the service that she hopes the minister believes his religious principles (7). Throughout the novel, Esther will make herself "anxious about the past or the future," and she will confront "the problems which have convulsed human thought from the earliest recorded time." Esther has this seriousness of purpose in common with earlier generations of Americans.

New to New York society, St. John's new minister, Stephen Hazard, is curious about Esther. Although Strong attempts to describe the young woman to his friend, the best description of Esther is given by the artist, Wharton. Upon learning that the artist saw Esther at the first service, Hazard exclaims, "Ah! Then you could see Miss Dudley!" (16). Wharton's response is a bit strange. Rather than explaining the circumstances that made it possible for him to see Esther, Wharton tells Hazard, "I can always see Miss Dudley" (16). Wharton's reply calls attention to Hazard's inability to see Esther. Though "the preacher seemed to be made up of two eyes and a voice, so slight and delicate was his frame" (5), he is unable to see her in the church. As the novel unfolds, we shall see that the preacher's literal inability to see Esther will take on metaphorical meaning.

Wharton goes on to explain that he is always able to see Esther because she is "interesting." "Miss Dudley is one of the most marked American types I ever saw" (16). As a painter trained in Europe, Wharton has unique perspective on America. This perspective causes Wharton to "hesitate before every thing American" (16). Nonetheless, he is curious about the future of this American type—much like Alexis de Tocqueville was curious about the future of democracy in America. Levenson notes Adams's interest in concrete examples even while contemplating theoretical exposition in his historical and biographical writings. I would add that Adams also contemplates concrete examples while engaging in theoretical exposition in his novels. Wharton tells his friends, "I want to know what she can make of life" (17). His further description of Esther echoes Tocqueville's descriptions of Americans: "[T]o take tradition only as information, and current facts only as a useful study for doing otherwise and better; to seek the reason for things by themselves and in themselves alone to strive for a result without letting themselves be chained to the means, and to see through the form to the foundation: these are the principal features that characterize what I shall call the philosophic method of the Americans. . . . I discover that in most of the operations of the mind, each American calls only on the individual effort of his reason."[14] Wharton describes Esther's mind in a similar way: "She never read a book, I believe, in her life. She tries to paint, but she is only a second rate amateur and will never be anything more, though she has done one or two things, which I give you my word I would like to have done myself. She picks up all that she knows without effort and knows nothing well, yet she seems to understand whatever is said" (17). Despite Esther's (and Americans') seeming mediocrity, there is much to regard in this type. There is a certain native intelligence to Esther. Wharton is taken by the "subtlety" of her mind and of her painting: "I have passed weeks trying to catch it. The thing is too subtle, and it is not a grand type, like we are used to in the academies" (17). In addition to this subtlety, Wharton cannot help admiring Esther's resiliency. She takes his harsh criticisms and continues to paint.

In his treatment of Henry Adams's novel, William Merrill Decker suggests that "in *Esther*, he [Adams] strives to create a symbol of a baffled, but aspiring, instinctively idealistic, American character" (210). Recalling passages from Adams's *The History of the United States during the Administrations of Jefferson and Madison*, Decker notices a similarity between the young American republic and Esther: "[I]n Wharton's description of Esther, we see reflections of what the historian identifies as the national dilemma in 1800, when the country's 'paucity of means' contrasted sharply with 'the immensity' of the task (A II 23). Esther Dudley [is] distinguished by quick intelligence, a piece of native quickness that allowed the American people to solve their pressing material problems and to hold their own in the War of 1812" (212). Decker goes on to remind his readers of Wharton's curious description of Esther: "She gives one the idea of a lightly-sparred yacht in mid-ocean; unexpected; you ask yourself what the devil is she doing there. She sails gaily along, though there is no land in sight and plenty of rough weather coming" (*Esther*, 17). Decker smartly connects this description of Esther to Adams's discussion of the American schooner in his history: "'Beautiful beyond anything then known in naval construction,' notorious for *her* effectiveness in raids on British merchantmen, the Yankee schooner emerges a triumphant instance of American thought, the vessel marking 'the first time when in competition with the world, on an element open to all,' Americans 'proved their capacity to excel'" (213; emphasis added). Decker concludes, "In this isolated instance of splendid realization, American character appears superlatively female" (213).

A further comparison between Mistress Dudley and Esther Dudley may be drawn. The distinctive characters of the British colonial subject and the "most marked American type" are both left alone, or nearly alone, in the world, and each finds protection from the political regimes of her day. Hawthorne tells us that Mistress Dudley is "the daughter of an ancient and once eminent family, which had fallen into poverty and decay, and left its last descendant no resource save the bounty of the King" (227). Like Mistress Dudley, Henry Adams's young Esther Dudley is "orphaned" in the course of the novel. Although Adams's character is not left in poverty or decay, her father does not properly provide for her future. Certain that his death is near, Mr. Dudley regrets having chased away his daughter's suitors because, he admits, Esther's marriage would have disturbed his own comfort. Just as Mistress Dudley was sheltered and protected by those who ruled the British colony, so Esther Dudley will be protected by those who rule New York. During the colonial period, it was the royal governors who ruled Massachusetts. At the close of the nineteenth century, it is the American people who rule New York City. Of course, the American public is comprised of different kinds of people. Working together, they determine the course of American democracy and protect the independent and intelligent American type from the princes, who would threaten her freedom.

Tocqueville had explained the significance of women to democracy: "There have never been free societies without mores, and as I said in the first part of this work, it is woman who makes mores. Therefore, all that influences the condition of women, their habits, and their opinions has great political interest in my eyes" (563). Adams also understands the importance of women to the American regime. In *Esther*, the American public is feminine. In addition to Esther, the American people are represented in Adams's novel by Mrs. John Murray of Fifty-third Street, Esther's aunt (as well as Strong's aunt). Mrs. Murray is married to the nearest example of a public figure that we have in Adams's second novel (Mr. Murray is a lawyer and often appears in court). Adams describes Mrs. Murray as having "the air of a woman who knew her own mind and commonly had her own way" (8). Mrs. Murray has singular influence (though not too much influence!) on her young niece: "Her Aunt Sarah . . . was the only person of whom she was a little—a very little—afraid" (12). It is no wonder that George Strong tells Hazard, "You know that a half a dozen women run this city, and my aunt, Mrs. Murray is one of the half-dozen" (14). As the novel gets under way, we learn that Mrs. Murray is "always doing something for somebody" (22). Although Mrs. Murray seems always willing to help others, she also seems inclined to allow other people their freedom, as her disposition to Esther's future demonstrates.

Recognizing that he has not properly provided for his daughter's future, Mr. Dudley asks Mrs. Murray to watch over Esther and see that she makes an appropriate choice for a husband. However, Mr. Dudley need not worry about his daughter. Esther is an example of the independent, self-governing character of American girls described by Tocqueville: "In the United States, the doctrines of Protestantism come to combine with a very free constitution and a very democratic social state; and nowhere is the girl more promptly or more completely left to herself" (563). The American girl is not vulnerable in her independence: "Thus the vices and perils that society presents are not slow to be revealed to her; she sees them clearly, judges them without illusion, and faces them without fear; for she is full of confidence in her strength, and her confidence seems to be shared by all those who surround her" (Tocqueville, 563). Mrs. Murray can assure the dying man that there is no reason to be anxious about his daughter: "Esther can take care of herself. Perhaps she will marry, but if not, she has nothing to fear. The unmarried women nowadays are better off than the married ones" (23). As further proof of Mr. Dudley's sense of humor, and of Esther's independence and good character, Mr. Dudley quips that he is not worried about Esther, but about her husband (23). The matchmakers have to admit that Esther's prospects are few. Stephen Hazard, who will be the most serious contender for Esther's hand, has only just arrived in

New York: "[T]aking out the dancing men, who don't count, I see nobody who would answer, except perhaps Cousin George, and to marry him would be cold-blooded" (24). Mrs. Murray must agree that George's travels as a paleontologist would prevent him from being a good husband to Esther. Without any further possibilities, Mrs. Murray suggests the two leave the matter alone and "let Esther take care of her own husband" (25).

Wishing to leave Esther to make her own choices, Mrs. Murray is pressed to explain her position to Mr. Dudley: "Women must take their chance. It is what they are for. . . . If Esther is sensible, she will never marry; but no one is sensible, so she will marry without consulting us" (25). Mrs. Murray does not elaborate her reasons for wishing that Esther will not marry. She does, however, continue to express her dread of becoming involved in matchmaking: "As for bringing about a marriage, I would almost rather bring about a murder" (25). It is not clear that Mrs. Murray is simply opposed to Esther marrying. Mrs. Murray's reluctance seems to be due at least in part to her unwillingness to interfere with Esther's independence or freedom. Because the American girl enjoys so much freedom, the decision to marry is especially serious. Tocqueville had observed, "In America the independence of woman is irretrievably lost within the bonds of marriage" (565). The sacrifice of her freedom must be made very judiciously and freely: "When the time has come to choose a spouse, the cold and austere reason that has been enlightened and steadied by a free view of the world indicates to the American woman that a light and independent spirit within the bonds of marriage is a subject of eternal trouble, not of pleasure; that the amusements of a girl cannot become the relaxations of a wife, and that for woman the sources of happiness are within the conjugal dwelling. Seeing clearly in advance the sole path that can lead to domestic felicity, she enters on it with her first steps and follows it to the end without seeking to turn back" (Tocqueville, 566). Mr. Dudley respects Mrs. Murray's position. Yet, he fears that Esther will be sad and lonely after his death. As a result, she will be quick to marry and, quite likely, make a bad match. "Keep an eye on her," Mr. Dudley tells Mrs. Murray; "Your principles will let you prevent a marriage, even though you are not allowed to make one" (25). Mrs. Murray returns home feeling the weight of her responsibility for Esther.

Although Mrs. Murray, the pillar of New York society, has been left to watch over "the most marked American type," she is not without help. Soon the "wild girl from the prairie," Catherine Brooke, arrives in New York.

Catherine is the daughter of one of Mrs. Murray's old friends. Just before she is to come of age, Catherine is orphaned, and Mrs. Murray agrees to be her temporary guardian. However, it soon becomes clear that Catherine is in little need of protection from Mrs. Murray and, indeed, is quite capable of protecting not only herself but also Esther from the new threats of tyranny posed by the preacher, the scientist, and the artist. Catherine has been raised in Colorado. As the westward expansion, which began with the Louisiana Purchase during the Jefferson administration, continues in the second half of the nineteenth century, Catherine represents a new generation of Americans. "She is as natural and as sweet as a flower," and "her pure complexion" has "the transparency of a Colorado sunrise" (28).

In addition to being fresh and honest, she proves to be rather clever. Assuming that the "wild girl from the prairie" is an easy target for his worldly sophistication, the scientist George Strong needles her with patronizing questions: "What kind of a revolver do you carry? . . . [D]o you like yours heavy, or say a 32 ball?" (28). Seemingly nonplussed, Catherine answers such questions sweetly and innocently: "'Oh, but I am not strong enough to use heavy shooting-irons,' replied Catherine quite seriously, 'I had a couple of light ones in my room at home, but father told me I could never hurt anything with them, and I never did'" (28). And, just to keep Strong on his toes, Catherine adds, "One night I took one of our herders for a thief and shot at him, but I missed, and just got laughed at for a week" (28). The Sage Hen, which Catherine reveals to Strong is her "very pretty name in Sioux," disarms the sophisticated scientist: "Strong felt a little doubt whether she was making fun of him or he of her, and she never left him in perfect security on this point" (28).

Catherine is a spirited young woman, and, in this regard, she is a nice and a necessary complement to Esther. Curious about Wharton's paintings, Catherine asks Strong why they are so dark and dismal. In a mischievous manner, Strong suggests the moody artist explain his work himself. "What criticism do you make, Miss Brooke?" Wharton challenges the Sage Hen. "Catherine was in mortal terror, but stood her ground like a heroine" (35). Catherine repeats to the artist that she believes the painting would be improved if it were lighter. "Although Catherine pleaded guilty to this shocking heresy, she did it with so much innocence of manner that, in a few minutes, Wharton was captured by her sweet face" (35). Catherine's willingness to confront the would-be tyrant is in contrast to Esther's own hesitation: "Esther, like most women, was timid, and wanted to be told when she could be bold with perfect safety. . . . To be steadily strong was not in Esther's nature. She was audacious only by starts, and recoiled from her own audacity" (38). Catherine's cleverness and boldness demonstrate her ability to withstand the tyrants. She will be an important ally to Mrs. Murray as Mrs. Murray rescues the "most marked American type" from the threats posed by the preacher and the scientist as they try to persuade her to marry.

Despite Catherine's fresh, bold personality, she is not without serious shortcomings. She may benefit from Esther's guidance as much as Esther enjoys Catherine's protection. Catherine seems to lack the "religious instinct" that Adams considers so important to the intellectual and moral life of earlier generations of Americans. Like the Americans that Adams will later describe in the *Education*, Catherine seems to "have persuaded [herself] that all the problems which had convulsed human thought from the earliest recorded time, were not worth discussing" (*Education*, 34). In the days following her father's death, Esther begins to grapple with "the problems which had convulsed human thought," and she makes the minister her confidant: "Then Catherine sat by and dozed while Esther talked mysticism with Hazard" (91). Although intimacy develops between Esther and Hazard, Esther does not share his religious beliefs, and she knows that this incompatibility would make her an unsuitable wife for the minister. When Esther expresses her concerns to Catherine, Catherine replies, "Why should you care what he preaches?" (98). As Esther's anxiety over what Hazard preaches grows, Catherine is happy for "an excuse for escaping to gayer houses and seeing brighter society" (91)—brighter society peopled by "the dancing men" who were considered unsuitable for Esther. When the time comes for Esther to reject Hazard's marriage proposal and to escape his hold on her, Catherine is willing to help Mrs. Murray: "She was tired of the long strain on her sympathies and feelings, and was glad to be made useful in a way that pleased her practical mind" (134). Catherine is motivated by a desire to see her friend happy, not by a recognition of Hazard's potential for tyranny or any particular belief of the superiority of science. The new face of America, whose complexion has "the transparency of the Colorado sunrise," seems indifferent to the waning influence of religion and the waxing authority of science. Adams offers us some hint that Catherine benefits from Esther's more serious contemplations. In joining Esther's flight from the minister, Catherine is also fleeing the romantic intentions of a dancing man, and Catherine is delighted by the notion of her and Esther eluding their suitors (128). Though Esther is a distinctive American type who seems to represent the seriousness of purpose of past generations that is now fading, she remains important if the promise of America is to be fulfilled by a younger, bolder generation of Americans.

We can see that Esther Dudley's tale diverges significantly from Mistress Dudley's tale. Mistress Dudley, on the one hand, has only the shades of the passing colonial period to keep her company. Esther, on the other hand, spends her time with Catherine—the representative of the young, vibrant, promising generation of Americans. Because Esther keeps company with the new, spirited generation of the American people and because she enjoys the concern of the older, wiser generation of Americans, Esther may be spared her namesake's fate. Although the reign of religion will give way to the reign of science, the American type will not languish for the sake of the old, corrupted regime. However, the passing of that regime comes at a profound loss for Esther, and it does not seem that the reign of science can provide the same fulfillment that Esther had hoped religion could.

The Princes of Religion, Art, and Science

Before turning to the events that threaten American self-governance, more should be said about the princes of religion, art, and science. After all, the arts and the sciences were meant to be the flowers of freedom and Americans are rightly attracted to their princes. Upon her arrival in New York, Catherine is also "greatly excited at the idea of knowing people as intellectual as Mr. Hazard and Mr. Wharton" (34). However, her excitement is misguided: "She thought them a sort of princes, and was still ignorant that such princes were as tyrannical as any in the Almanach de Gotha, and those who submitted to them would suffer slavery. Her innocent eagerness to submit was charming, and the tyrants gloated over the fresh and radiant victim who was eager to be their slave" (34). Sensing the danger posed by these princes, Catherine "appealed to the scientist, George Strong, who had not the air of being their accomplice, but seemed to her a rather weak-minded ally of her own" (34). These princes are at once competitors and accomplices of each other. Science, which would seem to be opposed to religion, and maybe to art, is no different.

As the novel opens, Henry Adams's readers eavesdrop on two observers in the new St. John's church. We soon learn that these observers are Esther and her cousin George Strong. A friend to both the minister and the artist who is painting the inside of the church, Strong tells Esther that the minister and the artist have turned everything "upside down" and that it will be left to the church committee "to pay for whatever damage is done" (5). From the start of the novel, the minister is allied not with his fellow believers, but with the artist. Furthermore, this alliance seems to have disrupted the order and the beauty of the church.

We also learn during this first service in the new church that the minister counts science as the friend of religion. In his first sermon, Hazard tells his flock that the hostility between religion and science has disappeared, at least on the part of religion: "There have been times when the church seemed afraid, but she is no longer. Analyze, dissect, use your microscope or your spectrum till the last atom of matter is reached; reflect, refine till the last thought is made clear; the church knows with the certainty of science what she once knew only by faith" (7). Although it is not clear that Strong sees the relationship of religion and science in the same way, he does serve as the accomplice of the minister. Immediately following the first service, Strong arranges to bring Esther and Hazard together, knowing that Esther's acquaintance will be important for the minister. Mrs. Murray, Strong tells his friend, expects Esther to take her place among the "half a dozen women who run this city. . . . I want you to know my Uncle Dudley and my cousin. I am going to have a little tea-party in my rooms and you must help me with it" (14). As the novel unfolds, Esther is engaged to Hazard. Although Strong's and Esther's aunt, Mrs. Murray, opposes the match, Strong will continue to assist the prince of religion in his conquest. It is only due to the education and guidance that he receives from the people that the prince of science discontinues his alliance with the tyrannical prince of religion and begins to work to preserve American independence.

The princes of religion, art, and science are not necessarily tyrannical. Indeed, they may cultivate the flowers of freedom as Henry Adams's great-grandfather had once envisioned and as Catherine assumes upon meeting the three intellectuals. However, these three particular princes are corrupted by what Adams identifies as their self-assertion. It is this self-assertion that has the potential to make them tyrannical. Robert F. Sommers observes that for Wharton and for Hazard, "the objective of art and of religion is to affirm the self."[15] We should not mistake the self-assertion of the princes with our contemporary understanding of self-esteem or self-confidence. Self-assertion privileges the individual over something that is greater than oneself and leads a person to bend others to his or her will. As Hazard begins his first sermon in the new church, "an almost imperceptible shiver passed through Esther's figure." Strong responds by assuring Esther, "Wait! he will slip in the humility later" (5). Humility, a central tenet of Christian faith, is relegated to an afterthought. The narrator tells us, "On the contrary, the young preacher seemed bent on letting no trace of humility slip into his first sermon" (5–6). Rather, Hazard confidently "took possession of his flock with a general advertisement that he owned every sheep in it . . . and to show that there could be no doubt on the matter, he added a general claim to right of property in all mankind and the universe" (6). Leaving little doubt about the tyrannical nature of Hazard's claims, Adams tell his readers, "He did this in the name and on behalf of the church universal, but there was self-assertion in the quiet air with which he pointed out the nature of his title, and then, after sweeping all human thought and will into his strong box, shut down the lid with a sharp click, and bade his audience kneel" (6).

Esther and her father have reputations as freethinkers and are known to question religion. As such, they are a particular challenge to the tyrant: "Hazard's instincts told him that his success, to be lasting, depended largely on overcoming the indifference of people like the Dudleys. If he could not draw to himself and his church the men and women who were strong enough to have opinions of their own, it was small triumph to draw a procession of followers from a class who took their opinions, like their jewelry, machine made" (37). Almost immediately upon meeting the American ideal, the tyrant seeks to bring her under his control: "He meant that Miss Dudley should come regularly to church, and on his success in bringing her there, he was ready to stake the chances for his mission in life" (37).

In a similar vein to Hazard, Wharton's potential for tyranny also lies in his self-assertion. Ironically, Wharton's corruption, which is so similar to Hazard's, is pointed out by Hazard himself. Having been brought together by Strong, Hazard suggests to Esther that she paint Catherine's portrait. Hazard recognizes Wharton's self-assertion in his painting style, and he warns Esther against it: "He covers a canvas with paint and then asks you to put yourself into it. He might as well hold up a looking-glass to you" (36). Hazard suggests that art is corrupted by the egotism of the viewer. Wharton is dangerous not because he would make others submit to him, but because he seeks to cultivate the other person's egotism, in this case the viewer of art. He will also seek to cultivate Esther's egotism as a painter. In both instances, the subject or the truth is distorted. Hazard goes on to suggest that a great work of art lies in the artist's ability to capture the subject. Hazard encourages Esther to capture Catherine's unique spirit while painting her model: "Give to her the soul of the Colorado plains! Show that the beauty of the subject is the right idea! You will annihilate Wharton and do an immortal work" (36). As the plot unfolds, Wharton will try to alter Esther's distinctive painting style in order to make it more similar to his own egoistic style. Although Wharton displays a propensity for self-assertion similar to Hazard's, the prince of art does not exercise his influence over Esther in order to make her submit to his tyranny. Rather, the prince of art attempts to bring out Esther's instinct for self-assertion at the expense of Catherine. The American tradition of self-governance must be on guard against tyranny—both the vulnerability to tyranny as well as the instinct for power.

Although Strong's inclination for self-assertion does not seem as pronounced as Hazard's and Wharton's, I would suggest that he also sees his profession in a selfish manner: "He was rich, and his professorship was little more to him than a way of spending money" (13). Sommers summarizes the ways in which the flowers of freedom have been corrupted by Hazard, Wharton, and Strong: "Their extensive knowledge of the past, emphasized early in the novel in contrast to Esther's apparent ignorance is concerned with dogma, icons, and fossils, and they tend to see the information they accumulate only in relation to themselves rather than its contexts" (139). Just as Strong seems to have taken up his profession for the sake of his amusement, his willingness to help the preacher make a romantic conquest of the American type also seems to be motivated by his amusement: "Hazard's knack of fixing influence wherever he went had long been the wonder of Strong, but had never more surprised or amused him more than now, when he saw Esther, after a moment's hesitation, accept this idea" (36). Having brought Esther, Catherine, and his friends together, Strong steps back to observe the work of the princes of religion and art, but he does not yet take part in the struggle.

With the suggestion that Esther paint Catherine's portrait, Hazard begins his attempt to gain influence over Esther: "Esther labored over the portrait with as much perseverance as though Hazard were right in promis-

ing that it should make her immortal" (37). At first, Esther does not allow
anyone to see her work, but one evening she allows Hazard to look at it. And
it turns out that his suggestions are quite good. So Esther allows Hazard to
see her work regularly and to offer his advice. "Before long, Hazard began
to dominate her will. She felt a little uneasy until he had seen and approved
her work. More than once he disapproved, and then she had to do it over
again. She began at length to be conscious of this impalpable tyranny, and
submitted to it only because she felt her own dependence" (38).

Hazard gains sway over Esther in a second way. He protects her from
the irritable prince of art. Upon completion of the work, Wharton is, of
course, critical of Esther's portrait of Catherine: "It happened that Wharton
attacked parts of the treatment for which Hazard was responsible, and when
Hazard stepped into the lists avowing that he had advised the work and
believed it to be good, Esther was able to retire from the conflict and to leave
the two men fighting a pitched battle over the principles of art" (39). Despite
Hazard's just barely perceptible tyranny over Esther, she is grateful for his
defense of her painting: "When he had reduced Wharton to silence, which
was not a difficult task, for Wharton was a poor hand at dispute or argument,
and felt rather than talked, Mr. Hazard turned to Esther who gave him a
look of gratitude such as she had rarely conferred on any of his sex. . . . 'I
never knew before what it was to have a defender,' said she simply" (39).

Wharton may have lost this particular battle, but he is not prepared to
yield his influence over Esther to the preacher. Wharton suggests that Esther join him in painting the interior decorations of the church. Catherine
will once again serve as Esther's model. Wharton intends to bring Esther
under his direction, but he also brings Esther further under the influence of
Stephen Hazard. The minister of the church will certainly have something
to say about the content of the paintings. Hazard suggests a painting of St.
Cecilia. She is the patron saint of church music. She was also an early Christian martyr. Sommers draws a comparison between St. Cecilia and Esther.
As we shall see by the novel's end, Esther, like St. Cecilia, will not accept
the faith or the rituals of a religious doctrine that she does not believe.
Sommers reminds us that St. Cecelia "suffered persecution under Marcus
Aurelius and Commodus, Alexander Severus, or Diocletian; it is not known
which" (135). With the exception of Marcus Aurelius, all of the men listed
by Sommers are tyrants. Hazard, the man who would compel her to accept
religious principles, is compared to ancient Roman tyrants.

Arriving at the church to begin their work, Catherine wonders if Esther is to paint her in a similar manner as Wharton has painted the other saints—as an "ornery saint," "lean and dingy, in a faded brown blanket" (44). Determined not to be portrayed as "lean and dingy," Catherine "applied all her energies and feminine charms to the task of preventing this disaster, and her first effort was to make a conquest of Wharton" (44). As we have already seen, Esther's painting style is different from Wharton's. In painting St. Cecilia, Esther attempts to capture the beauty of her subject and model. As a result, Esther suffers much criticism from Wharton. But Esther is not left to face the tyrant alone: "Catherine, being encouraged by the idea that Esther was partly struggling for her sake, often understood to join in the battle and sometimes got roughly handled for her boldness" (45). Wharton instructs Esther: "I want you to be above your subject, whatever it is. Don't you see? You are trying to keep down on a level with it. . . . I want to make St. Cecilia glow with your soul, not with Miss Brooke's" (45). Wharton's criticism of Esther's work is that Esther has preserved the equality between the artist and the subject, between Esther and Catherine. With Catherine's support, Esther stands her ground against the tyrant's instructions, and she refuses to use her painting of Catherine as an opportunity for self-assertion: "No woman would ever have done it. I don't like it. I prefer her as she is and as I made her" (46).

Although the minister was inclined to let Wharton have his way, he allows Esther to paint St. Cecilia in her own style, winning favor with the American type. "Esther liked to have her own way. She had the instinct of power, but not the love of responsibility, and now that she found herself allowed to violate Wharton's orders and derange her plans, she became alarmed" (57). The American type retreats from the temptation for power and seeks protection among the American people, represented in this instance by Catherine Brooke. Esther "asked no more favors, stuck closely to her work, and kept Catherine always at her side" (57). Esther's painting of St. Cecilia is completed. Although she may not be entirely happy with her work, it is done in her style, rather than in Wharton's. The objective of her painting is not to affirm herself, but to affirm her subject. Esther, with Catherine's help, is able to escape to resist the corrupting influence of the prince of art and to quiet her own instinct for power.

While Esther seems to have escaped the corruption encouraged by the prince of art, she comes more and more under the influence of the prince of religion. It soon becomes clear that Stephen Hazard is the most serious contender for her hand in marriage. In order to escape Hazard's tyranny, Esther will require the help of Mrs. Murray, as well as Catherine. The American type can only be saved with the help of her fellow Americans.

A Case of the Survival of the Fittest

As Mr. Dudley predicted, his death puts quite a strain on his daughter. Stephen Hazard is on hand to help Esther when the difficult time comes: "The only person outside the family whom she saw was Hazard. He was either at the house in some way or near her almost every day. He took charge of the funeral services, and came to make inquiries, to bring messages, or to suggest some occupation, until he was looked upon as one of the household" (90). It is under these circumstances that Hazard falls in love with Esther. In the weeks following Mr. Dudley's death, Esther comes to see the physical part of life as the lesser part of existence and concentrates on the spiritual: "Her illusions were not serious; perhaps she had for this short instant a flash of truth, and by the light of her father's deathbed, saw life as it was; but, while the mood lasted, nothing seemed real except the imagination, and nothing true but the spiritual" (90). The minister believes he has found a mate to share his greatest hopes and is overwhelmed by his love for his absent parishioner: "His great eyes shone with the radiance of paradise, and his delicate thin features expressed beatitude, as he discussed the purity of soul, the victory of the spirit over matter, and the peace of infinite love" (90–91). Declaring his love for Esther, Hazard is met with some resistance from her. She must admit that she does not share his conviction for his work: "I am not good enough for you. You must love some one who has her heart in your work" (93). Hazard is undeterred and willfully demands Esther's love: "I have more faith in us both. Promise to love me and I will take care of the rest" (93).

The apparent submission of "the most marked American type" to the tyranny of the prince of religion attracts the attention and concern of the people. Esther's romantic connection to Stephen Hazard is a matter of gossip even before he declares his love for her. "People are talking about it," a concerned Mrs. Murray tells her husband; "It really is a matter of public discussion" (93). Recalling her promise to Mr. Dudley, Mrs. Murray knows that she must intervene to prevent Esther from making a bad marriage.

Though Mrs. Murray is a member of the church, she recognizes the submission that would be required of Esther in becoming the minister's wife. She calls upon George Strong to aid her. After all, Strong is primarily to blame, having brought the two lovers together. Typical of Strong, he is amused by the ensuing struggle between Esther and the preacher. He tells Mrs. Murray that he does not want to prevent the match: "It's a case of the survival of the fittest. If Hazard can manage to convert Esther, let him do it. If not, let her take him in charge and convert him, if she can. I'll not interfere" (103). A longtime observer of Hazard, Strong explains that he has often been the accomplice of the prince of religion. Nonetheless, in this contest, the prince of science will place his wager on the American type: "He has done what he has liked with us all his life. I have worked like a dog for him and his church because he was my friend. Now he will see whether he has met his match. I double you up all round on Esther" (103). Although he favors the American type in the contest for her freedom, the scientist's detachment prevents him from working to ensure his cousin's freedom. As the reign of the prince of science ascends, it is not clear that he has a moral commitment to American self-rule.

At this point, Mrs. Murray expresses her frustration with the prince of science and his accomplices: "You and he [Hazard] and all your friends are a sort of clever children. We are always expecting you to do something worth doing, and it never comes. You are a sort of water-color, worsted-work, bric-à-brac, washed out geniuses, just big enough to want to do something and never carry it through. I am heartily tired of the whole lot of you, and now I must set to work and get these two girls out of your hands" (104–5). The minister, the artist, and the scientist were meant to cultivate the flowers of freedom, but their self-absorption has prevented them from making full use of their democratic legacy, and they do not achieve anything great. These princes of religion, art, and science are a disappointment to the older generation of Americans. It falls to the generation represented by Mrs. Murray to educate the prince of science and to save the American type.

Rather than remain an amused bystander, Strong decides to come to the aid of his friend once again. He decides that he must talk to Esther and try to alleviate some of her anxiety concerning the church's doctrine. Although Strong laughs at the church's doctrine, he thinks that he can understand it. Echoing Hazard's first sermon at the new St. John's church, Strong compares science to religion. However, in contrast to Hazard, who claims religion and science are similar in their certain knowledge, Strong considers the two similar in their demand for faith: "Mystery for mystery science beats religion hallow. I can't open my mouth in my lecture-room without repeating ten times as many unintelligent formulas as ever Hazard is forced to do in his church" (107). Strong tries to calm Esther's nerves by pointing out this similarity. Esther is not easily persuaded, and Strong feels the strength of his opponent. The accomplice to the would-be tyrant must be more forceful with "the most marked American type": "If you have faith enough in Hazard to believe in him, you have faith enough to accept his church. Faith means submission. Submit!" (113). Ironically, the prince of science, "the freest of the free thinkers" (122), who would seem to be the greatest challenge to the prince of religion, turns out to be his accomplice.

Despite the efforts of the scientist and the preacher to ensure that Esther marry Hazard, public opinion is stronger than the two tyrants. Esther cannot bear the thought of submitting to the church and the expectations imposed on the minister's wife. She breaks the engagement. Hazard is undeterred and asserts his will on Esther: "For us to part is impossible. You and I are one. You cannot get yourself apart from me, though you may make us both unhappy; and even if you go away forever you will still belong to me" (129). Although Esther has broken her engagement to Hazard and this American type seems to have freed herself from tyranny, she is still vulnerable.

Knowing that Esther would remain vulnerable to the tyrant after the engagement is broken, the American people are at the ready to protect the American ideal. Mrs. Murray is primarily responsible for rescuing Esther from the new threat of tyranny: "The time had come for her to take command, and she did it without fretfulness or unnecessary words" (133). However, Mrs. Murray cannot do it alone. Having summoned George to her, she asks for the assistance of the prince of science. Although he seems to have been working for the benefit of the prince of religion, he agrees to help Mrs. Murray. He will take Esther's mind off of the minister during a spontaneous trip to Niagara Falls—on the condition that Mrs. Murray will educate the prince of science on the right course of action: "'I will do anything that you want,' said Strong, 'on the condition that you tell me what you are about'" (127). In addition to the help from the prince of science, this older, wiser, more privileged representative of the American people requires the help of the younger generation of American people. She enlists Catherine to help

take Esther away from New York City and out of the reach of Stephen Hazard: "'You are the only person I know with a head,' said she to Catherine.
'You have some common sense and can help me'" (133). Catherine quickly
consents to Mrs. Murray's proposed alliance, recognizing the older and
wiser woman has the authority that she lacks: "'I will run it all if you will
take care of Esther,' replied Catherine. 'I'm not old enough to boss her'"
(133). The American people are comprised of people with different, but
complementary virtues. Together they cooperate effectively to preserve the
freedom of the American type.

Before leaving New York City, Strong visits the minister to tell his
friend of their plans. The alliance between the prince of religion and the
prince of science is faltering. Hazard recognizes Strong's influence on Esther and considers it a threat to his own power over the young woman:
"'The real struggle is just coming,' said [Hazard]. 'If you keep out of the
way, I shall win. So far I have never failed with her. My influence over her
today is greater than ever, or she would not try to run away from it. If you
interfere I shall think it unkind and unfriendly'" (140). Still, the scientist
tries to maintain his preferred neutrality: "I don't mean to interfere if I can
help it, but I can't persecute Esther, if it is going to make her unhappy. As
it is, I am likely to catch a scoring from my aunt for bringing you down on
them, and undoing her work" (141). Although Strong would like to maintain
his detachment, he dreads the disfavor of his aunt or more broadly the
American people that she represents. Furthermore, Strong is concerned
about Esther's happiness. As he leaves the minister, Strong acknowledges
a growing attachment to her. George thinks to himself: "What a trump
that girl is, and what a good fight she is making! I believe that I am getting to be in love with her myself" (141). Working together, Mrs. Murray
and Catherine are able to take the American type out of the reach of the
tyrant, the prince of religion. Mrs. Murray has chosen Niagara Falls as the
place of their retreat, an unlikely destination in February: "Hour after hour
dragged on, the little excitement of leaving Albany was long past, and the
train wandering through the dullness of Central New York, when at last a
faint suspicion of dim light appeared in the landscape, and Esther returned
to her window. If anything could be drearier than the blackness of night,
it was the grayness of dawn, which had all the cold terror of death and all
the grim repulsiveness of life joined in an hour of despair" (138). But the
harsh winter landscape takes on brilliance in the light of day: "The sun was

high above the horizon; the sky was bright and blue; the snowy landscape flashed with the sparkle of diamonds, when Esther woke, and it was with a cry of pleasure that she felt her spirits answer the sun" (138). The trip has its desired effect on Esther. Though she is sad, she is no longer in the anxious state into which the impending marriage to Stephen Hazard put her.

Mrs. Murray makes an astute choice in Niagara Falls as their destination due to Esther's unfulfilled metaphysical longings. Niagara Falls fills Esther with a sense of awe and wonder: "She fell in love with the cataract and turned to it as a confidant, not because of its beauty or power, but because it seemed to tell her a story which she longed to understand" (143). Esther's new disposition to the falls may not be the "religious instinct" that Adams will later write about in *The Education of Henry Adams*, but it does have something in common with that. Niagara Falls seems to remind Esther that "all the problems of the universe," "all the problems which had convulsed through human thought from the earliest recorded time," were indeed worth discussing and seems to offer her a way to do that. Ironically, it is the scientist—who continually insists he does not believe in anything— who helps Esther to articulate her metaphysical longings. In doing so, the prince of science demonstrates that he is worthy of the American type: "If you can get hold of one true thought, you are immortal as far as thought goes. The only difficulty is that every fellow thinks his thought the true one. Hazard wants you to believe in his, and I don't want you to believe in mine, because I've not got one which I believe in myself. . . . We may some day catch an abstract truth by the tail, and then we shall have our religion and our immortality" (150–51). Esther responds to Strong: "Does your idea mean that the next world is a sort of great reservoir of truth, and that what is true in us pours into it like raindrops? . . . After all I wonder whether that may not be what Niagara has been telling me!" (151).

The prince of religion appears in Niagara Falls to make one final effort in his conquest of "the most marked American type." However, Esther has been fortified by her time away from New York and her new reflections on universal problems. Esther is no longer afraid to stand up to this tyrant: "Are all men so tyrannical with women? You do not quarrel with a man because he cannot give you his whole life." Revealed to be a tyrant, Hazard exerts himself more forcefully than ever: "'I own it!' said Hazard warmly. 'I am tyrannical! I want your whole life, and even more. I will be put off with nothing else'" (161). Esther overcomes her fear and identifies the corrupt character of Hazard's religious principles. Just as Wharton asks his viewers to put themselves in his art, so Hazard asks Esther to put herself in the immortal. Esther is repulsed: "I despise and loathe myself and yet you thrust self at me from every corner of the church as though I loved and admired it. All religion does is pursue me with self even into the next world" (164). Esther goes on to condemn Hazard's teaching: "Why must the church always appeal to my weakness and never to my strength! I ask for spiritual life and you send me back to my flesh and blood" (165). Esther is able to free herself from the tyrant.

It is at this moment that Strong enters the room. The angry prince of religion accuses the prince of science of disloyalty: "'Have you been trying to supplant me in order to put yourself in my place?' demanded Hazard, still in the tone of a master." Strong denies this charge, "half inclined to laugh" (165). The prince of religion knows that his reign has come to an end and that it is to be followed by the reign of the prince of science. Like Mistress Dudley, who lived to see "a new race of men" supplant colonial rule, Esther Dudley witnesses science supplant the rule of religion.

As the novel comes to an end, it is unclear how the prince of science will exert his influence on "the most marked American type." Impressed by his cousin's defiance of the tyrant, Strong proposes to Esther: "You have fought your battle like a heroine. If you will marry me, I will admire and love you more than ever a woman was loved since the world began" (166). Esther's ambivalent response leaves the reader wondering if this seemingly benevolent prince will make a conquest of the American type: "Esther looked at him with an expression that would have been a smile if it had not been infinitely dreary and absent; then she said simply and finally: 'But George, I don't love you, I love him'" (166). Although the scientist has offered Esther a means by which to ponder "all the problems of the universe," a match between the scientist and "the most marked American type" would be cold-blooded and sadly lacking, as Mrs. Murray had feared.

Henry Adams's novel *Esther* demonstrates the capacity of American people to overcome the new threats to American democracy. "The most marked American type," with the help of the American people, has escaped submission to the prince of religion and has resisted the inclination to tyranny or self-assertion as it was encouraged by the prince of art. It remains to be seen how and to what extent the American regime will be influenced by science. This concern will occupy Adams for the rest of his life.

Notes

1. Richard Brookhiser, *America's Dynasty: The Adamses, 1735–1918* (New York: Free Press, 2002), 213.

2. Earl N. Harbert, *The Force So Much Closer to Home: Henry Adams and the Adams Family* (New York: New York University Press, 1977), 52. Hereafter cited parenthetically.

3. Henry Adams, *Esther* (New York: Penguin, 1999), 34. Hereafter cited parenthetically.

4. Henry Adams, *Letters of Henry Adams, 1858–1891*, ed. Worthington Chauncey Ford (Boston: Houghton Mifflin, 1930), 468.

5. See, for example, Millicent Bell, "Adams' Esther: The Morality of Taste," *New England Quarterly* 35, no. 2 (June 1962): 147–61; and Patrick Wolfe, "The Revealing Fiction of Henry Adams," *New England Quarterly* 49, no. 3 (September 1876): 399–426.

6. James P. Young, *Henry Adams: The Historian as Political Theorist* (Lawrence: University Press of Kansas, 2001), 130–35.

7. William Merrill Decker, *The Literary Vocation of Henry Adams* (Chapel Hill: University of North Carolina Press, 1990), 7. Hereafter cited parenthetically.

8. For thoughtful comparisons between Adams's novel and Hawthorne's *The Scarlet Letter*, see William Merrill Decker, *The Literary Vocation of Henry Adams;* and Robert F. Sommer, "The Feminine Perspectives of Henry Adams' *Esther,*" *Studies in American Fiction* 18, no. 2 (Autumn 1990).

9. Nathaniel Hawthorne, *Twice-Told Tales*, with an introduction by Rosemary Mahoney (New York: Modern Library Classics, 2001), 227. Hereafter cited parenthetically.

10. To avoid confusion, I refer to Hawthorne's character as Mistress Dudley and to Adams's character as Esther Dudley or Esther.

11. Henry Adams, *The Education of Henry Adams* (New York: Modern Library, 1999), 34. Hereafter cited parenthetically.

12. J. C. Levenson, *The Mind and Art of Henry Adams* (Boston: Houghton Mifflin, 1957), 19.

13. John Ernest, "Henry Adams's Double: Recreating the Philosophical Statesman," *Journal of American Culture* 14, no. 1 (1991): 32.

14. Alexis de Tocqueville, *Democracy in America,* translated, edited, and with an introduction by Harvey C. Mansfield and Delba Winthrop (Chicago: University of Chicago Press, 2000), 403. Hereafter cited parenthetically.

15. Sommer, "The Feminine Perspectives of Henry Adams' *Esther,*" 138. Hereafter cited parenthetically.

PART II

The Search for Lost Faith

CHAPTER 6

Henry Adams

Henry Steele Commager

"IT WOULD BE FUN to send you some of my examination papers," wrote Professor Adams to his friend Charles Milnes Gaskell. "My rule in making them up is to ask questions which I can't myself answer."[1] It was a report and a prophecy. All his life Henry Adams made it a rule to ask questions he couldn't answer—questions that were, perhaps, quite unanswerable. In the beginning, when Adams was merely a teacher, there was something whimsical about it, and faintly perverse. Later on, it became part of a literary technique, an inverse method of stating a fact or suggesting an idea. In the end, it was a serious business, a desperately serious business. In the end, he asked questions because he wanted answers—because, indeed, "a historical formula that should satisfy the conditions of the stellar universe weighed heavily on his mind."[2] But his true function was to ask questions, not to answer them; his true function was to provoke speculation, not to satisfy it.

What Adams did, then, was relatively unimportant; but what he signified was immensely important. At Harvard, the teacher was more interesting than the subject; in his Washington study, the author was more interesting than the books. In the end, Adams abandoned the effort to eliminate the personal equation and recognized that, insofar as he was concerned, insofar as his generation was concerned, the Education of Henry Adams was the crucial question. He recognized that no questions Adams could ask were quite as interesting as the questions that he inspired, that no facts summoned from the historical past were quite as illuminating as the facts of his own intellectual history. He recognized, quite impersonally, that if the historian expected to find a formula that would explain American character, if he expected to find a formula that would reduce history to a science, if he expected to find a formula that would satisfy the conditions of a stellar universe, he must find a formula to explain Henry Adams.

Obviously, then, it is not as a teacher or as a historian, or even as a philosopher, that Adams is chiefly significant, but as a symbol. Adams himself regarded his teaching experience as a failure, his historical work as negligible, and his philosophical speculations as suggestive rather than final; and Adams's critical acumen was so sharp, his judgment so sound, and his sincerity so unimpeachable that it would be insolent to differ with him. And Adams was very positive about this matter. Lodge and Laughlin and Taylor and half a dozen others might recall that he was the most inspiring of teachers, that his learning was prodigious and his interpretation profound; but he himself "was content neither with what he had taught nor with the way he had taught it"; and he was sure that Harvard University, "as far as it was represented by Henry Adams—produced at great waste of time and money results not worth reaching."[3] Nor was he less dogmatic about the value of his books—he who was so rarely dogmatic. Adams "had even published a dozen volumes of American history," he confessed, "for no other purpose than to satisfy himself whether, by the severest process of stating, with the least possible comment, such facts as seemed sure, in such order as seemed rigorously consequent, he could fix for a familiar moment a necessary sequence of human movement. The result had satisfied him as little as at Harvard College. Where he saw sequence, other men saw something quite different, and no one saw the same unit of measure."[4] Nor was this the perversity of old age or an effort to outwit criticism. Even as he was publishing the stately volumes of his *History*, he wrote to Elizabeth Cameron: "There are not nine pages in the nine volumes that now express anything of my interests or feelings; unless perhaps some of my disillusionments. So you must not blame me if I feel, or seem to feel, morbid on the subject of the history. I care more for one chapter, or any dozen pages of *Esther* than for the whole history."[5] And to Dr. J. F. Jameson he confessed: "I would much rather wipe out all I have ever said than go on with more."[6] And as for the dynamic theory of history, the rule of phase applied to history, the law of entropy, and the law of acceleration, Adams was too good a historian not to see the fallacy of analogies from science to society, too good a scientist not to know that the science of today is the superstition of tomorrow. He was concerned indeed—the conclusion seems inescapable—with urging the necessity of formulating some philosophy of history, some science of society; he was concerned with asking questions and pointing to the consequences of all conceivable answers.[7]

Adams dismissed his own historical labors in a paragraph, and it would perhaps be discourteous for us to insist that they deserve more than this inattention. But even if we should agree that Adams's teaching was futile and his historical writing irrelevant, we would still be eager to discover the cause of that futility, the meaning of that irrelevancy; we would still be inclined to ask questions. Here are the volumes, standing soberly on our shelves, eloquent witnesses to the unwilling conformity of an Adams: *The Writings of Albert Gallatin*,[8] *The Life of Albert Gallatin*,[9] *John Randolph*,[10] *The History of the United States of America during the Administrations of Jefferson and Madison*.[11] Why, it may be asked, did Adams write these books? Why did he write them in conventional, what he called "old-school," form? Why, having written them, did he profess to think them worthless? Adams himself could not answer these questions in any satisfactory way, and it is not to be supposed that we can do better than he was able to do. We could say that he wrote them because he could think of nothing better to do, but that would be to adopt consciously the paradox that is pointless if deliberate. We could say that he wrote them to satisfy his own curiosity about the Adams family and the role it played in the evolution of the American nation; and Adams, who was never unconscious of his family, would readily accept this explanation. Certainly he felt that the history of the Adams family was central to the history of the American people, and that the problem presented by the victory of Jefferson over John Adams and of Jackson over John Quincy Adams was as fascinating as any problem in history. We could say that he wrote them in order to clarify in his own mind the meaning of American history, in order to prepare the way for the formulation of historical laws. He observed:

> The scientific interest of American history centered in national character, and in the workings of a society destined to become vast, in which individuals were important chiefly as types. Although this kind of interest was different from that of European history, it was at least as important to the world. Should history ever become a true science, it must expect to establish its laws, not from the complicated story of rival European nationalities, but from the economical evolution of a great democracy. North America was the most favorable field on the globe for the spread of a society so large, uniform, and

isolated as to answer the purposes of science. . . . The interest of such a subject exceeded that of any other branch of science, for it brought mankind within sight of its own end.[12]

These histories and biographies conformed to a pattern, and the pattern was not without either beauty or symmetry. They satisfied certain requirements both of form and of substance; they were thorough, accurate, scholarly, critical, impartial; they were distinguished in thought and in style. It is not an exaggeration, indeed, to insist that *The Life of Albert Gallatin* is the best political biography, the *Administrations of Jefferson and Madison* the finest piece of historical writing, in our literature. They stated "such facts as seemed sure, in such order as seemed rigorously consequent"; they "fixed for a familiar moment" a sequence of human movement. But the result, we must remember, satisfied Adams as little as had teaching. The history was good history—better history had not been written. Everyone agreed that it was good history; but no one, least of all Adams, knew what it was good for. It was good for facts, of course; but Adams himself confessed that "I never loved or taught facts, if I could help it, having that antipathy to facts which only idiots and philosophers attain."[13] It was good for what it told of American character, for what it prophesied of American democracy; but the character changed and the prophecies were invalid, for Adams's ideal ploughboy was less likely in 1900 than in 1800 to "figure out in quaternions the relations of his furrows." It was good for the purposes of philosophy, insofar as it "fixed a sequence of human movement"; but Adams came to doubt that it was a necessary sequence and was satisfied that "the sequence of men led to nothing, and that the sequence of their society could lead no further, while the mere sequence of time was artificial, and the sequence of thought was chaos."[14]

But if, by his own valuation, Adams's historical labors contributed nothing to history, we can turn perhaps to his philosophy with hope of more satisfactory results. It is something to say that Adams is the only American historian who has ever seriously attempted to formulate a philosophy of history. He was not unaware of the difficulties; but no Adams had ever been frightened by difficulties, and Henry Adams, certainly, had nothing to lose. So in 1894, three years after he had published the last volume of that history that he regarded with such indifference, he addressed a letter to his colleagues in the American Historical Association on the tendency of history to become a science: "That the effort to make history a science may fail is possible, and perhaps probable; but that it should cease, unless for reasons that would cause all science to cease, is not within the range of experience. Historians will not, and even if they would they can not, abandon the attempt. Science itself would admit its own failure if it admitted that man, the most important of all its subjects, could not be brought within its range."[15] But alas, the generation of Comte and Buckle was past, and historians did not even undertake the attempt that Adams had announced as inevitable.

But, however derelict his professional colleagues, Adams would not be derelict. Years earlier, in drawing the brilliant Mrs. Lightfoot Lee, he had written sympathetically of the intellectual curiosity that looked for first causes: "Here, then, was the explanation of her restlessness, discontent, ambition,—call it what you will. It was the feeling of a passenger on an ocean steamer whose mind will not give him rest until he has been in the engine-room and talked with the engineer. She wanted to see with her own eyes the action of primary forces; to touch with her own hand the massive machinery of society; to measure with her own mind the capacity of the motive power."[16] Adams experienced the same discontent, the same restlessness in the face of the riddles of history. "To the tired student, the idea that he must give it up seemed sheer senility. . . . Every man with self-respect enough to become more effective, if only as a machine, has had to account to himself for himself somehow, and to invent a formula of his own for his own universe, if the standard formulas fail."[17] That the standard formulas had failed, none would deny; and Adams invented one of his own.

The result of Adams's speculations can be read in the concluding chapters of the *Education,* in the "Letter to American Teachers of History,"[18] and in the essay on the "Rule of Phase Applied to History." "If history ever meant to correct the errors she made in detail," he had written, "she must agree on a scale for the whole";[19] and these essays constituted an attempt to formulate a scale for the whole. The scale was to be large enough to be inclusive. The problem was to bring human history in harmony with the organic laws of the universe, and the formula that Adams hit upon was the Law of the Dissipation of Energy.

The formula had many ramifications and was supported by an impressive array of scientific data; for from those early years, when he had hobnobbed with Sir Charles Lyell and with the *Pteraspis,* Adams had prided himself on his knowledge of science. Those who will, can read the evidence and ponder the conclusions; the argument, for all its bewildering mathematical formulas, is simple enough. The Second Law of Thermodynamics announced that energy was constantly being expended without being replaced. The idea of progress, therefore, was a delusion; and the evidence customarily adduced to substantiate the idea sustained, instead, a very different conclusion. Civilization itself had been brought about by the operation of the Law of Entropy—the law of the dissipation of energy by the constant degradation of its vital power, rather than the reverse. Society, as an organism, is subject to the law of degradation precisely like any other organism, and faces therefore the prospect of running down indefinitely until at last total stagnation is reached. And the period of stagnation, Adams continued, is not in some remote future but in the present. In the first quarter of the twentieth century, thought "would reach the limit of its possibilities," and the honest historian might logically "treat the history of modern Europe and America as a typical example of energies indicating degradation with 'headlong rapidity' towards 'inevitable death.'" "Already," Adams concluded desperately, "History and Sociology gasp for breath."[20] We are not concerned, here, with the validity of this argument except insofar as it constitutes Adams's contribution to the philosophy of history, and Adams himself has furnished us the most pertinent comment on that contribution. "Historians," he observed, "have got into far too much trouble by following schools of theology in their efforts to enlarge their synthesis, that they should willingly repeat the process in science. For human purposes a point must always be soon reached where larger synthesis is suicide."[21] In this case, certainly, the larger synthesis was suicide. Suggestive, provocative, brilliant, and profound the dynamic theory of history indubitably was; but the most interesting thing about it was that Adams should have advanced it.

But if Adams had damned his formal contributions to history as insignificant and characterized his historical synthesis as intellectual suicide, we are left with only one alternative. If we can consider neither the history nor the philosophy, we must fall back on a consideration of Adams himself. Such an approach has, fortunately, the warrant of excellent precedent; for it is precisely what Adams himself did in the circumstances. "One sought," he tells us, "no absolute truth. One sought only a spool on which to wind the thread of history without breaking it. Among indefinite possible orbits, one sought the orbit which would best satisfy the observed movement of the runaway star Groombridge, 1838, commonly called Henry Adams."[22]

And there is no more convenient spool upon which to wind the thread of history than Henry Adams. For Adams was not only a historian: he was himself a historical fact—he was, indeed, to use a term too often used, a significant fact. Of Adams alone, among the major historians, can it be said that what he was is more significant than what he wrote. Of Adams alone can it be said that, given a choice between what he wrote and what he was, we should inevitably choose the latter. For it is no merely capricious judgment that has preferred *Mont-Saint-Michel and Chartres*[23] and the *Education* to the *History* or the biographies; and as for Adams's philosophical speculations, the most thoughtful of American historians has justly observed that "Adams was worth a wilderness of philosophies."[24]

It is an exaggeration, of course, to suggest that we can interpret the whole of American history in the person of Henry Adams, but it is no very shocking exaggeration to insist that to the student of American history, the contemplation of Adams is the beginning of wisdom. For whether we confine ourselves to the mere outward aspects of Adams's career or embrace the history of the entire family that he recapitulated, or penetrate to his own intellectual and psychological reactions to his generation, we will find that Adams illuminates, better than any of his contemporaries, the course of American history.

He explains for us the shift in political power from New England to the West, from agriculture to industry, from the individual to the mass, and the change in the nature of political power from intelligence to instinct, from reason to force. He reveals the decline of the intellectually aristocratic tradition and of the family tradition, the futility of intellectual discipline, the impotence of moral integrity, and the irrelevance of fastidiousness, in politics. He emphasizes what Brooks Adams called the "degradation of the democratic dogma" and the failure of eighteenth-century concepts of democracy to effect a compromise with nineteenth-century society. Intellectually he represents the transition from transcendental faith to pragmatic acquiescence, from evolutionary optimism to mechanistic pessimism, from unity to multiplicity, from order to chaos. He illustrates the rejection of the Victorian idea of progress for the idea of entropy, the rejection of a teleological universe for a mechanistic universe, the substitution of science for philosophy, of the machine for man, of force for faith, of the dynamo for the Virgin, and, at the same time, the convulsive effort to discover a philosophy that would satisfy the requirements of both instinct and reason. And he was never unaware of his significance as a symbol and as an experiment, never unconscious of the larger meaning that could be read out of his intellectual and spiritual biography, and never unwilling to undertake himself the task of interpretation.

No one who has ever turned the leaves of the *Education* will forget Adams's description of the Grant administration,[25] no one who has ever read the scintillating pages of *Democracy* will fail to remember the picture of political corruption in the Washington of the seventies.[26] Anonymity could not conceal, or objectiveness disguise, the intensely personal character of these reflections. But it is a singular distinction of Adams that where he was most personal he was most general. The failure of Henry Adams to adjust himself to the politics of the Grant administration illustrated the failure of eighteenth-century democracy, of the democracy of Gallatin and John Quincy Adams, to effect such an adjustment. The indifference of the politicians of postwar America to the talents and the ideals of Adams represented the indifference of a new, industrialized America to the discipline and the ideals of the past. Adams was at pains, here, to account for his own failure; but had that been the whole of the matter, he would have dismissed the experience as cavalierly as he had dismissed Harvard College or the *North American Review*. It was because he understood the pertinence of his own experience to the experience of the American people, because he appreciated the moral implicit in his story, that he dignified this episode in his life with elaborate analysis and interpretation. So, too, with *Democracy*, that sprightly commentary on American politics and society in the Gilded Age. As a novel it is thin, and as an analysis of the forces behind American political corruption it is thinner still; but even its brittle thinness, its dilettantism and exoticism, may be taken to reflect certain qualities in the American mind.

Adams himself furnished the best criticism of *Democracy*. The authorship of the book had been well concealed, and it amused Adams to impute it to his friend John Hay. He wrote to the long-suffering Hay: "I repeat that your novel. . . . is a failure because it undertook to describe the workings of a power in this city, and spoiled a great tragic subject such as Aeschylus might have made what it should be. . . . The tragic element, if accepted as real, is bigger here than ever on this earth before. I hate to

see it mangled *à la* Daudet, in a tame-cat way. Men don't know tragedy
when they see it."[27] Could anything better illustrate the futile liberalism of
the postwar years than this confession that a great tragic subject had been
treated, deliberately, as a joke, or, what was worse, as an essay in cynicism?
It is suggestive that the author of *Gallatin*, of the *Jefferson and Madison
Administrations*, should also be the author of *Democracy*; suggestive that
the historian of democratic idealism should be the critic of the degradation
of the democratic dogma. It is even more suggestive that that mind that had
celebrated so magnanimously the idealism of Jefferson should be reduced
by Blaine and Conkling to a cynicism that was frivolous and a satire that was
frustrated. It was personal perhaps, but no one who recalls the impotence of
the genteel tradition as represented by Godkin and Gilder and Curtis can
doubt that it was more than personal.

Yet, it would be unjust to imply that Adams and his generation of liberals
were defeated by the political pygmies who strut and fret their way through
the pages of the *Education* or *Democracy*. Nothing as trivial as a phalanx of
Blaines, Conklings, Camerons, and Butlers could account for the failure of
an Adams. These men, after all, were the proper objects of satire and, where
they did not render even satire ridiculous, could be disposed of easily enough.
Nor was it even the more powerful Goulds and Vanderbilts and Whitneys and
Morgans who made the existence of Adams irrelevant, if not impertinent.
These were but the instruments of larger forces—objects, as Adams showed,
of scientific study, not of moral indignation. What silenced Adams was precisely the realization that "modern politics is, at bottom, a struggle not of
men but of forces. The men become every year more and more creatures of
force, massed about central powerhouses. The conflict is no longer between
the men, but between the motors that drive the men, and men tend to succumb to their own motive forces."[28] It took, after all, cosmic forces to account
for the tragedy of John and John Quincy Adams, and the indifference of a
modern world to the existence of a Henry Adams was less humiliating when
it was seen to be the inevitable consequence of scientific forces over whose
operation man exercised no control. The failure of Henry Adams to achieve
his education was indeed a failure of so cataclysmic a character that it was
necessary to invoke the whole of science and philosophy in order to explain it.

But here, again, the experience of Adams was the experience of his
generation, though Adams alone seemed to appreciate it. For when Adams
began that long pilgrimage that was to end, so curiously, before the altar of

Chartes, he had no need of faith other than faith in the beneficient workings of the laws of the universe. Darwin and Lyell had taught him evolution, and everyone knew that evolution meant progress. Science and sociology joined hands to justify the findings of the historian; and it was clear that the dreams of Rousseau and Condorcet, of Jefferson and Gallatin, fell short of realities, and that the intuitive truths of transcendentalism were to be justified by the experimental truths of the laboratory. "Then he had entered gaily the door of the glacial epoch, and had surveyed a universe of unities and uniformities."[29] But science was a slut, and treated Adams as shamefully as she had treated his grandfather, John Quincy Adams. Parrington says: "In the nineties the clouds drew over the brilliant Victorian skies. With the substitution of physics for biology came a more somber mood that was to put away the genial romanticism of Victorian evolution, substitute a mechanistic conception for the earlier teleological progress, and reshape its philosophy in harmony with a deterministic pessimism that denied purpose or plan in the changing universe of matter."[30] Of all Americans, Adams most fully comprehended the change, and he most fully illustrated it. Not for him the heavenly vision of truth that was revealed to John Fiske in his youth: "When we have come to a true philosophy, and make *that* our standpoint, all things become clear. We know what things to learn, and what, in the infinite mass of things to leave unlearned—and then the Universe becomes clear and harmonious."[31] Alas for Adams, his true philosophy taught him only infinite confusion and chaos and left him naked and defenseless in a world that had "neither joy, nor love, nor light, nor certitude, nor peace, nor help for pain."

It would be misleading, of course, to interpret this tragedy as intellectual merely. Indeed, it might almost be said that the whole of Adams's intellectual career was an effort to find some impersonal meaning in the tragedy that had shattered his life. For when he returned home that bleak December morning to find Marian Hooper dead, he entered the wastelands; and for twenty years he walked in desolation until at last he had convinced himself that the universe was but desolation.

To an intimate, he might reveal his anguish; and to Elizabeth Cameron he confessed: "The light has gone out. I am not to blame. As long as I could make life work, I stood by it, and swore by it as though it was my God, as indeed it was."[32] But in his more formal writing he preserved his immaculate impersonality:

The child born in 1900 . . . found himself in a land where no one had ever pen-
etrated before; where order was an accidental relation obnoxious to nature;
artificial compulsion imposed on motion; against which every free energy
of the universe revolted; and which, being merely occasional, resolved itself
back into anarchy at last. He could not deny that the law of the new universe
explained much that had been most obscure, especially the persistently fiendish treatment of man by man; the perpetual effort of society to establish law,
and the perpetual revolt of society against the law it had established; the
perpetual building up of authority by force, and the perpetual appeal to force
to overthrow it; the perpetual symbolism of a higher law, and the perpetual
relapse to a lower one; the perpetual victory of the principles of freedom,
and their perpetual conversion into principles of power; but the staggering
problem was the outlook ahead into the despotism of artificial order which
nature abhorred. . . .

All that a historian won was a vehement wish to escape. He saw his education complete, and was sorry he ever began it. As a matter of taste, he greatly
preferred his eighteenth-century education when God was a father and nature a mother, and all was for the best in a scientific universe.[33]

Adams was right, of course, in generalizing his own tragedy; that
tragedy was more immediate, more catastrophic even, than the tragedy
of others who wandered in the wastelands of the new century; but that it
was universal, rather than merely personal, no one can doubt. Twentieth-
century America was a nation adrift from its moorings, skeptical of its past,
uncertain of its future. The old faiths were gone, the muscular Calvinism
of the seventeenth century, the enlightened deism of the eighteenth, the
romantic and buoyant transcendentalism of the nineteenth. Pragmatism
was a sorry substitute for faith, and the drift from Jefferson to Emerson and
from Emerson to Dewey was as heartbreaking as the drift from Newton to
Darwin and from Darwin to Haeckel.

No one better illustrated this drift than did Adams himself, and no
one was more sensitive to its significance. To Jefferson and his followers
the destiny of America, the destiny of mankind, was plain, and they did not
doubt the ability of man to control that destiny; but Adams knew that he
was the creature, the victim, of forces that he but faintly understood and
over which he could exercise no control, and he knew that he was unique
only in the extent to which he understood his impotence. Intellectually
Adams recognized the chaos, the multiplicity, of the twentieth century; and

he even went so far as to furnish us with the most illuminating study of that multiplicity in our literature. But intellectually he had recognized, too, the inevitable defeat of "his eighteenth century, his Constitution of 1789, his George Washington, his Harvard College, his Quincy, and his Plymouth Pilgrims. . . . He had hugged his antiquated dislike of bankers and capitalistic society until he had become little better than a crank. . . . He had known for years that he must accept the régime, but he had known a great many other disagreeable certainties—like age, senility, and death—against which one made what little resistance one could."[34] Recognition and acquiescence were very different matters, and there was rebel blood in the Adams veins. "The soul," he wrote, "has always refused to live in peace with the body. The angels, too, were always in rebellion." As a matter of taste, he had said, he much preferred a philosophy in which "God was a father and nature a mother, and all was for the best in a scientific universe."[35]

His revolt against the chaos of modern science threw him back on the unity of the church. It was not a matter of taste merely. Force for force, as he never tired of observing, the Virgin was as intelligible as the dynamo, and as powerful. So Adams, "happy in the thought that at last he had found a mistress who could see no difference in the age of her lovers,"[36] turned to the adoration of the Virgin. It was in part an emotional reaction, an act of faith; but Adams could not be satisfied with a reaction merely emotional: he had to rationalize his faith in the power and the grace of the Virgin as John Quincy Adams had rationalized his faith in a democracy. He who had lived, passionately, the life of reason, who had inherited from generations of Adamses a reverent respect for reason, made this gesture of faith an exercise in historical logic.

Abélard had been silenced, and St. Thomas had formulated a philosophy that explained the universe as a unity; but Adams found unity not as the conclusion of a syllogism, though he was fascinated by the syllogism, but in the life and thought and emotion of generations of men. He was persuaded not by the *Summa theologiae* but by the Merveille of the cathedral of St. Michel, by the rose window of Chartres, by the *Chanson de Roland*, and by the miracles of the Virgin.

The Virgin was not rational, but she was the most rational thing in an irrational universe. Faith was above law and scorned logic; and Adams, who had discovered that law was chance and logic bankrupt, preferred to take his chances with the Virgin rather than with science.

Mary concentrated in herself the whole rebellion of man against fate; the whole protest against divine law; the whole contempt for human law as its outcome; the whole unutterable fury of human nature beating itself against the walls of its prisonhouse, and suddenly seized by a hope that in the Virgin man had found a door of escape. She was above law; she took feminine pleasure in turning Hell into an ornament; she delighted in trampling on every social distinction in this world and the next. She knew that the universe was as unintelligible to her, on any theory of morals, as it was to her worshipers, and she felt, like them, no sure conviction that it was any more intelligible to the Creator of it.[37]

Uprooted and demoralized, his life a broken arch, his past without meaning and his future without hope, tortured by a restlessness that found no repose in thought and no purpose in action, resigned to the bankruptcy of reason and the futility of knowledge, disillusioned of progress and of evolution, reconciled to the degradation of energy, the exhaustion of society, and the fall of man, lost in a universe that was mechanistic and chaotic, Adams turned in desperation to the one symbol of unity that seemed to have meaning, and found there such solace as he could. "Her pity," he knew, "had no limit";[38] and it was not only Adams but his generation that needed limitless pity.

Notes

Reprinted from *The Marcus W. Jernegan Essays in American Historiography,* ed. William T. Hutchinson (Chicago: University of Chicago Press, 1937), 191–206, by permission of the University of Chicago Press.

1. Worthington C. Ford, ed., *Letters of Henry Adams, 1858–1891* (Boston, 1930), 211.
2. H. Adams, *The Education of Henry Adams: An Autobiography* (1918; Boston, 1930), 376.
3. Ibid., 304.
4. Ibid., 382.
5. *Letters,* February 13, 1891, 468.
6. *American Historical Review* 26:9. See also *Education,* 325.
7. *Education,* 474–98.
8. 3 vols. (Philadelphia, 1879).
9. Philadelphia, 1880.

10. Boston, 1882.

11. 9 vols. (New York, 1889–91).

12. Adams, *History*, bk. 9, 222, 225.

13. H. Adams to H. O. Taylor in 1915, quoted by J. T. Adams in his *The Adams Family* (New York, 1930), 340, 348; *Education* 37, 301–2.

14. *Education*, 382.

15. "The Tendency of History," *American Historical Association Annual Report, 1894* (Washington, 1895), 18.

16. H. Adams, *Democracy: An American Novel* (New York, 1880), 10.

17. *Education*, 472.

18. Adams, *The Degradation of the Democratic Dogma* (New York, 1919), 137–209.

19. Ibid., 267–311; *Education*, 434.

20. *The Degradation of Democratic Dogma*, 243, 261. See also 142, 154, 308.

21. *Education*, 401–2.

22. Ibid., 472.

23. Washington, 1904.

24. Carl L. Becker, *Everyman His Own Historian: Essays on History and Politics* (New York, 1935), 156.

25. *Education*, chaps. 17 and 18.

26. *Democracy: An American Novel*, passim.

27. *Letters*, March 4, 1883, 348.

28. *Education*, 421–22.

29. Ibid., 400.

30. V. L. Parrington, *The Beginnings of Critical Realism in America* (New York, 1930), 190–91.

31. Quoted by John S. Clark in his *The Life and Letters of John Fiske*, 2 vols. (Boston and New York, 1917), 1:255.

32. *Letters*, January 2, 1891, 458.

33. *Education*, 457–58.

34. Ibid., 343–44.

35. Ibid., 458.

36. Ibid., 470.

37. *Mont-Saint-Michel and Chartres*, 241; see also 286.

38. Ibid., 83, 244.

CHAPTER 7

The Politics of Scientific History

Richard Samuelson

Henry Adams vs. the American Historical Association

FOR MORE THAN A century, America's historians have quarreled with Henry Adams. Herbert Baxter Adams, one of the founders of the modern historical discipline in America, concluded that "we ought never to have elected Henry Adams president" of the American Historical Association (AHA). A few years ago, Gordon Wood celebrated the centennial of the *American Historical Review* with an apologia for the American Historical Association. The subtitle of Wood's essay was "How Henry Adams Got It Wrong." The feeling was mutual. Henry Adams called Herbert Baxter Adams his "bête noir."[1] We can only speculate about what Adams would make of Wood's remarks.

Yet Henry Adams is one of America's greatest historians, and he always thought of himself as a historian. His *The History of the United States of America during the Administrations of Thomas Jefferson and James Madison* may very well be the best work of history written by an American. Even after he ceased to work in the field, Adams still styled himself a historian. In his autobiographical *Education of Henry Adams,* Adams repeatedly turns to the perspective of the "historian." On his time in London during the Civil War: "Within the narrow limits of this class, the American Legation was fairly at home; possibly a score of houses, all liberal, and all literary, but perfect only in the eyes of a Harvard College historian." On his writings on civil service reform during the Grant administration: "Material furnished by a government seldom satisfies critics or historians, for it lies always under suspicion." At the Chicago Exposition of 1893: "For the historian alone the Exposition made a serious effort." Adams adds many other such references in the *Education*. Formally speaking, of course, "historian" was Adams's profession. The only regular job he ever held was his assistant professorship at Harvard from 1871 to 1877. Adams remained comfortable in the role, even if he left the classroom behind.[2]

Wherefore, then, the mutual hostility and disrespect between Adams and his brother historians? Adams's Presidential Address to the American Historical Association sheds some light on the matter. Sandwiched between Adams's *History of the United States* on one side, and his famous literary works *Mont-Saint-Michel and Chartres* and *The Education of Henry Adams* on the other, this short piece can be read as Adams's valedictory to the field. Perhaps because of the shadow cast by Adams's major works, his Presidential Address has received relatively little attention.[3] Yet the piece repays close reading, as it sheds light on Adams's move out of the field of history, at least as the discipline came to understand itself under the direction of the American Historical Association.

Before we turn to the contents of the Address, we should note the difficulty of interpreting it. The Address is short and, at times, elliptical. Moreover, Adams admitted that he did not explain himself fully: "In these remarks, which are only casual, and offered in the paradoxical spirit of private conversation, I have not ventured to express any opinion of my own; or, if I have expressed it, pray consider it as withdrawn" (233).[4] In the Address, Adams was making suggestions, and giving hints. That being the case, our job is to read Adams with care, and with a due appreciation of the difficulties he presents us.

Even during his own tenure as president of the American Historical Association, Adams distanced himself, both literally and figuratively, from his brother historians. He made sure not to be present to give the address in person. In late September 1894, Adams wrote his friend John Hay: "I arrived here [in Washington, D.C.] happy in the thought that the Historical Association had met, as announced, at Saratoga, Sept. 12, and had by this time merrily gone its path, led by a new and, I need not say, a less capable President. My namesake [Herbert Baxter Adams] coppered me neatly. I find a circular postponing the occasion till Dec. 27, *at Washington.* Really, he has put me in a tight place, but if [Clarence] King will go to Mexico, I may escape." In the event, Adams did manage to be out of town.[5]

The contents of Adams's Presidential Address to the AHA indicate that there was more than a physical distance separating Adams from the other leaders of the historical profession in America. Adams disagreed with the AHA about the nature and purpose of scientific history. Addressing the AHA, he wrote: "That the effort to make History a Science may fail, is possible, and perhaps probable; but that it should cease, unless for reasons that would cause all science to cease, is not within the range of experience. Historians will not, and even if they would they cannot, abandon the attempt. Science itself would admit its own failure, if it admitted that man, the most important of all its subjects, could not be brought within its range" (229). When Adams penned his Address, the American Historical Association was less than a decade old. It was organized as part of an effort to turn the study of history into a modern, scientific discipline, following the rules of evidence and interpretation used in the natural sciences. In that sense, history was a stand-in for social science more generally. The creation of the American Historical Association represented the effort to study man scientifically. In the seventeenth century, men like Galileo and Newton had made the study of the heavens scientific; meanwhile Bayle and his peers had done likewise for chemistry. In the eighteenth and nineteenth centuries, Buffon, Darwin, and others had applied the scientific method to the animal kingdom. The rise of social science, and with it the rise of the social science Ph.D. and social science organizations like the AHA, represented the effort to apply the same ideas to the study of human beings.

Adams believed that historians should either take the scientific method as seriously as did natural scientists, or admit that their science was not science at all—at least not in the sense that chemistry was. Just as no one doubted the truth of Boyle's law, Adams suggested, so too would no one doubt the laws of history, once science had discovered them: "a Science cannot be played with. If an hypothesis is advanced that obviously brings into a direct sequence of cause and effect all the phenomena of human history, we must accept it, and if we accept it, we must teach it. . . . The rest of society can reject or ignore, but we must follow the new light, no matter where it leads" (232). Similarly, he added, "any Science of History must be absolute, like other Sciences, and must fix with mathematical certainty the path which human society has got to follow" (231). Historical science could not work with half measures. If historians wished to have an equal place in the university with the natural sciences, they had to have the same exacting standards of proof. Like Galileo, Adams said, they must say, "in secret if not in public: 'E pur si mouve!'" (232).

In his contribution to the first issue of the *American Historical Review*, Adams tried to shed further, albeit ironic light on the question of scientific history. To help the American Historical Association launch its signature publication, Adams sent in an essay that did little more than correct an error he had discovered in his *History*. Adams had misidentified Count Edward de Crillon, an adventurer who appeared in Washington during Madison's administration. As Professor Wood suspects, Adams was suggesting that it would always be hard to interpret the past because it is full of people who are less than honest, who distort or hide the truth, and who may themselves not know what they intend to do. Beyond that, Adams was pointing to the problem of turning history into a science. Were history truly to be a science, Adams was suggesting, factual accuracy would have the same importance in history as it did in chemistry. That very idea was problematic: unlike a lump of coal, a human being can try to deceive us, rendering important facts debatable at best. In short, Adams wondered whether the subject matter of history was, in fact, suited to the scientific method.

Even as he highlighted the problem of factual accuracy, Adams also pointed to deeper questions, asking what kinds of truths science discovered. "Any Science," he wrote in the Address, "assumes a necessary sequence of cause and effect" (231). Yet, Adams found, one could not know, in an absolute sense, whether the assumption upon which the science rested was true. The problem was that, on one hand, correlation and causation were different things, and, on the other, that the scientific method is a method for discovering nothing more than correlations. In the *Education*, Adams drew out the implication still further. "Historians," he wrote,

> undertake to arrange sequences,—called stories, or histories—assuming in silence a relation of cause and effect. These assumptions, hidden in the depths of dusty libraries, have been astounding, but commonly unconscious and childlike; so much so, that if any captious critic were to drag them to light, historians would probably reply, with one voice, that they had never supposed themselves required to know what they were talking about. Adams, for one, had toiled in vain to find out what he meant. He had even published a dozen volumes of American history for no other purpose than to satisfy himself whether, by the severest process of stating, with the least possible comment,

such facts as seemed sure, in such order as seemed rigorously consequent, he could fix for a familiar moment a necessary sequence of cause and effect. . . . He cared little about his experiments and less about his statesmen, who seemed to him quite as ignorant as himself and, as a rule, no more honest; but he insisted on a relation of sequence, and if he could not reach it by one method, he would try as many methods as science knew.[6]

Between the lines, Adams was suggesting, once again, that history might not be a good candidate for the scientific method. Beyond that, he pointed to the problem of cause and effect. What were they? Could they ever be proven in history the same way as they were proven in chemistry? History, after all, was not amenable to controlled experiments. Ultimately, Adams was suggesting that brother historians acted in bad faith. They knew that their discipline could never be a science in the same way that the natural sciences were, and yet they went on creating a professional organization, and a journal, as if the natural sciences were a proper model for history. Similarly, most historians disregarded epistemological questions. Such questions belonged in a department of philosophy, not a history department. That's what Adams meant when he suggested that historians did not really know what they were talking about. Is it any wonder that Adams and his brother historians had a rocky relationship?

The Burden of History

Despite his strictures on historical science, Adams took the responsibilities of the historical profession quite seriously. Adams suggested that historians had a peculiar burden in the modern age. Given the peculiar ideological contours of the modern age, Adams found, only history could give direction to science in general. Moreover, he thought such a task was necessary, given the dangers that civilization faced.

Adams combined two concerns that most of us think of as separate: the fear that technology would overwhelm man, and the need to make history a science. In 1862, he wrote his brother Charles: "Man has mounted science, and is now run away with. I firmly believe that before many centuries more, science will be the master of man. The engines he will have invented will be beyond his strength to control. Some day science may have the existence of mankind in its power, and the human race commit suicide, by blowing up the world."[7] Adams's observation was shrewd, and, after the twentieth century it is easy for us to understand. Adams's solution to the problem—making history scientific—looks downright odd to us.

Because science, a human invention, was responsible for the dangers that men faced, Adams concluded that scientists had a duty to help find a solution. Near the end of the Address, Adams noted that Western civilization seemed to be moving toward a crisis, and "our Universities, at all events, must be prepared to meet it. If such a crisis should come, the Universities throughout the world will have done most to create it, and are under most obligation to find a solution for it" (233). Because the universities, and the science that they invented, had done so much to produce a crisis, it was their duty to search for a solution to the crisis.

Among all the disciplines in the modern university, Adams held, history alone was capable of providing leadership. At the beginning of his Address, Adams admitted that historians might have a hard time leading public opinion, but, he found, it would ultimately become necessary: "that we should ever act on public opinion with the weight of one compact and energetic conviction, is hardly to be expected; but that, one day or another, we shall be compelled to act individually, or in groups, I cannot doubt" (229). Near the end, Adams said that the historians "may at any time in the next fifty years be compelled to find an answer: 'Yes' or 'No'" (233). Regardless of historians' ability to give their fellow men wise counsel, the historians would have to say something.

Of all the social sciences, why was history the only one that could provide answers? According to Adams, the effort to control science, or to control the men who used the results of science, was the goal of scientific history. "Four out of five serious students of history who are living today, have, in the course of their work, felt that they stood on the brink of a great generalization that would reduce all history under a law as clear as the laws which govern the material world." Such a man "hope[s] that he might find the secret which would transform these odds-and-ends of philosophy into one self-evident, harmonious and complete system. . . . Scores of times, he must have dropped his pen, to think how one short step—one sudden inspiration,—would show all human knowledge . . . would bring him on the high-road of science. Every professor who has tried to teach the doubtful facts which we now call History, must have felt that, sooner or later, he or another would put order in the Chaos and bring light into the darkness"

(229–30). A grand synthesis would complete the work of making history scientific. Modern science is predictive. By studying the world, it generates laws that allow men to predict the direction in which things will go in the future. That's what set history apart from the other social sciences. By describing a line of progress, history might allow society to control itself by discovering a principle with which to discriminate among means and ends. It would allow the scientist to determine which questions are and are not worth asking. Modern science was not supposed to explore ends, Adams knew, but that was precisely the problem. How could one use the scientific method to tell us how to distinguish right from wrong, when to go to war and when to make peace, and how to live? By describing a line of change over time, from the past to the future, history might offer an answer.

Once again, some of Adams's comments in the *Education* shed further light on this point. Adams called himself a "child of the seventeenth and eighteenth centuries." That meant that he was born to a tradition that wanted to put reason in charge of society. James Young notes that Adams traced modernity to Francis Bacon. Bacon and others, notably Bacon's one-time secretary Hobbes, hoped that science could bring an end to the religious wars that plagued Europe in their day. Bacon, Adams wrote, "urged society to lay aside the idea of evolving the universe from a thought, and to try evolving thought from the universe. The mind should observe and register forces—take them apart and put them together—without assuming unity at all." Because "the idea of evolving the universe from a thought" had led men to war over competing ideas (and the religions they bred), Bacon advised men to study the world as they confronted it, noting its multiplicity and using what they studied to serve their own, material ends. The quest for more bread would end the religious circus. Reasonable agreements about interests would replace religious wars over belief. The new science of politics that inspired Adams's great-grandfather and the other Federalists of 1788 and 1789 was based, in part, on that foundation.[8] For a while, the project of science seemed to be working. Man's control over nature grew greater and greater, and men ceased to fight about religion.

The problem Adams highlighted in his Address was that science had two uses. Even as it produced inventions that relieved man's lot on earth, it also gave man bigger and bigger guns and bombs. Alas, Adams found, imperfect men, under the direction of imperfect human sciences, were still in charge of things. Science had not overcome free will, or the abuse of it. The result, Adams feared, was a near mathematical certainty that men would, eventually, use their new weapons and cause great evil. There was no turning back from science, and yet it was unclear whether science would teach men to control themselves. The crisis to which Adams alluded would come when men needed a means to save them from the evils that science made possible.

Having been built in opposition to religion, science would demand a scientific means of control. In the modern world, few men—at least few educated men—took religion seriously, but elites did defer to science. Modern religious thinkers tended to be orthodox, affirming truth strictly as a matter of faith uninformed by reason. In *Chartres,* Adams wrote that "amid the philosophy of his age, Pascal wearily replied that it was not God he doubted, but logic." In Pascal, Adams found, "the French language rose, perhaps for the last time, to the grand style of the twelfth century. . . . It belongs; to a century of faith and simplicity; not to the mathematical certainties of Descartes and Leibniz and Newton." Pascal "forced himself to disbelieve in himself rather than admit a doubt of God."[9] Pascal's solution, as Adams described it, was not viable in the late nineteenth century. It was too late in the day to dismiss the language of science. The solution to the problems science caused must be scientific.

The effort to make history scientific was the only way Adams discovered by which man could be given ethical direction within the canons of science. Perhaps it is more accurate to say it was the only way Adams discovered of controlling the powers unleashed by science within the language of science. Modern science was very good at tracing lines of power over time. It could describe the acceleration of a ball rolling downhill, or the pull of gravity on a heavy man. So too, Adams suggested, could it describe the trajectory of an idea in society. Perhaps it could even describe the path that a society as a whole would follow. That could only be done historically. All other human sciences were partial, allowing for multiplicity. They described human behavior within a limited compass. Only historical science could provide unity of purpose. That's why Adams spoke of history creating "one self-evident, harmonious and complete system" that would "put order into Chaos and bring light into darkness." Only history could govern. For that reason, Adams seemed to be saying, historical thinking would inevitably come to dominate all the social sciences. In the modern age, Adams thought, historians became prophets.[10] Judged from Adams's high standard, the conventional distinction between religion and science broke down. The belief that either one could lead society forward built upon a leap of faith.

Politics by Other Means

The effort to make history scientific would be both dangerous and difficult, Adams found: "I ask myself what shape can be given to any Science of History that will not shake to its foundations some prodigious interests?" (231). Adams listed the church, the state, property, and labor among other interests that could conflict with history. "If it pointed at a socialistic triumph, it would place us in an attitude of hostility towards existing institutions" (231). Property would not take that kindly, and might refuse to fund history. "If, on the other hand, the new Science required us to announce that the present evils of the world—its huge armaments, its vast accumulations of capital, its advancing materialism and declining Art—were to be continued, exaggerated, over another thousand years, no one would listen to us with satisfaction" (232). "If finally, the Science should prove that society must, at a given time, revert to the Church, and recover its old foundation of absolute faith in a personal Providence and a revealed Religion, it commits suicide" (232). The three potential courses Adams discovered were suggestive. The only programmatic solution that history could find was socialism. The idea that history was moving the world in the direction of peace, plenty, and harmony had a natural appeal to modern historians, and to others who were weaned on a Christian understanding of benevolence. But, in the near term, if historians found that socialism was the wave of the future, they put themselves at war with their society as it was then organized. The other possible discoveries were less inspiring. If historians found that civilization was stuck in modernity, they could not do anything other than sit, watch, and wait. "No one, except Artists and Socialists, would listen, and the conviction which we should produce on them could lead only to despair, and attempts at anarchy, in Art, in Thought and in Society" (232). Finally, if they concluded that an old-fashioned faith must ultimately triumph, they signed their own death warrant as scientists. Were that the case, Clio must ultimately return to the character she had in the time of Thucydides.

At first glance, Adams appeared to give no indication of which path forward he thought historical science would discover. Because it was the only positive vision that would be discovered, socialism would be the easiest one for historians and other intellectuals to accept. Yet that conclusion, Adams suggested, would make historians rather unpopular, at least for a while. In addition, Adams despaired of its truth, and perhaps of its goodness as well. The prospect that the world will muddle along as it was, was, and still is, a grim prospect, however likely it might be. Adams's comment that only artists and socialists would listen, and that attempts at anarchy would ensue is very suggestive in the year that he began to call himself a "Conservative, Christian, Anarchist."[11] That Adams billed himself a "Christian" anarchist might suggest that Adams concluded that civilization must eventually return to faith.

Adams's comments point to the explicitly political dimension of scientific history. Consider his comments about the church. That the church and science would conflict was nothing new. Science, in the modern sense, became important as part of the effort to overcome the evils that the church had caused. By listing the church as simply one among many interests, Adams suggested something larger. Science was supposed to be disinterested, which meant it should also be apolitical. Following Bacon's method, scientists would do no more than describe what they saw. Science was not supposed to be in the business of making moral distinctions among parties or causes. Yet, Adams noted, it was, in fact, doing that very thing.

To emphasize the arbitrary quality of scientific history, Adams pointed to the moral qualities that history would inevitably have. "A change has come over the tendency of liberal thought since the middle of the century," Adams wrote. "Darwin led an intellectual revival much more hopeful than any movement that can now be seen in Europe, except among the socialists. Had History been converted into a science at that time, it would perhaps have taken the form of cheerful optimism which gave Darwin's conclusions the charm of a possible human perfectibility." Unfortunately, "of late years, European thought has been distinctly despondent. . . . If a Science of History were established today . . . I greatly fear it would take its tone from the pessimism in Paris, Berlin, London and St. Petersburg" (231). If the mood of the Western intelligentsia would play an essential role in the nature of the history that becomes a science, what did that say about the science? What kind of science left so much room for emotions and passions? Perhaps one that was made by, for, and about men.

Ultimately, Adams implied, truth could not be the acid test of scientific history. History was too complicated to submit to such a simple test. Near the end of his Address, Adams noted that the older generation of historians "are not likely to accept any new theory that shall threaten to disturb our repose. We should reject at once, and probably by a large majority, a hypothetical science that must obviously be incapable of proof. We should take the same attitude that our fathers took toward the theories and hypotheses of Darwin" (232–33). The test of the validity of a historical science was its ability to command assent. The science would inevitably be conjectural or "hypothetical." It would appear to be "self-evident," to borrow a term from earlier in the Address, only because a large majority accepted it.

The historian who made the discipline scientific would, according to Adams, be a legislator in the classical sense. He would bring the world to order and give modern society its unifying principle. That had once been Adams's ambition. In the 1870s, he wrote, "The American statesman or philosopher who would enter upon this great debate must make his appeal, not to the public opinion of a day or of a nation, however large or intelligent, but to the minds of the few persons who, in every age and in all countries, attach their chief interest to the working out of the great problems of human society under all their varied conditions." When he moved to Washington to begin work on the *History*, Adams wrote, "I am writing for a continent of a hundred million people fifty years hence." When he was operating as a political reformer and as an American historian, Adams's ambition had focused on his own nation. The ambition of the scientific historian was broader, reaching across the borders of all the Western nations. In his Presidential Address, Adams points to Rousseau, Adam Smith, and Darwin as philosophers whose ideas seeped through society, making the extent of their influence almost impossible to determine.[12] The ambition to make history a science was similar. The first scientific historian would be the modern prophet, giving direction to science itself. The goal of the new, professional, historical guild might be to take politics out of history, rending the study cold, clinical, objective, and scientific. Adams's Address put it back in.

The Rest Is Science

What did Adams think of all that? He was never quite sure how seriously to take it. On one hand, his logic was, he thought, impeccable, at least as applied to the idea of turning history into a science, and to the deep political problems of his age. By taking those very ideas so seriously, Adams also tried to show their limits, perhaps their absurdity. But if Adams was correct, what should historians do? Perhaps Adams's confession that he was speaking only "in the paradoxical spirit of private conversation" offers some wisdom here. That very comment took aim at the notion that history could be an exact science. It also, probably not coincidentally, suggests that Adams had no good answer to give. Yet answers would be necessary, and historians would have to give them.

Philosophically speaking, the basic theoretical problem Adams found was that science was, or had become, a faith. Practically speaking, the scientific method allowed men to understand how nature appeared to work in many ways, and it also allowed them to do considerable work relieving man's estate on earth. At the same time, the tools science helped men create included modern weaponry. But the belief that science could render politics and statesmanship—with the attendant haggling, coalition building, and wars—unnecessary was, Adams implied, a vain hope. That was the case because in order to address the problem of human error, or perhaps wickedness, science needed to attain both theoretical and practical certainty.

To suggest this conclusion, Adams capitalized the words "History" and "Science" in his Address. He did not always capitalize them. He only did so when he was speaking of history as a science. That he also capitalized "Science" sometimes in the Address suggests that he was distinguishing this historical science from other sciences. The distinction between "history" and "History" was the distinction between the idea that history was simply the study of the past and the belief that History could be a modern, scientific, academic discipline. In short, history was an ancient discipline; History was a religion. But if Adams was correct both that history was a poor fit for the scientific method, and that History was, as a practical matter, well suited to give direction to Science, the distinction was still important. To be successful, the prophet of History would have to make a plausible case that his conclusions were truly scientific. Once he did so, common people, and perhaps even intellectuals, might become content to dismiss ideas not because they were "wrong," but rather because they were passé, proper for a different time period, or "out of date."[13]

Though science, in practice, could direct scientists, at the same time, it would have to deny that it was doing so. In his 1910 "Letter to American Teachers of History," Adams wrote that "Science has shut and barred every known exit." Because of its epistemological foundation, science did not, and by nature could not, disprove the possibility of revelation. Yet most scientists, and most other modern intellectuals, acted as if that were not the case. Science was a faith that defined itself as "reason." For that reason, it would be particularly difficult to break the spell. In this context, consider another passage from the *Education*:

> Chaos was the law of nature; Order was the dream of man.
>
> No one means all that he says, and yet very few say all they mean, for words are slippery and thought is viscous; but since Bacon and Newton, English thought had gone on impatiently protesting that no one must try to know the unknowable at the same time that everyone went on thinking about it. The result was as chaotic as kinetic gas; but with the thought a historian had nothing to do. He sought only its direction. For himself he knew, that, in spite of all the Englishmen that ever lived, he would be forced to enter supersensual chaos if he meant to find out what became of British science—or indeed of any other science. From Pythagoras to Herbert Spencer, everyone had done it, although commonly science had explored an ocean which it preferred to regard as Unity or a Universe, and called Order. Even Hegel, who taught that every notion included its negation, used the negation only to reach a "larger synthesis," till he reached the universal which thinks itself, contradiction and all. The Church alone had constantly protested that anarchy was not order, that Satan was not God, that pantheism was worse than atheism, and that Unity could not be proved as a contradiction. Karl Pearson seemed to agree with the Church, but everyone else, including Newton, Darwin and Clerk Maxwell, had sailed gaily into the supersensual, calling it: "One God, one Law, one Element, / And one far-off, divine event, / To which the whole creation moves."
>
> Suddenly, in 1900, science raised its head and denied.[14]

Followers of the scientific method, since Bacon's day, understood that, strictly speaking they only described nature as it appeared to the senses. That being the case, science did not, and could not, know Truth in any ultimate sense. That's what it meant to say, "one must not try to know the unknowable." Similarly, because of its very nature, modern science could not tell men how to live. And yet, Adams noted, from the time of Bacon, men went on living as if those questions could be answered scientifically. Few people, in other words, took science as literally as Adams did for neither they nor their societies could function if they did. Adams worried, perhaps thanks to developments in modern physics, that the contradiction was growing too great to ignore. Were science to turn on itself, the result might be a nasty form of nihilism.

Though he remained skeptical of the outcome of the work, Adams kept pushing ahead in scientific history because he could not think of where else to turn for answers. Late in life, he wondered whether his use of Darwin had been misguided. Responding to the Darwinianism of his brother Brooks, Henry noted that Darwin did not say evolution was progressive. "Darwin called it fittest; and, in one sense, fittest is the fittest word. Unfortunately it is always relative and therefore liable to misunderstanding." Darwinian science was tautological. A change lasted because it was better suited to the environment; it was better suited to the environment because it lasted. Adams applied the same logic to the realm of culture and ideas. But suppose one wanted to know what made a society good? Perhaps, Adams hoped late in life, Kelvin would be a better model than Darwin. "Kelvin was a great man," Adams wrote Charles Milnes Gaskell in 1909, "and I am sorry I did not know enough of mathematics to follow him instead of Darwin who led us all wrong." As he neared the end of his life, Adams placed his hopes for the future in physics: "The future of Thought, and therefore of History, lies in the hands of the physicists, and that future historian must seek his education in the world of mathematical physics. Nothing can be extracted from further study on the old lines."[15] Newtonian physics had ordered science in the eighteenth century; perhaps Kelvinian science would do the same in the twentieth century. That Adams capitalized "History" here suggests the direction of his true thoughts about physics.

Adams never found a solution that he thought would command assent. As he brought his address to a close, Adams quoted Heine:

> So we persistently question
> Till with a handful of earth
> Our mouths are finally stopped—But is that an answer?[16]

That was a strange passage for the president of the recently created American Historical Association to quote to his peers. Adams seemed to be saying that the true academic life was a life devoted to questioning. The trouble was that the world, particularly the world created by modern science, needed answers, and Adams had none to give. That brings us back to Adams's topic:

that the university and science, having brought civilization to a crisis, must help their fellow men to find a solution.[17]

Man mounted science with the best of intentions, Adams knew. Science would help man turn away from religious war. At the same time, it would ease our physical estate on earth. Unfortunately, that very same science produced new dangers of its own. These dangers were so great that Adams could not say whether man was truly better off as a result.[18] Yet civilization could not turn back. For that reason, Adams chose silence: "The situation seems to call for no opinion, unless we have some scientific theory to offer" (233). Adams did not wish to repeat the errors of the past. He did not wish to offer a solution unless he was certain that the cure would not be worse than the disease.

Adams ended his Address by asking his brother historians not to despair. They should "consider the matter in a spirit that will enable us, should the crisis arise, to deal with it in a kindly temper, and a full understanding of its serious dangers and responsibilities" (233). If and when society demanded an answer of them the scholars would have to provide one, even though the answer would inevitably be partial and fraught with danger. Acting on imperfect information, alas, was part of the human condition. No science could save us from that condition. There was no final solution. The human condition was given to us by our maker. We may complain and quail all we want, but in the end we must forgive ourselves for our limitations. That was not a message many of Adams's brother historians wanted to hear.

Notes

1. Herbert Baxter Adams in *The Letters of Henry Adams*, ed. J. C. Levenson et al., 6 vols. (Cambridge: Belknap Press of Harvard University Press, 1982), 4:228 n.2; Gordon Wood, "A Century of Writing Early American History: Then and Now Compared; Or How Henry Adams Got It Wrong," *American Historical Review* (June 1995): 678–96; HA to John Hay, September 26, 1894, *Letters*, 4:214.

2. Henry Adams, *The Education of Henry Adams* (Boston: Houghton Mifflin, 1918), 202, 271, 341. In 1877, Adams reflected that he had moved beyond the cut and thrust of politics, and, instead, had taken on the mantle of the historian: "I hob-nob with the leaders of both parties, and am very contented under my cloak of historian. I am satisfied that literature offers higher prizes than politics, and I am willing to look on at my friends who differ with me on that point of theory"

(Adams to Charles Milnes Gaskell, April 14, 1877, *Letters*, 2:303). Adams was also the editor of the *North American Review* while he was teaching at Harvard, but that was not a full-time job.

3. James Young, for example, dismisses the Address for being thin (*Henry Adams: The Historian as Political Theorist* [Lawrence: University Press of Kansas, 2001], 209).

4. Adams's Presidential Address to the American Historical Association is reprinted in *Letters*, 4:228–34. Hereafter cited parenthetically.

5. HA to Hay, September 26, 1894, *Letters*, 4:214. Adams fled to Central America; the Presidential Address was delivered in the form of a letter.

6. *Education*, 382.

7. HA to CFA II, April 11, 1862, *Letters*, 1:290.

8. *Education*, 4, 484–85; Young, *Henry Adams*, 211. See also HA to CFA II, October 23, 1863: "Two years ago I began on history; our own time. I labored at financial theories, and branched out upon Political Economy and J. S. Mill. Mr. Mill's works, thoroughly studied, led me to the examination of philosophy and the great French thinkers of our own time; they in their turn passed me over to others whose very names are now known only as terms of reproach by the vulgar; the monarchist Hobbes; the atheist Spinoza and so on" (*Letters*, 1:401). For the similarity of John Adams and *Publius*, see John P. Diggins, *Lost Soul of American Politics* (New York: Basic Books, 1983). Diggins also gives a very good reading of Henry Adams. On the importance of John Adams's political thought to Henry Adams, see my "Henry Adams' Debt to John Adams," in *Henry Adams and the Need to Know*, ed. William Decker and Earl Harbert (Boston: Massachusetts Historical Society, 2005), 18–44.

9. Adams treats the question of faith, science, and reason in his novel *Esther.* HA, *Mont-Saint-Michel and Chartres* (New York: Penguin, 1904), 304.

10. This also may have something to do with democracy. Tocqueville notes that in democratic ages history tends to describe broad trends rather than individual actions (*Democracy in America*, 2:1, 20). When he was a young man, Adams wrote, "I have learned to think De Tocqueville my model, and I study his life and works as the Gospel of my private religion" (HA to CFA II, May 1, 1863, *Letters*, 1:350). On the importance of Tocqueville's historical ideas, see my "The Real Education of Henry Adams," *Public Interest* (Spring 2002). Richard Brookhiser also mentions this aspect of Tocqueville in his *The Adamses, 1735–1918: America's First Dynasty* (New York: Free Press, 2002), 189. This account of the connection between the rise of the modern historical profession in America, the modern scientific method, and certain modern ideas about history sheds light on the ideas discussed by Dorothy Ross in her essay "Historical Consciousness in Nineteenth-

Century America," *American Historical Review* 89 (1984): 910. Ross devotes much more space to Herbert Baxter Adams than to Henry Adams.

11. Recall Adams's comment about Marx in June 1894: "Did you ever read Karl Marx? I think I never struck a book which taught me so much, and with which I disagreed so radically in conclusion" (HA to Charles Milnes Gaskell, June 15, 1894, *Letters*, 4:194–95). Adams coined the term "Conservative, Christian, Anarchist" in 1894 (ed. note in *Letters*, 4:151). Interestingly, J. G. A. Pocock concludes that Americans, unlike Europeans, did not embrace historicism in the nineteenth century, adding, "What would succeed that perspective is hard to imagine—the indications of the present point inconclusively toward various kinds of conservative anarchism" (*The Machiavellian Moment* [Princeton: Princeton University Press, 1975], 545).

12. Henry Adams, "The Session," *North American Review* 111 (July–October 1870): 62; HA to Charles Milnes Gaskell, February 3, 1884, *Letters*, 2:535. And in his preface to the *Education*, Adams identified with Rousseau, saying "Jean Jacques was a very great educator in the manner of the eighteenth century" (xxiii).

13. Thomas Jefferson expressed this idea when he suggested that "it is too late in the day for men of sincerity to pretend they believe in the Platonic mysticisms that three are one" (TJ to John Adams, August 22, 1813, *Adams-Jefferson Letters*, ed. Lester J. Cappon [Chapel Hill: University of North Carolina Press, 1955], 368).

14. "Letter to American Teachers of History," in *Degradation of the Democratic Dogma*, ed. Brooks Adams (New York: Peter Smith, 1949), 191. Young quotes this passage from *Education* (451–52) in *Henry Adams* (215).

15. HA to BA, April 2, 1898, *Letters*, 4:557. In his 1910 "Letter to American Teachers of History," Henry Adams reiterated this point. Darwin did not believe evolution was progressive, but he was taken to mean that: "Darwin might perhaps have said that he was never a Darwinian, but his popular influence lay in the law that evolution had developed itself in unbroken order from lower to higher" (*Degradation of the Democratic Dogma*, 161; HA to Gaskell, June 6, 1909, *Letters*, 6:251; HA, "The Rule of Phase Applied to History," in *Degradation of the Democratic Dogma*, 283). For more on Adams's science of history, see Keith P. Burich, "'Our Power Is Always Running Ahead of Our Mind': Henry Adams's Phases of History," *New England Quarterly* 62 (1989): 163–86, esp. 182.

16. Adams quotes the German (Address, 233). The translation is in *Letters*, 4:234 n.3.

17. In this context, we should recall that Ernest Samuels called the "Letter to American Teachers of History"—Adams's effort to apply the Second Law of Thermodynamics to history—a "Socratic missile." *Henry Adams* (Cambridge: Belknap Press of Harvard University Press, 1989), 418. In his essay on Adams in

this volume, Henry Steele Commager does not quite get to the ironic heart of Adams's commentary on modern historians. Commager notes that "pragmatism was a sorry substitute for faith" (page 149 of this volume). From Adams's perspective, however, pragmatism was a perverse kind of faith—a faith whose basic premise was that it was no such thing. Commager also asserts that Adams, in the end, "turned to the adoration of the Virgin" (page 150 of this volume). Again, I suspect that he does not quite grasp the depths of Adams's irony. For my interpretation of Adams and the Virgin, see my "Henry Adams' Debt to John Adams" (cited above). To his brother Brooks, Adams called the letter to history teachers "a jibe at my dear historical association,—a joke which nobody will know enough to understand" (HA to Brooks Adams, January 30, 1910, *Henry Adams: Selected Letters*, ed. Ernest Samuels [Cambridge: Belknap Press of Harvard University Press, 1992], 523).

18. In this, Adams echoed Thomas Jefferson. Reflecting upon the depredations the French and English had visited upon America during their presidencies, and implicitly upon the ravages of the Napoleonic wars then going on in Europe, Jefferson stated, "if science produces no better fruits than tyranny, murder, rapine and destruction of national morality, I would rather wish our country to be ignorant, honest and estimable as our neighboring savages are" (TJ to JA, January 21, 1812, *Adams-Jefferson Letters*, 291). In the *History of the United States*, Adams suggested that that idea was the key to Jefferson's statecraft. Jefferson refused "to build up a new nationality merely to create more navies and armies, to perpetuate the crimes and follies of Europe" (*History I*, 101).

CHAPTER 8

Mont-Saint-Michel and Chartres: From Unity to Multiplicity

Patrick J. Deneen

WRITING IN *THE EDUCATION of Henry Adams* of his decision to devote himself to the study of the medieval cathedrals and theology of France and Europe, Henry Adams wrote in the chapter entitled "The Abyss of Ignorance" that his ambition was to use the twelfth century as a point of reference for comparison to the dawning twentieth century. He wrote: "eight of ten years of study had led Adams to think he might use the century 1150–1250, expressed in the Amiens Cathedral and the works of Thomas Aquinas, as the unit from which he might measure motion down to his own time, without assuming anything as true or untrue, except relation. . . . Setting himself to the task, he began a volume which he mentally knew as 'Mont-Saint-Michel and Chartres: a Study of Thirteenth-Century Unity.' From that point he proposed to fix a position for himself, which he would label: 'The Education of Henry Adams: a Study of Twentieth-Century Multiplicity.' With the help of these two points of relation, he hoped to project his lines forward and backward indefinitely, subject to correction from anyone who should know better."[1] His ambition—stated throughout the *Education*—was to identify the point of lost unity, and the rise of modern multiplicity.

Most critics have accepted that this was the basic ambition of Adams, and that the two books written as companion volumes aim—and, to some extent, even succeed—in delineating a kind of descent from medieval religious or fideistic unity to modern scientific multiplicity. Adams himself wrote that modern science failed to offer "a vestige of proof, or a theory of connection of its forces, or any scheme of reconciliation between thought and mechanics," while the theological mind of St. Thomas Aquinas "at least linked together the joints of his machine," arguing that "the cause of all form and sequence in the universe" was ultimately derivable from "the intelligent prime motor"—God. Adams's failure to achieve an education in modern America derived from modernity's fundamental inability to provide a unifying explanation of all phenomena; by contrast, immersion in the world of twelfth- and thirteenth-century France provided the very essence of unity in the form of faith and belief.

Indeed, a number of critics have understood *Mont-Saint-Michel and Chartres* not only to identify the highest point from which the decline of Western civilization can be traced, but also to elucidate a genealogy of decline within the span of the twelfth century that it studied. The organization of *Mont-Saint-Michel and Chartres*, it is argued, takes the form of a triptych, a tripartite structure in which the central and most important chapter—on the Virgin of Chartres—is bordered by the discussion of the masculine Archangel Michael and his cathedral of Mont-Saint-Michel (and the accompanying discussion of the warrior Roland) and the concluding discussion of the developments in late-twelfth-century theology, from Abelard to the mystics and culminating in the final discussion of St. Thomas Aquinas's efforts to reconcile these disparate theologies. A leading and widely shared interpretation of the text of *Mont-Saint-Michel and Chartres* understands the high point of twelfth-century medieval unity to have occurred during the central period described by Adams, those decades during which Mariolatry was at its apogee, and that the descent into the scholasticism of the twelfth and thirteenth centuries represents a loss of unity and constitutes a harbinger of the rise of modern science.

For instance, John McIntyre, S.J., has argued that the three parts of the book trace a "decline" leading to Adams's "futilitarianism."[2] Indeed, McIntyre notes quite arrestingly that a *literal* decline takes place from the first line to the concluding sentences of the book, from its dramatic opening sentence, "The Archangel loved heights," to its eloquent, suggestive conclusion: "The pathos of its self-distrust and anguish of doubt is buried in the earth as its last secret."[3] Following in this vein, Michael Colacurcio wrote in a persuasive and insightful article of the decline from the "prerational" unity that accompanied worship of the Virgin—unity that "simply was"—to the disintegration of this intuitive unity with the rise of scholasticism.[4] Noting that Adams's depiction of Aquinas's language comes to resemble the mechanistic features of modern science—particularly Adams's translation of *"movens"* as "motor," not "Mover"—Colacurcio discerns in Adams's portrayal of the medieval philosophical and theological controversies a rise of divisiveness and the beginnings of the modern scientific dissolution of meaning.[5] The conclusions that "logic is divisive" and "reason inevitably destroys faith" constitute the underlying argument of *Chartres,* suggesting that, for Adams, unity was and could only be the result of an unconscious, "feminine" adherence to simple unreflective faith.[6]

Robert Mane concurs, relying on Colacurcio's analysis, arguing that "'Will,' that is, the energy of Mary, who alone, thanks to her feminine intuition, could embrace all contradictions and unify the world, disappears, killed by St. Thomas' ruthless 'logic.'"[7] T. J. Jackson Lears, in his fine concluding chapter on Adams in his study *No Place for Grace,* similarly observes that the "genuine (though precarious) unity of Chartres gave way to the spurious unity of the *Summa Theologica.* In Adams's scheme, scholasticism was a portent of modernity."[8] And, confirming these readings, James P. Young understands Adams to have turned Aquinas "into a modern scientist, or perhaps an electrical engineer" who insists upon "hierarchy," while it is the Virgin who represents a "heretical, anarchic" spirit "whose propensity to subvert authority, not to mention her care for the downtrodden, points toward ultimately democratic sympathies."[9] For each of these eminent interpreters of Adams's difficult text, there is clear and persuasive evidence that it traces a trajectory of decline and fragmentation, one that anticipates the "multiplicity" of the modern age depicted in the *Education.*

Adams clearly intended the two works to be read and considered together, and believed that it would be evident through the course of reading the two books what was meant by "unity" and "multiplicity." Again and again in both works, he alludes to the unity of the Middle Ages, contrasting that condition explicitly with the multiplicity and divisions he finds evident in nearly every aspect of his contemporary era. "True, the Church alone had asserted unity with any conviction . . . ; but the only honest alternative to affirming unity was to deny it; and the denial would require a new education" (*Education,* 430). By contrast with the "asserted unity" of the Middle Ages, in his own day "the scientific synthesis commonly called Unity was the scientific analysis commonly called Multiplicity. The two things were the same, all forms being shifting phases of motion. What was Unity? Why was one forced to affirm it?" (*Education,* 431). It seems evident that multiplicity has to do with the variety and divergent understandings of the universe that informs the scientific undertaking, in contrast to the unified faith and belief that undergirded the Middle Ages.

But further reflection suggests that this can't be altogether correct. Adams notes in this passage that the scientific project itself is intent upon achieving "a larger synthesis," a blanket and comprehensive explanation for all phenomena. In this sense, one might conclude—here in marked contrast to the theological divisions that he describes in the last part of *Mont-Saint-Michel and Chartres*—that it is, in fact, the *modern era* that is defined more by the effort to achieve some form of unity. What Adams notes in this passage is that the very effort to achieve this "larger synthesis" in fact results in greater chaos for humans: "Science seemed content with its old phrase of 'larger synthesis,' which was well enough for science, but meant chaos for man" (*Education*, 431). It is evidently not the *philosophical* or *theological* unity—or multiplicity—that Adams thus believes to mark the nature of the two different historical eras, but the respective effects on humankind. Thus, one might refine Adams's formulation to be an exploration of how unity derived from a multiplicity of views in the Middle Ages, and—by contrast—how a multiplicity of experience arose from a unity of scientific understanding in the modern age. Far from describing a "descent" from unity to multiplicity in the pages of *Mont-Saint-Michel and Chartres*, Adams depicts a deeper unity amid the multiplicity of competing and various understandings of man's relation to God that can only be ascertained through a consideration of all its iterations. This "unity from multiplicity" he contrasts with the "multiplicity from unity" of the modern scientific and technological age. His study of the Middle Ages invites us to achieve a kind of elevated unity of understanding, one only possible through an effort to perceive the deeper continuity of the disparate elements of belief in the century he explores, a deeper continuity that resulted in a unified lived experienced—reflected, above all, in the grandeur and order of the cathedrals. In effect, amid the multiplicity of contending beliefs, he sees a singular capacity to find meaning; whereas amid the uniformity of scientific theory in modernity, he perceives a scattering of meaning, even the specter of "nihilism" (430). He dated this decline of actual church unity to 1450, well after the thought of Thomas Aquinas, suggesting that Aquinas—far from being blameworthy for the rise of modernity—is in some respects the crowning moment of unity achieved amid multiplicity. The book depicts an ascent, not a descent: as in the structure of a cathedral itself, we enter through the lower part, but our gaze is drawn inexorably upward.

Modernity: Multiplicity through Unity

Early in the *Education*, Adams states that the central challenge of education consists in the achievement of unity: "From cradle to grave this problem of running order through chaos, direction through space, discipline through freedom, unity through multiplicity, has always been, and must always be, the task of education" (*Education*, 12). Shortly thereafter, Adams notes that his education had been a failure as a result of the conditions of modernity that prevented such an achievement of unity—an observation he continues to repeat throughout the long work: "Pondering on the needs of the twentieth century, he wondered whether, on the whole, the boy of 1854 stood nearer to the thought of 1904, or to that of the year 1. He found himself unable to give a sure answer. . . . The education he had received bore little relation to the education he needed. Speaking as an American of 1900, he had as yet no education at all" (53).

It becomes evident during the course of Adams's reflections on his own education that it is the very dynamism at the heart of modern life that makes education of the form he first describes nearly impossible, that is, achieving unity through multiplicity. The whole trajectory of modernity was one of increasing multiplicity: "The movement from unity to multiplicity, between 1200 and 1900, was unbroken in sequence, and rapid in acceleration. Prolonged one generation longer, it would require a new social mind" (*Education*, 498). Adams describes a series of unsuccessful attempts to achieve the fruits of education, pursuing what always seems to be just out of reach, and leading eventually to his conclusion that he lives in the midst of constant and increasing acceleration of change and multiplicity. In such a circumstance, he suggests, education recedes from the grasp of not only Adams, but everyone. Unity is an impossibility in the modern world.

Yet, it should be simultaneously noted that what Adams everywhere describes as "multiplicity" is in material and scientific fact a form of ever greater homogeneity and standardization. What jars about Adams's constant invocation of rising and accelerating "multiplicity" are the numerous descriptions throughout the *Education* of increasing *sameness* in modernity, particularly those achieved through scientific and technological achievement, or in the realm of science through comprehensive explanatory theories such as Darwinism. In short, the modern times he describes as distinguished by "multiplicity" seem in fact to be noteworthy for their uniformity—particularly the uniformity of scientific and material "progress." This apparent discrepancy deserves further reflection.

One source of the elimination of the "medieval" character of Europe—specifically Germany, in this case—that Adams observed in his time, "floundering between worlds passed and worlds coming"—was the rise of the "coal-power and railways" (*Education*, 83). The rise of this new configuration of human society—based upon the harnessing of fossil fuels—was rapidly displacing the settled ways of life that had long defined human experience. "The last ten years had given to the great mechanical energies—coal, iron, steam—a distinct superiority in power over the old industrial elements—agriculture, handiwork, and learning" (*Education*, 238). The single task of erecting a rail system was practically reshaping the whole of society into a singular, uniform model: "This relatively small part of its task was still so big as to need the energies of a generation, for it required furnaces, shops, power-houses, technical knowledge, mechanical population, together with a steady remodeling of social and political habits, ideas, and institutions to fit the new scale and suit the new conditions" (*Education*, 240). The world was being remade—not simply one part, but its entirety—in one uniform and comprehensive model.

At the same time, Adams's world was also being reduced to a form of uniformity of scientific understanding through the ascendance of Darwinism as an explanatory theory for biological life. The attraction of Darwin's theory, Adams argued, was at once its capacity for self-flattery and its attraction as a unified explanation.

> Unity and Uniformity were the whole motive of philosophy, and if Darwin, like a true Englishman, preferred to back into it—to reach God *a posteriori* —rather than start from it, like Spinoza, the difference in method taught only the moral that the best way of reaching unity was to unite. Any road was good that arrived.
>
> Life depended on it. One had been, from the first, dragged hither and thither like a French poodle on a string, following always the strongest pull, between one form of unity or centralization and another. The proof that one had acted wisely because of obeying the primordial habit of nature flattered

one's self-esteem. Steady, uniform, unbroken evolution from lower to higher seemed easy. (*Education*, 226)

Adams understood the attraction to Darwin's theory not for its truth—he regarded it as patently and absurdly fallacious, purely a matter of "dogma," observing wryly that "the progress of evolution from President Washington to President Grant, was alone evidence enough to upset Darwin" (*Education*, 231, 266)—but for its flattery of human pride, particularly the temptation to believe in the ever-increasing improvement of the species, "the promise of ultimate perfection" (*Education*, 231). Adams rejected Darwinism not only for its evident falsehood—not only in the fossil record, but, in moral terms, against such evidence as the recently concluded savagery of the Civil War (*Education*, 229, 230–31)—but, further, because it posited a false uniformity on all living phenomena: "the idea of one Form, Law, Order, or Sequence had no more value for him [Adams] than the idea of none; that what he valued most was Motion, and that what attracted his mind was Change" (*Education*, 231).

What Adams was witnessing was the remaking of the world he was born into—the nineteenth century—and its transformation into a homogeneous and monotonous machine. The "dynamo" that would come to represent for him the very essence of modernity generated change, perhaps, but change that pointed toward the promise of ultimate uniformity. Sensitive to the trajectories of the logic of consolidation and centralization to which the new industrialized and economic system pointed, he lamented the "centralizing and mechanical" tendencies of the modern economic order and "the whole mechanical consolidation of force, which ruthlessly stamped out the life of the class into which Adams was born, but created monopolies capable of controlling the new energies that America adored" (*Education*, 345). What Adams anticipates is the creation of an industrial and economic monoculture, the homogenization engendered by the unleashed force of industrial modernity. Far from seeing multiplicity in the physical dimensions of life, or its scientific theories, he detected the evisceration of actual diversity and distinctive cultures before the leveling power of the machine.

His lamentation over the homogenization and standardization effected by modern forces is laced throughout the *Education,* and there are few passages that express this process more poignantly than the one quoted below from his chapter "Teufelsdröckh":

> In 1858 the whole plain of northern Europe, as well as the Danube in the
> south, bore evident marks of being still the prehistoric highway between
> Asia and the ocean. The trade-route followed the old routes of invasion, and
> Cologne was a resting-place between Warsaw and Flanders. Throughout
> northern Germany, Russia was felt even more powerfully than France. In
> 1901 Russia had vanished, and not even France was felt; hardly England or
> America. Coal alone was felt—its stamp alone pervaded the Rhine district
> and persisted into Picardy—and the stamp was the same as that of Birming-
> ham and Pittsburgh. The Rhine produced the same power, and the power
> produced the same people—the same mind—the same impulse. . . . From
> Hammerfest to Cherbourg on one shore of the ocean—from Halifax to Nor-
> folk on the other—one great empire was ruled by one great emperor—Coal.
> Political and human jealousies might tear it apart or divide it, but the power
> and empire were one. Unity had gained that ground. (*Education*, 415)

The power derived from coal—a concentrated form of energy accumulated
over millennia—now allowed humans to transcend the particularities of
place and culture, to reshape the world for uniform economies, governments,
and humans. The hallmark of modernity, based upon a philosophy, science,
and economics of progress, was toward *unity* and unification, manifested
especially in a flattening uniformity in the wake of obliterated particularity.

Why, then, did Adams describe the modern age to be "a movement
of unity to multiplicity" and suggest that the subtitle of his autobiography
should be "a Study of Twentieth-Century Multiplicity"? (*Education*, 498,
435). Given the stress upon the unifying nature of modern science, technology, economics, and politics, what was "multiple" about his age? In fact, it is
actually not altogether easy to discern what Adams precisely means by the
"multiplicity" of the modern age. If the religious faith of the Middle Ages
represented one form of unity, then why does not the scientific faith of the
modern age—and its concomitant reshaping of the world in an ever more
homogenized form—represent a competing (but no less a form of) unity?

Adams speaks of an increasingly singular and unified manner of understanding the world—through evolution—and its increasing homogeneity
under the transformative energies of industrialization. At the same time, he
speaks of the modern world being one that had caused history to break down,
that induced meaninglessness, that generated chaos, that was "a multiple"
(*Education*, 301, 368, 382, 455). One can somewhat schematically picture
his diagnosis of the modern condition as he portrays it in the *Education*

as two kinds of unity giving rise to multiplicity: a unified system of belief (modern science) coincident with the rise to an increasingly homogeneous world (industrialization) that in turn generates chaos and multiplicity. Why this latter case is so is not intuitively obvious, however.

Most obviously, the scientific theories associated with Darwinism have long been understood to undermine philosophies or theologies that ascribe a natural or divine meaning to creation. The Darwinist acceptance of a certain randomness to the evolution of species leads to a breakdown in the belief in a narrative of meaning and leaves in its wake an understanding of the world in which chance, power, contingency, and randomness govern. Nature ceases to be conceived as an unchanging order, but rather is seen as the quintessence of change and even disorder. The "multiplicity" of which Adams speaks can certainly be understood to derive from the triumph of Darwinism, although this conclusion is hardly original to Adams.[10]

There is a deeper and more original point submerged in Adams's belief in the recognition of the multiplicity induced by modernity. Adams does not actually hold that it was Darwinism that introduced the rise of modern "chaos" and multiplicity: rather, the existence of "multiplicity" is a permanent condition of existence that was simply unveiled most fully by developments in modernity. As he wrote in his chapter entitled "The Grammar of Science": "Since monkeys first began chattering in trees, neither man nor beast had ever denied or doubted Multiplicity, Diversity, Complexity, Anarchy, Chaos. Always and everywhere, the Complex had been true and the Contradiction had been certain. Thought started by it. Mathematics itself began by counting one—two—three" (*Education*, 455). Our experience of the reality of the world was, in fact, multiple: separation and division were the brute facts of our reality, from our separation of humankind from nature to our distinctiveness from one another. Adams suggests that thought itself derives from the sheer fact of our separation: absent distinctions, thought would be unnecessary, superfluous. Modernity does not generate "multiplicity": it is, in some senses, a consequence of the composition of the world.

However, Adams goes on in this passage to note that simultaneous with the inception of thought as a consequence of division is the impetus of thought to contain, arrange, order, and unify that very multiplicity: "Chaos was a primary fact even in Paris—especially in Paris—as it was in the book of Genesis; but every thinking being in Paris or out of it had exhausted thought in the effort to prove Unity, Continuity, Purpose, Order, Law, Truth, the Universe, God, after having begun by taking it for granted, and discovering, to their profound dismay, that some minds denied it. The direction of mind, as a single force of nature, had been constant since history began. Its own unity had created a universe the essence of which was abstract Truth; the Absolute; God!" (*Education*, 455–56). Coincident with human recognition of diversity and multiplicity comes the effort to provide order and unity. Adams contends that this effort is, at its heart, the very activity of education: "from cradle to grave this problem of running order through chaos, direction through space, discipline through freedom, unity through multiplicity, has always been, and must always be, the task of education" (*Education*, 12). Modernity thus represents the disruption of this basic and fundamental undertaking of human beings, one at the heart of what it is to be human. A curious contradiction results: a more pervasive uniformity imposed upon the world disrupts the capacity of humans to achieve unity through thought. Materially imposed unity results in mental disunity. In particular, the exertion of energy aimed at mastering and transforming the world seems to eviscerate the possibility of the exertion of energy necessary to achieve unity through thought. Energy, according to Adams, seemed capable of enforcing external and material uniformity, or "intellectual" unity. As he would write in *Mont-Saint-Michel and Chartres*, "the attempt to bridge the chasm between multiplicity and unity is the oldest problem in philosophy, religion and science, but the flimsiest bridge of all is the human concept, unless somewhere, within or beyond it, an energy not individual is hidden" (*Chartres*, 302). In making energy everywhere visible and transformative, the modern age disrupted this more internal form of unifying intellectual energy, creating uniformity but reinforcing multiplicity of meaning. The problem, as ever for Adams, lay in the uses and sources of energy.

Modernity thus represents a deep rupture with the past—including the capacity of humans to forge unity out of multiplicity—and suggests why Adams ultimately becomes attracted to the study of history. This theme of rupture appears in the earliest moments of the *Education*, in which Adams first observes the obstacles that lie in the path of his receiving an education (or putting the activity of thought toward the attainment of unity): "He and his eighteenth-century, troglodytic Boston were suddenly cut apart—separated forever—in act if not in sentiment, by the opening of the Boston and Albany Railroad; the appearance of the first Cunard steamers in the bay; and the [advent of] telegraphic messages" (5). Multiplicity is not itself the result of modernity; it is a permanent feature of the human condition. However, Adams suggests, modernity makes the theological or philosophical activity of attaining some understanding of the underlying or transcendent unity of that multiplicity impossible. And that obstacle, at some level, is the result of the advent of a transformation of the modern world under the unifying and homogenizing force of modern technology. The manifestation of *physical* and technological unity makes impossible the human capacity for *intellectual*—philosophical and theoretical—unity. The result is a historical rupture—a rupture that can only be understood by an investigation of history—whether premodern, one's nation's, one's own life, or the nature of history itself.

Adams intimates that we need the actual confrontation with multiplicity to achieve unity, and that what the modern world represents is the effort to erase multiplicity from the world. The result is increasing scientific and material unity but our incapacity to achieve a kind of higher unity *precisely because such higher and intellective unity arises from multiplicity*. The imposition of technologically achieved unity dispels the conditions necessary for higher unity. Brought to a mundane level, the existence of the multiple cultures that dotted the landscape of Europe—the existence of multiplicity—is a necessary precondition for coming to inquire about and achieve some understanding about the underlying unity of all human cultures and their relationship to the reality of the natural world. The transformation of the world into an industrial monoculture dispels the precondition of evident multiplicity that permits the attainment of an understanding of a higher unity, one intimated in the longing to understand and know the Divine.

Above all, what Adams intimates is that the effort to impose a material unity on the world through unleashed *forces* of industrial civilization makes impossible the kind of philosophical and theological reflection upon unity that once informed the Middle Ages. For Adams to be able to articulate what was lost, he necessarily turns to an examination of an age that, for him, most perfectly represented the apogee of human thought and activity aimed toward forging unity out of multiplicity.

The Middle Ages: Unity through Multiplicity

Toward his effort to ascertain what had been lost to modern man, Adams described his work on the medieval cathedrals, poetry, culture, politics and

theology as "a study of Thirteenth-Century Unity" (*Education*, 435). Yet, as
we have noted earlier, many of the most prominent interpreters of Adams's
work understand it to be a portrayal of thirteenth-century disunity, a kind
of descent from unity in its middle phase—particularly during the height
of worship of the Virgin—into incipient modern multiplicity. While one can
credit that Adams is not without criticism of aspects of scholasticism, the
view that *Mont-Saint-Michel and Chartres* portrays a steady descent into
modern disunity is belied by the "disunity" that seems to define its very
organization. The work is organized as a tripartite investigation of various
aspects of medieval belief and life—namely, the celebration of "the Church
Militant" manifested through Mont-Saint-Michel, the archangel Michael,
and *La chanson de Roland;* the cult of the Virgin Mary as represented in
the achievement of Chartres and the centrality of female characteristics
that were the object of adoration and admiration; and the disputations of the
theological schools of the thirteenth century, culminating in Aquinas's great
effort of synthesis. If we are to understand these various and distinctive
aspects of the medieval church and world as constituting "unity," it is at best
a peculiar kind of unity and not one that is self-evident to a casual reader.
Indeed, considering the kind of "unity" that Adams seems to describe to lie
at the heart of the modern project, one might even wonder if Adams had
simply made an error in transcription. His portrayal of the Middle Ages
defies easy summation as one of unity.

The studies of the two cathedrals—Mont-Saint-Michel and Chartres—
can be seen as posing a deep duality, one inherent in the human creature,
above all, the divergence between male and female. Adams depicts Mont-
Saint-Michel as a bastion of masculinity and militarism, beginning with its
description as "the Church and State, . . . both militant" (*Chartres*, 1), and
subsequently in pairing the Cathedral of St. Michael with the great medieval poem of one of its greatest soldiers, Roland. The identification of the
church and the soldier's song are near complete: "The poem [*La chanson de
Roland*] and the church are akin; they go together and explain each other.
Their common trait is their military character, peculiar to the eleventh century. The round arch is masculine. The 'Chanson' is so masculine that, in
all its four thousand lines, the only Christian woman so much as mentioned
was Alda . . . to whom one stanza, exceedingly like a later insertion, was
given, toward the end" (*Chartres*, 22–23).

Moving to the long central section of the book, covering the architecture of Chartres, the cult of the Virgin Mary, and three queens of the twelfth and early thirteenth centuries, Adams explores the powerful role of the feminine in shaping the beliefs and forms of worship during the heart of the twelfth century. Beginning his study of this period, he wrote, "among the unexpected revelations of human nature that suddenly astonish historians, one of the least reasonable was the passionate outbreak of religious devotion to the ideal of feminine grace, charity, and love" (*Chartres*, 50). Expanding on his depiction of the distinctive aspects of femininity, later he connects Mary to "the eternal woman"—represented in "Astarte, Isis, Demeter, Aphrodite, and the last and greatest deity of all, the Virgin," as well as Eve, reflection upon whom "lays bare the whole subject of sex" (*Chartres*, 198). He depicts Mary as the embodiment of "the spirit of love and grace" and of "mercy," as well as "by essence illogical, unreasonable and feminine" (71, 196, 261). Femininity was not only distinct and separate from the masculinity—of the sort represented in the structure and worship of Mont-Saint-Michel or *La chanson de Roland*—but it was superior to its opposite: "The superiority of the woman was not a fancy but a fact. Man's business was to fight or hunt or feast or make love. The man was also the travelling partner in commerce, commonly absent from home for months together, while the woman carried on the business. The woman ruled the household and the workshop; cared for the economy; supplied the intelligence, and dictated the taste. Her ascendancy was secured by her alliance with the Church, into which she sent her most intelligent children; and a priest or clerk, counted socially as a woman" (Chartres, 199).

Many interpreters of these sections understand Adams's praise and attraction to the Virgin to be animated by his belief that Mariolatry represented the high point in intuitive, self-abnegating, prerational, and hence unified belief. John P. McIntyre, S.J., speaks for many when he writes that "in the context of [Adams's] thought the Virgin yields her meaning, for she expresses an infinite energy, capable of unifying an entire civilization through her power of love."[11] Yet, while Adams certainly describes the Virgin at various points as a major unifying force in twelfth-century society, he has already previously depicted Mont-Saint-Michel and the masculine ideal *also* as unitive. "The whole Mount . . . expressed the unity of Church and State, God and Man, Peace and War, Life and Death, Good and Bad; it solved the whole problem of the universe. . . . God reconciles all. The world is an evident, obvious, sacred harmony" (44–45). He will also go on to praise Aquinas as well as achieving a unitive philosophical and theological synthesis: "An economic civilization troubles itself about the universe much as a hive of honey-bees troubles itself about the ocean, only as a region to be avoided. The hive of Saint Thomas sheltered God and man, mind and matter, the universe and the atom, the one and the multiple, within the walls of an harmonious home." At the same time, Adams also describes the Virgin as noteworthy for her *absence* of unity: "The Mother alone was human, imperfect, and could love; she alone was Favour, Duality, Diversity. Under any conceivable form of religion, this duality must find embodiment somewhere, and the Middle Ages logically insisted that, as it could not be in the Trinity, either separately or together, it must be in the Mother. If Trinity was in its essence Unity, the Mother alone could represent whatever was not Unity; whatever was irregular, exceptional, outlawed; and this was the whole human race" (*Chartres*, 263).

Already from the first two parts of *Mont-Saint-Michel and Chartres* it is evident that what is supposed to pass for medieval *unity* in fact is already marked by remarkable multiplicity. The differences between the two cathedrals—and their respective animating spirits, the masculine Archangel and the feminine Virgin—appear to reflect more the spirit of multiplicity that Adams claimed to define the modern age, an age that has many of the hallmarks of being an age of *unity*. But it is not until the concluding section of Adams's book on medieval cathedrals—a section devoted to an exploration of debates within medieval theology—that the full dimensions of the age's multiplicity come out. With the disagreements ranging between Abelard and William of Champeaux, the mysticism of the Franciscans and Bernard, and the synthesis attempted by Thomas Aquinas, one sees in the realm of ideas the intellectual diversity that was reflected in the material realm in the difference between the various cathedrals.

Indeed, the organization of the final section of *Mont-Saint-Michel and Chartres* appears to be an echo in the intellectual realm of the very same divisions that Adams has explored in the preceding sections on the respective cathedrals of Mont-Saint-Michel and Chartres. In focusing on the debate between the "realism" (and ultimately, the pantheism) of William of Champeaux and the nominalism of Abelard, Adams seems to portray in the fierce dialectical combativeness of Abelard a similar militant spirit as that which animated the Archangel and Roland. Abelard is described as an "adventurer," a description not out of keeping with that of the Archangel's qualities as "ambitious, restless, striving for effect" or the masculine military character of Roland (303, 8). While the slashing and parrying of the sword is replaced by the swift stabs of Abelard's logic and dialectic, the characters are undeniably masculine in their agonistic and combative spirits.

By contrast, the mystics treated in the following chapter are the very opposite of the logicians just explored. Intellectually, the mystics exhibit a unity of faith and feeling similar to what Adams depicts in the central section of the book when describing the feminine qualities embodied above all in the Virgin. Indeed, Adams explicitly regards the theological development of mysticism to be no less a transition in the intellectual realm than the building of Chartres represents in architecture: "In essence, religion was love; in no case was it logic. . . . Saint Francis of Assisi had affirmed it loudly enough, even if the voice of Saint Bernard had been less powerful than it was. The Virgin had asserted it in tones more gentle, but any one may still see how convincing, who stops a moment to feel the emotion that lifted her wonderful Chartres spire up to God" (325–26). The second of the theological movements described by Adams—the mystics, themselves a response to and rejection of the slashing and masculine logic of Abelard's nominalism—corresponds intellectually to the architectural spirit that animated Chartres. Intellectually, Abelard echoes Mont-Saint-Michel, while the mystics echo Chartres. Multiplicity appears to be the defining feature of the Middle Ages, Adams's claims notwithstanding.

This puts Aquinas in a unique position in the book as a whole: Aquinas represents the effort to integrate the disparate elements of the theological tradition—and the respective differences in the architectural traditions—that appear to show the deep and pervasive multiplicity at the heart of the medieval tradition. Indeed, Aquinas was responsible for the construction of what may be the most integrative "cathedral" of all those discussed in the book, the one that incorporates the otherwise disparate elements that lie at the heart of the respectively masculine and feminine cathedrals previously explored: "Saint Thomas's architecture, like any other work of art, is best studied by itself as though he created it outright; otherwise, a tourist would never get beyond its threshold. Beginning with the foundation which is God and God's active presence in His Church, Thomas next built God into the walls and towers of his Church, in the Trinity and its creation of mind and matter in time and space; then finally he filled the Church by uniting mind and matter in man, or man's soul, giving to humanity a free will that rose, like the fleche, to heaven. . . . After the eleventh-century Romanesque Church of Saint Michael came the twelfth-century Transition Church of the Virgin, and *all merged and ended* at last in the thirteenth-century Gothic Cathedral of the Trinity" (*Chartres*, 350–51; emphasis added). Aquinas's effort to achieve *theological*—which is to say, intellectual—synthesis represents the unique and culminating effort of the era studied by Adams in *Mont-Saint-Michel and Chartres* to achieve unity out of multiplicity.

Adams, in particular, is attentive to Aquinas's effort to retain the "realism" of William of Champeaux (contra the nominalism of Abelard) without falling into a near-inevitable resulting pantheism. The danger of aspiring to "unity"—beginning not with the assumption of the multiplicity of the world that was afforded some unity only through the "naming" (hence "nominalism") as a human construct—was to disallow any true separation or distinction between things, above all, the distinction between God and his Creation. Hence, the kind of unity sought by William—or Aquinas— seemed inevitably to elicit a crude but logically inevitable form of pantheism.

Adams admired Aquinas's logical exposition of the unity that emanated from God throughout the created order, praising the "fusion" achieved by Aquinas "of the universal with the individual, of unity with multiplicity, of God and nature, which had broken the neck of every philosophy ever invented" (*Chartres*, 360). It "broke their necks" because of the impossibility of avoiding pantheism—the heresy and falsehood that there was no real difference between God and man or anything else for that matter, a conclusion that "had ruined William of Champeaux and was to ruin Descartes" (*Chartres*, 360). Aquinas insisted upon the "reality" of matter and of corresponding individuation of human persons. Adams labors to describe the delicate balance that Aquinas attempts to achieve in his own struggle to avoid the pantheistic logic of his argument of the fundamental unity of existence, and—Adams contends—Aquinas is able to achieve this delicate balance by means of a subtle and not easily maintained "equilibrium" that can only be compared to the finest achievements in architecture: "Thomas and his master Albert were almost alone in imposing on the Church the compromise so necessary for its equilibrium. The balance of matter against mind was the same necessity in the Church Intellectual as the balance of thrusts in the arch of the Gothic cathedral. Nowhere did Thomas show his architectural obstinancy quite so plainly as in thus taking matter under his own protection. . . . He insisted on keeping man wholly apart, as a complex of energies in which matter shared equally with mind. The Church must rest firmly on both" (*Chartres*, 365). Adams labored mightily to describe exactly the contours of this philosophical and theological "equilibrium"—an explanation that McIntyre regards to be "an imaginative construct" and a "fiction"— but in the end was unable to do so in any way that could be regarded as conclusive or wholly explanatory.[12] Indeed, Adams must finally—and perhaps appropriately—invoke a kind of faith that Aquinas had achieved what he set out to accomplish: "The theology turns always into art at last, and ends in aspiration. The spire justifies the church." The continuity of lines, leading upward, reflects finally the human aspiration to make the many One while preserving the Many, leaving Aquinas and his successors unable finally to "distinguish where God's power ends and man's free will begins. All they saw was the soul vanishing into the skies. How it was done, one does not care to ask; in a result so exquisite, one has not the heart to find fault with 'adresse'" (*Chartres*, 379). Having spent the culminating chapter of the lengthy study of medieval unity on an exploration and explication of the thought of Thomas Aquinas, Adams concludes "about Saint Thomas's theology we need not greatly disturb ourselves. . . . The essence of it—the despotic central idea— was that of organic unity both in the thought and the building." More than that, Adams suggests, we can't really understand. The very kind of intuitive or accepting faith of the sort he praises among the Virgin's believers is the sort we need in finally approaching the thought of Aquinas. There seems to be no final logical explanation for the delicate balance of unity from multiplicity that it achieved; it is enough to recognize the accomplishment.

Adams finally reveals his great attraction to the unitive quality of medieval thought above all because it achieves unity not through the demolition of actual multiplicity—as he saw clearly in the trajectory of modern thought and practice—but in the preservation of multiplicity through which a greater or higher unity was achieved. In the preservation of multiplicity that was undestroyed by this higher unity there was finally more possibility for human liberty and true human diversity: "A Church which embraced, with equal sympathy, and within a hundred years, the Virgin, Saint Bernard, William of Champeaux and the school of Saint-Victor, Peter the Venerable, Saint Francis of Assisi, Saint Dominic, Saint Thomas Aquinas, and Saint Bonaventure, was more liberal than any modern State could afford to be.

Radical contradictions the State may perhaps tolerate, though hardly, but never embrace or profess. Such elasticity long ago vanished from human thought" (*Chartres*, 361).

This last thought reveals most fully why Adams was content to classify himself—with accustomed understatement that nevertheless revealed a deep radicalism—a "conservative Christian anarchist" (*Education*, 405).[13] His conservatism derived from his resistance to the advances of modern "progress"; his Christianity from his attractions to the ancient achievements of unity that in practice preserved multiplicity, the recognition of a created order that indicated both its derivation from a unified source and the reality of the manyness of that created order; and his anarchism in his strenuous defense of local and diverse liberty that predated the transformations of modern rationalization, centralization, and imposed order. His attraction to the dizzying diversity of the Middle Ages was its capacity to preserve diversity amid a broader conception of a unified source. If his great study of the Middle Ages made him at least theoretically the object of suspicion by "the Judges" who might "burn me according to law," it was because his apostasy was in a source of belief that contradicted the modern faiths. Against the grain of his age, he defended the liberty of a pluralistic unity against the enforcement of modern unity that demolished diversity and sowed meaninglessness and uncertainty in its wake. His attraction to an ancient faith was born of his suspicion of the universally held modern faith. And regarding his suspicions toward the logic of modern homogenization of monolithic order imposed by the extension of the project of human mastery from the vantage of our own more advanced age, one can only marvel at Adams's prescience and foresight, and wonder anew whether a return to the contemplation of more ancient forms of unity might be the path to a renewal of actual diversity in our increasingly flattened and uniform age.

Notes

1. Henry Adams, *The Education of Henry Adams*, ed. Ernest Samuels (1918; Boston: Houghton Mifflin, 1973), 435. Hereafter cited parenthetically.

2. McIntyre, "Henry Adams and the Unity of *Chartres*," *Twentieth Century Literature* 50, no. 4 (1962): 168, 169.

3. Henry Adams, *Mont-Saint-Michel and Chartres* (1913; Princeton: Princeton University Press, 1982), 1, 383. Hereafter cited parenthetically.

4. Michael Colacurcio, "The Dynamo and the Angelic Doctor," *American Quarterly* 17, no. 3 (1965): 696–712.

5. Ibid., 701.

6. Ibid., 706.

7. Robert Mane, *Henry Adams on the Road to Chartres* (Cambridge: Harvard University Press, 1971), 220.

8. T. J. Jackson Lears, *No Place for Grace* (Chicago: University of Chicago Press, 1981), 283.

9. James P. Young, *Henry Adams: The Historian as Political Theorist* (Lawrence: University Press of Kansas, 2001), 152, 155.

10. For the widespread response to Darwin that echoes this concern for the loss of narrative meaning, see, for instance, A. N. Wilson's *God's Funeral: The Decline of Faith in Western Civilization* (New York: W. W. Norton, 1999).

11. McIntyre, "Henry Adams and the Unity of *Chartres,*" 167.

12. Ibid., 162, 169.

13. Writing to his friend Charles Milnes Gaskell on December 20, 1904, Adams wrote of *Mont-Saint-Michel and Chartres* that "it is my declaration of principles as head of the Conservative Christian Anarchists; a party numbering one member. The Virgin and St. Thomas are my vehicles of anarchism. Nobody knows enough to see what they mean, so the Judges will probably not be able to burn me according to law" (*Letters of Henry Adams, 1892–1918*, ed. Worthington Chauncey Ford [Boston: Houghton Mifflin, 1938], 2:444).

CHAPTER 9

History, Science, and Politics: A Lifetime's Education

James P. Young

MORE THAN JUST AN autobiography, *The Education of Henry Adams* is both a tale of a lifetime of education and a theory of history.[1] It is a deeply personal book, as personal in its way as *Chartres,* and the education in question is that provided by the events of his life as filtered through his often quirky mind. Some disagree. The idea that it is less personal than its predecessor no doubt stems from the fact that Adams writes about himself in the third person, thus attempting to generate a sense of detachment from his own life.[2] Instead, I suggest that rather than being impersonal, the story of his career reveals different sides of the very complex Adams persona, more guarded and more ironic than in the utopian enthusiasm of *Chartres.* But there is no doubt that a clearly personal portrait emerges—brilliant, wry, sometimes acidic, but always a recognizable self, though perhaps not one as likable as the author of his great exploration of medieval France. "He was," as Andrew Delbanco says, "between Whitman and Mailer, the most self-conscious of our major writers, I think, defiantly asserting that the most interesting literary subject he could find was the action of his own mind."[3] Michael Rogin also notes the similarity of Adams to Norman Mailer, a comparison Adams probably would not have relished. *The Time of Our Time,* Mailer's anthology of his own work, both fiction and nonfiction, designed to tell the history of our time, may seem to be the sort of "monument to the ego" that Adams rejected, but "the *Education* did not so much 'efface the ego' (Adams's claim) as to make it the measure not just of American but of eschatological history."[4] And it is no small ego that presents its own life as history itself.[5] The story Adams tells represents not only his life but also the history of his family, his class, and indeed his country, not to mention, in his later years, the fate of the Western world. It also shifts the focus away from the "world of joy" in *Chartres* to a "world of power."[6] He explores this world as it was represented by his life, or at least a sublimated, abstracted, aestheticized version of it.

Considered as an autobiography, the book is full of twists and turns and is indeed rather odd. But Adams did not call his book an autobiography. That label was attached by the publisher after his death. This is a book that omits twenty of the most productive and, at first, happiest years of his life. Of course, the omission is due to the pain of writing about his marriage and the suicide of his wife, Marian. When the narrative resumes in 1892, Adams refers to it as his "posthumous life." The book was first printed and circulated to friends in 1907. The public edition appeared after his death in 1918, with an "Editor's Preface" written by Adams but bearing the signature of Henry Cabot Lodge. In it, he treats the *Education* as the sequel to *Mont-Saint-Michel and Chartres* and suggests Saint Augustine's *Confessions* as a model. This obviously is no mean standard.[7]

The Education of Henry Adams offers what Adams wanted his public to think about. It is not by any means a standard autobiography. For that, it is much better to turn to the enormously voluminous and brilliantly written letters.[8] As I have suggested, what Adams had in mind was something altogether more ambitious than a mere autobiography, no matter how great, since, with no little display of ego, he took his life to be emblematic of all American history in the nineteenth and early twentieth centuries. His book is another take on his theory of American historical development and his philosophy of history. The one feeds the other. And his education begins at the beginning.

Education as an Adams

Even the simple statement of Adams's birth in the famous opening paragraphs is portentous. It is clear that he saw that being an Adams conveyed both advantages and disadvantages. Born in Boston, "under the shadow of the State House," and christened by his uncle, the minister of the First Church, he could not have been more marked, or handicapped, "had he been born in Jerusalem under the shadow of the Temple and circumcised in the Synagogue by his uncle the high priest under the name Israel Cohen."

A hundred years before, this heritage would have secured his future, but by 1838, the Boston associations, "so colonial—so troglodytic," posed problems for a boy required to "play the game" in the twentieth century.[9]

Education began with Henry's eighteenth-century inheritance.

> The atmosphere of education in which he lived was colonial, revolutionary, almost Cromwellian, as though he were steeped, from his greatest grand-mother's birth, in the odor of political crime. Resistance to something was the law of New England nature; the boy looked out on the world with the instinct of resistance; for numberless generations his predecessors had viewed the world chiefly as a thing to be reformed, filled with evil forces to be abolished, and they saw no reason to suppose that they had wholly succeeded in the abolition; the duty was unchanged. That duty implied not only resistance to evil, but hatred of it. . . . The New Englander, whether boy or man, in his long struggle with a stingy or hostile universe, had learned also to love the pleasure of hating; his joys were few.

In Massachusetts, politics was as "harsh as the climate," Adams observed, the systematic organization of hatreds.[10]

Perhaps no other passage captures the mood of the Adams political heritage quite so well—the reformist zeal, the hatred and contempt for the opposition, the deep distrust of any form of orthodox party politics, and the conviction that moral force can improve, though not transform, the world. (It must be said that Henry Adams would come to question the last point.) The Adamses were born to be political mavericks, whether they sought office or, in the case of Henry, chose to pursue reform with the pen. He was very much a product of the education provided by this family tradition.

And, of course, at the heart of that tradition were two presidents. With great charm he tells about sitting in church in Quincy looking at the bald head of his grandfather, the sixth president, John Quincy Adams:

> It was unusual for boys to sit behind a President grandfather, and to read over his head the tablet in memory of a President great-grandfather, who had "pledged his life, his fortune, and his sacred honor" to secure the independence of his country and so forth; but boys naturally supposed, without much reasoning, that other boys had the equivalent of President grandfathers. . . . The Irish gardener once said to the child: "You'll be thinking you'll be President too!" The casuality of the remark made so strong an impression on his mind that he never forgot it. He could not ever remember to have thought

on the subject; to him, that there should be a doubt of his being President was a new idea.[11]

This says a great deal. There is the well-deserved sense of familial pride; the sense of duty, if not destiny; and the seeds of disappointment when the youthful expectations were not met, a disappointment that turns into a general critique of American politics when those "obviously" best fitted to rule were unable to attain the heights of power. There is a sense of an aristocracy, perhaps even a Jeffersonian "natural aristocracy," that is central to the later generations of the Adams family. Henry explains that until 1850 and beyond, the professions ran New England. The men acted not as individuals but as representatives of their professional classes, "as though they were clergymen and each profession was a church. In politics the system required competent expression; it was the old Ciceronian idea of government by *the best* that produced the long line of New England statesmen." As a boy, he expected this system to be permanent. The system worked; even Germany wanted to try it. "England's middle-class government was the ideal of human progress." Three instruments worked for the human good: "Suffrage, Common Schools, and Press." Only Karl Marx expected radical change, as Adams so wryly remarked.[12]

It was as a boy in Quincy that Adams claims to have discovered the problem that became the center of his educational concerns and his lifelong obsession as well. It was the problem of order, but not order alone. "From cradle to grave this problem of running order through chaos, direction through space, discipline through freedom, unity through multiplicity, has always been, and must always be, the task of education, as it is the moral of religion, philosophy, science, art, politics, and economy."[13] And of course, as described earlier, he learned the power of firm, traditional, yet highly personal authority from his president grandfather, who silently marched him off to school against his will. It is also important to note that all these lessons were learned during summers in Quincy, not in Boston, which Adams came to detest, not least because it was the center of rising capitalist finance. Nor did he receive these lessons of education in school, for he believed his schooling from age ten to sixteen years to be time wasted. Pointing to the tremendous upheavals that were to come, he says, quite rightly, "Perhaps his needs turned out to be exceptional, but his existence was exceptional. Between 1850 and 1900 nearly everyone's existence was exceptional."[14]

Complexity began to enter this world of certainties when his father took twelve-year-old Henry to Washington to visit his widowed grandmother. There he made a pilgrimage to Mount Vernon. The roads were terrible, and from this he received a complete Virginia education. To a New Englander, good schools, good roads, and the like were part of the system of order. "Bad roads meant bad morals. The moral of this Virginia road was clear, and the boy fully learned it. Slavery was wicked and slavery was the cause of this road's badness which amounted to social crime—and yet, at the end of the road and product of the crime stood Mount Vernon and George Washington." Luckily, Adams tells us, boys accept contradictions as easily as their elders, or he "might have become prematurely wise." He was told, and accepted for life, that Washington stood alone, a polestar that was always steady. Jefferson, Madison, Marshall, Franklin, even John Adams could be seen in changing light, but Washington held still. "Mount Vernon always remained where it was, with no practicable road to reach it; and yet, when he got there, Mount Vernon was only Quincy in a Southern setting. No doubt it was much more charming, but it was the same eighteenth-century, the same old furniture, the same old patriot, and the same old President."[15] But still, the trip to the South introduces into the story a sense of the complexity that was to be central in Adams's thought.

Life remained fairly simple for a time. Faced with slavery, the boy simply stepped back from an eighteenth- to a seventeenth-century morality. He was more political than ever, but "slavery drove the whole Puritan community back on its puritanism." Still, he began to see that there might be some difficulty reconciling sixteenth-century principles with eighteenth-century statesmanship and nineteenth-century party organizations. Life became less simple, and old educational verities began to show signs of strain.[16]

Education at Harvard College

The early education in Quincy—since he never liked Boston—and the trip to Washington furnished Adams with the foundations of his view of the world. These ideas stayed with him, but already there is a hint that he felt that they unfitted him for the modern world in which he lived his life. The values of Quincy become a kind of lost utopia, which becomes all the more clear as he examines his Harvard education, the first of the "failures" that provide one of the main narrative lines of the *Education*.

Adams did not much like Harvard, though he thought it less hurtful than any other university of the time. The education it offered was certainly not distinguished, though it was mild and liberal and made possible a friendship with "Rooney" Lee, the son of Robert E. Lee, as well as with some of Rooney's Virginian friends. Adams liked the Virginians, but this did not stop him from looking down on them from the heights of his sense of Yankee superiority. As he puts it, "Strictly, the Southerner had no mind; he had temperament. He was not a scholar; he had no intellectual training; he could not analyze an idea, and he could not even conceive of admitting two; but in life one could get along very well without ideas, if only one had the social instinct."[17] Always assuming that Adams's recollections are accurate, one can see here the continuation of the condescension toward the prewar South that had begun in Mount Vernon and continued until after Emancipation.

Though he learned something about southern character, Adams saw the time spent at college as largely wasted. "Harvard College was a good school, but at bottom what the boy disliked most was any school at all." He complains that he simply was not taught anything about the two writers of his time who later influenced him most; thus, he never heard the name of Karl Marx or of *Capital*, nor was there any mention of Auguste Comte. Of course, one has to say that this complaint is more than a little unfair— a case of authorial license, one might say—since the first volume of *Das Kapital* was not published until 1867, nine years after Henry's graduation, and the first English translation of Comte was not published until 1853 and popularized only in 1865 by John Stuart Mill's little book *Auguste Comte and Positivism.*[18]

In the classroom, the one saving grace seems to have been Louis Agassiz in his course on the glacial period and paleontology, which was to prove helpful later, when Adams turned his attention to the theory of evolution. More importantly, perhaps, Agassiz was to have a major influence on Adams's style of thought regarding scientific matters. Agassiz was devoutly Christian and held an antirationalist attitude toward science, which had the effect of steering Adams away from experimental and biological sciences. The religion of Agassiz never captured Adams, but when he gave up his religious heritage, it was not replaced by naturalism or scientific materialism; instead, he adopted a quasi-idealist approach to the sciences. Thus, as William Jordy says, "Adams enjoyed the vivid generalizations of science far more than its methodical investigation."[19] Certainly this may help account for the freewheeling speculation, unanchored by much real evidence, of his late attempts to apply the laws of physics to history.

Nevertheless, Harvard had its influence. The New England certainties established in childhood began to waver, if only a little. Adams "was slipping away from fixed principles; from Mount Vernon Street; from Quincy; from the eighteenth century; and the first steps led toward Concord." But "he never reached Concord, and to Concord Church he, like the rest of mankind who accepted a material universe, remained always an insect, or something much lower—a man."[20] Thus, despite his wife's close familial connections to the transcendentalists, Emerson, Thoreau, and other major intellects of his time had little impact on his thought.

So transcendentalism did not take hold, and the New England values were simultaneously weakened, though the judgmental Puritan cast of mind never disappeared. This set up a lasting tension between the certainty of moral rectitude and the growing uncertainty about the foundations of that sense of right. But still, looking back, Adams thought that his education had not even begun. So he did what any well-to-do youth might have done; he went to Europe for two years. Although being in Europe doubtless deepened his aesthetic sensibilities, there is little sign that he was provided with the ideas necessary for the tumult of the last half of the nineteenth century, let alone the early twentieth, however long he might imitate Gibbon sitting on the steps of Santa Maria Ara Coeli in Rome.[21] The next real chance for education came with the Civil War and a close-up view of international diplomacy when he served in London as his ambassador father's private secretary.

War, Diplomacy, and Education

Following the election of 1860, Adams's father, then a congressman from Massachusetts, went to Washington, accompanied by the twenty-two-year-old Henry, to be present for the looming crisis.[22] Even after forty-four years, Henry's assessment of the impending situation was clear and blunt—treason was the only word to suffice. Confronting the southern radicals was a government that had an "air of social instability and incompleteness that went far to support the right of secession in theory as in fact; but right or wrong, secession was likely to be easy when there was so little to secede from. The

Union was a sentiment, but not much more."[23] Echoing his article on the secession winter, Adams finds the secessionists "unbalanced," like victims of "hallucinations," not to mention "stupendously ignorant of the world" and "provincial to a degree rarely known." By contrast, their New England opponents, in his rather Manichaean view of the world, "were sane and steady men, well-balanced, educated, and free from meanness or intrigue."[24] In spite of any friendship he felt for Rooney Lee, southerners as a group were to be avoided.

Of course, senators could not be avoided, but the institution they inhabited still met with Adams's withering contempt, even looking back from 1907. They were, he said, much given to "admiring in [the institution's] members a superiority less obvious or quite invisible to outsiders."[25] In this setting, the Puritan character of Representative Adams had to be supple, and though he was thick-skinned, like all the Adamses, all would have insisted "that they had invariably subordinated local to national interests, and would continue to do so, whenever forced to choose. C. F. Adams was sure to do what his father had done, as his father had followed the steps of John Adams, and no doubt thereby earned his epithets."[26] Thus, the family tradition, redolent of civic republicanism, would continue.

One thing was certain; Abraham Lincoln did not appear to be up to the job entrusted to him. In what Adams must surely have known, in retrospect, to be a bizarre misjudgment, only General Winfield Scott looked ready for the crisis. And Adams, who may have been unaware of it even as late as 1907, had misjudged Lincoln just as badly. All he could see at the Inaugural Ball was a "long, awkward figure; a plain, ploughed face; a mind, absent in part, and in part evidently worried by white kid gloves; features that expressed neither self-satisfaction nor any other familiar Americanism, but rather the same painful sense of becoming educated and of needing education that tormented a private secretary; above all a lack of apparent force. . . . No man living needed so much education as the new President . . . but all the education he could get would not be enough."[27] There is no clear sense of the famous Adams irony here. Of course, no one going into the war could have known how to cope, but Adams's lack of regard for the president, plus his own self-regard, makes it appear that at this crucial turning point in American history, Adams simply missed the significance of Lincoln.[28] Only very late in life did he offer a more positive, if brief, evaluation of Lincoln.

Certainly the important conclusion to the chapter dealing with the crisis in Washington as war fever increased gives no hint that Adams was not entirely serious in his estimate of Lincoln. Notice carefully what Adams says: "Not a man there knew what his task was to be, or was fitted for it; everyone without exception, Northern or Southern, was to learn his business at the cost of the public. Lincoln, Seward, Sumner, and the rest, could give no help to the young man seeking education; *they knew less than he;* within six weeks they were all to be taught their duties by the uprising of such as he; and their education was to cost a million lives and ten thousand million dollars, more or less, North and South, before the country could recover its balance and movement."[29]

The familiar Adams arrogance is striking here. Certainly it is true that no one knew what to expect from the Civil War. No one foresaw the awful carnage that was to come. What is disturbing here is that Adams, while protesting his lack of education, claims to know more than the other, much more senior, much more consequential figures he mentions. This defies all probability. His views on Reconstruction provide strong evidence that he never fully grasped what was at stake in the crisis over slavery. But this is an important passage, because it is an early instance of one of the most common rhetorical strategies in the *Education,* the pose of Socratic ignorance.[30] Throughout the book Adams protests his lack of knowledge and the failure of his education. But the reader clearly is intended to understand that despite this failure, Adams grasped ideas and events better than his contemporaries. Similarly, in the Platonic dialogues, Socrates, in spite of his protests, does in fact know more than his fellow conversationalists, and he knows that he does. What is troubling here is that in this passage, it is obvious that Adams is ignorant, but it is not at all clear that *he* recognizes that fact. His assessment of the coming crisis of the Civil War shows little of his characteristic irony. For a recognition of genuine failure, a failure that really taught him something important about the difficulty of understanding human affairs, we need to look at his experience as private secretary to his father during the war. In those years, Adams came to see the difficulties of interpreting men, motives, and events, and in coming to this understanding, he developed a deep sense of the true complexity of political action.

Diplomatic service in London, even in a minor capacity, proved to be both educational and deeply disconcerting for the young secretary.[31] On May 12, 1861, things seemed simple; he thought that the British government was a friendly one, "true to the anti-slavery principles which had been their steadiest profession. For a hundred years the chief effort of his family had aimed at bringing the Government of England into intelligent cooperation with the objects and interests of America. . . . The slave states had been the chief obstacle to good understanding. As for the private secretary himself, he was, like all Bostonians, instinctively English. He could not conceive the idea of a hostile England. He supposed himself, as one of the members of a famous anti-slavery family, to be welcome everywhere in the British Islands." But on May 13, the British recognition of Confederate belligerency was announced, and Adams suddenly learned "that his ideas were the reverse of truth; that in May, 1861, no one in England—literally no one—doubted that Jefferson Davis had made or would make a nation, and nearly all were glad of it. . . . The sentiment of anti-slavery had disappeared."[32] The great goal of American policy, under these surprising circumstances, became preventing the British from extending this position and extending diplomatic recognition to the Confederacy.

At the same time, leaving other expectations to one side, Henry writes, "Thanks to certain family associations, Charles Francis Adams naturally looked on all British Ministers as enemies; the only public occupation of all Adamses for a hundred and fifty years at least, in their brief intervals [from] quarreling with State Street, had been to quarrel with Downing Street."[33] On the British side, the two principals to contend with were Lord Palmerston, the prime minister, and Lord John Russell, the foreign secretary. In private, it was taken for granted, even by his friends, that Lord Russell was a liar. Palmerston was thought to be hardly better. "Other Prime Ministers may perhaps have lived who inspired among diplomats as much distrust as Palmerston, and yet between Palmerston's word and Russell's word, one hesitated to decide, and gave years of education to deciding, whether either could be trusted, or how far." Adams did not really mind this, saying quite realistically, "Diplomatists have no right to complain of mere lies; it is their own fault, if, educated as they are, the lies deceive them; but they complain bitterly of traps. Palmerston was believed to lay traps. He was the *enfant terrible* of the British government."[34]

Ambassador Adams believed that Palmerston wanted a quarrel and that he could better trust Lord Russell than he could the prime minister. The private secretary, for his part, believed that there was nothing to choose between the two British leaders.[35] Indeed, he went so far as to ask Thurlow Weed, a consummate Albany politician who joined the embassy staff, whether he thought that no politician could be trusted; Weed advised him that a young man should not begin by thinking so. Adams thought that this simply meant that Weed believed that youth needed illusions. But later, Weed's position appeared more complex to him: "Young men needed experience. They could not play well if they trusted to a general rule. Every card had a relative value. Principles had better be left aside. Adams knew that he could never learn to play politics in so masterly a fashion as this; his education and his nervous system equally forbade it, although he admired all the more the impersonal faculty of the political master who could thus efface himself and his temper in the game."[36]

Thus Adams had trouble taking Weed's advice. As he says, he "felt officially sure of dishonesty." But whom to distrust? Perhaps everyone? This decision depended on a knowledge of the genuine facts, which the ambassador died without knowing.[37] Charles Francis Adams went to his grave in 1886 believing Lord Russell's protestations of friendship. But in a biography of Russell, who had died in 1878, Spencer Walpole published a tale unknown to the senior Adams. By September 1862, when news of Lee's invasion of Maryland reached London, the idea of a Union in crisis was widespread. The fall of Washington or Baltimore was expected. Palmerston immediately wrote to Russell, asking whether, in such an eventuality, England and France should not intervene between North and South and suggest a separation. Had it reached the American legation, this letter would have surprised no one, given Palmerston's supposed diplomatic inclinations at the time. But, as Adams says, it is Russell's reply to Palmerston that bears careful analysis.

Russell, so trusted by Charles Francis Adams, argued that should mediation with a view to recognizing the Confederacy fail, England should indeed recognize the rebels unilaterally. "Here, then," Adams writes, "appeared in its fullest force, the practical difficulty in education which a mere student could never overcome; a difference not in theory, or knowledge, or even want of experience, but in the shear chaos of human nature. Lord Russell's course had been consistent from the first, and had all the look of rigid determination to recognize the Southern Confederacy 'with a view' to breaking up the Union." Besides having the appearance of forethought, the policy required the "deliberate dishonesty" not only of Palmerston and Russell but also of the previously unmentioned chancellor of the exchequer, William Gladstone. It would have been interesting to know the ambassador's reaction to these revelations, had he been privy to them, but, says Adams, it would have been even more interesting to know his father's response to Palmerston's reply to Russell, in which he urged caution just in case the Union forces won. Thus, "the roles were reversed. Russell wrote what was expected from Palmerston, or even more violently; while Palmerston wrote what was expected from Russell, or even more temperately." Not only was the private secretary's view wrong, but it turned out that the closest associates of the British leaders "knew little more about their intentions than was known in the Legation." Thus it emerged that only three members of the cabinet favored recognition of the Confederacy.[38]

Had these facts been known in the American embassy, there would have been great relief and a sense that the danger had passed, but this euphoria would have been mistaken. Enter William Gladstone, the Liberal leader. If there was a fixed point in the world, Adams thought, it was the British exchequer. But here, he tells us, is the education he received from observing Gladstone's actions. The chancellor indicated that he was glad to hear the prime minister's position because of the rapid progress of the southern forces and the risk of impatience in the Lancashire mill towns, which "would prejudice the dignity and disinterestedness of the proffered mediation." This letter to Palmerston was dated September 24, but on October 3, the news of the great Union victory at Antietam and the announcement of the Emancipation Proclamation reached London. Adams remarks of Gladstone's letter to Palmerston, "Had the puzzled student seen this letter, he must have concluded from it that the best educated statesman England ever produced did not know what he was talking about, an assumption which all the world would think quite inadmissable from a private secretary—but this was a trifle."[39]

It was a mere trifle because, on October 7, in spite of his knowledge of the Union victories, Gladstone delivered an amazing address. In it he proclaimed that the North would have to take its medicine, for "there is no doubt that Jefferson Davis and other leaders of the South have made an army; they are making, it appears, a navy; and they have made, what is more than either, they have made a nation."[40]

This was a startling pronouncement. From it, Adams "drew some harsh moral conclusions: Were they incorrect? Posed bluntly as rules of conduct, they led to the worst moral practices. As morals, one could detect no shade of difference between Gladstone and Napoleon except to the advantage of

Napoleon. The private secretary saw none." The evidence against Gladstone was overwhelming. One should never, says Adams, use the word "must," as Gladstone had in his speech. He knew perfectly well that the only hope for a southern nation rested in the hands of the British. Failing British action, his position was nonsense. "Never," says Adams, rising to a great height of indignation, "in the history of political turpitude had any brigand of modern civilization offered a worse example." Even Palmerston was outraged, since he had no thought of letting the chancellor force his hand. As for Russell, he followed Gladstone in favoring British intervention, but when Russell met with Ambassador Adams, he contended that intervention was still in doubt, insisting that Gladstone had been misunderstood. In spite of Gladstone's speech, the ambassador continued to believe in Russell. The "truth," when it was revealed thirty years later, showed Russell's position to be the reverse of what he had claimed while meeting the senior Adams. In fact, as it turned out, Gladstone had drawn his position from Russell's own policy. Palmerston disavowed Gladstone, but Russell never did. For the young Adams, "the lesson was to be crucial; it would decide the law of life. All these gentlemen were superlatively honorable; if one could not believe them, Truth in politics might be ignored as a delusion."[41]

Young Henry might have been distrustful—he only later learned the truth himself—but his father's belief in Lord Russell continued, as we have seen, to his death. Without pursuing further complications relating to this matter, such as the involvement of Napoleon III in pursuit of the goals of Russell and Gladstone, Adams drew some important lessons on which we too can build. Of the principal actors, Russell was the most interesting to Adams, simply because he was the most consistent and hence "statesmanlike." His every act showed a clear determination to break up the Union. He showed persistence, "supported, as was necessary, by the usual definite falsehoods." He said one thing and "habitually" did another.

Palmerston, so distrusted in the American embassy, tried to check Russell, scolded Gladstone, and discouraged Napoleon. "Palmerston told no falsehoods; made no professions; concealed no opinions; was detected in no double dealing. The most mortifying failure in Henry Adams's long education was that, after forty years of confirmed dislike, distrust, and detraction of Lord Palmerston, he was obliged at last to admit himself in error, and to consent in spirit—for by that time he was nearly as dead as any of them—to beg his pardon."

Gladstone was the "sum of contradictions." His confessions of 1896 "brought all reason and hope of education to a standstill." Gladstone simply confessed to "undoubted error." He even had the effrontery to assert that his statement that Jefferson Davis was making a nation was intended, though based on a "false estimate of the facts," as an act of "friendliness to all America." Doubtless out of a sense of filial piety, Adams does not comment on his father's repeated acceptance of Lord Russell's lies, which merited a more skeptical examination. There is no doubt that the senior Adams was regularly deceived.

From all these misperceptions, Adams concludes that he, the private secretary, had "seen nothing correctly at the time."[42] He is perhaps a little unfair to himself, since he indicates that he entertained a certain skepticism about British leadership as these events occurred. However, the situation points the way to what may be, for him, the central implication of this complex diplomatic situation. "Forty years afterwards," reading Gladstone's reports on cabinet meetings, "when everyone except himself, who looked on at this scene, was dead, the private secretary of 1862 read these lines with stupor, and hurried to discuss them with John Hay, who was more astounded than himself. All the world had been at cross-purposes, had misunderstood themselves and the situation, had followed wrong paths, drawn wrong conclusions, and had known none of the facts. One would have done better to have drawn no conclusions at all. One's diplomatic education was a long mistake."[43]

As usual, Adams's protestations of failed education go too far. In fact, they provide important lessons for scholars, journalists, politicians, and all others who hope to understand contemporary events. One thing that can surely be learned, or relearned, is that it is necessary for decision makers to do as well as possible under the prevailing circumstances, whatever they are. And these circumstances always include incomplete information. Frequently, perhaps usually, it is not possible to wait until all the facts are in, and when they are in, precisely what they are is likely to be disputed, as is their meaning. The most direct, close-up participants are likely to be deceived by the events going on around them, yet they must act in spite of their ignorance. This is an important lesson that Adams can teach.

Nor is this situation unique to the specific situation Adams was in. This is certainly part of the meaning of Tolstoy's account in *War and Peace* of the great Russian battles in the Napoleonic wars, in which he portrays scenes

of incredible confusion where no one has any real knowledge of what is
going on. But we need not limit ourselves to fiction. In his superb account
of U.S.-Soviet relations in the immediate postrevolutionary setting, George
Kennan observes something quite similar. His was the first study to go back
to the original sources to try to discern what had happened. The first volume is a minutely detailed study of events from the revolution in November
to the Russian withdrawal from World War I in March. Kennan's comments
on his work and what he found are amazingly reminiscent of Adams's. He
notes "the marvelous manner in which purpose, personality, coincidence,
communication, and the endless complexity of the modern world all combine to form a process beyond the full vision or comprehension of any single
contemporary." Then he concludes, "It is sobering to reflect that, imperfect
as this study is, there was none of the participants in the events recounted
here—indeed, there was no one alive in those years of 1917 and 1918—who
knew even the entirety of what is set forth in this volume."[44] Surely this
passage would have been relished by Adams, and I suggest that no serious
history or any contemporary study of politics can honestly avoid similar conclusions. The methodological lessons for history and political science today
are clear and profound.

One can hardly doubt that when he returned from England in 1868,
Adams combined his wartime experiences and the skepticism they bred
with the long-standing Adams family distrust of any orthodox party politics
of the sort abundantly on display in England. With this skepticism came a
growing sense of the ambiguity of agency and intention in politics. Doubtless these attitudes influenced his journalistic critiques of American politics
and society. These criticisms must be kept in mind while we consider some
of Adams's other intellectual interests, not least his growing concern with
scientific developments in his time, which often fed back into his conceptions of politics and history.

Darwinism and Education

Adams's interest in science carried on a long family concern, perhaps most
notably in the case of John Quincy Adams.[45] But the interest goes back as
far as John Adams, who perceived "laws of nature, not less without our
power, than beyond our comprehension."[46] But between the first and fourth
generations of the Adams dynasty, there was a significant difference.

The second president's beliefs reflected, and in turn encouraged, the socially engaged interests of a practicing statesman; the future historian's search for unalterable law reflected and encouraged his tendency to passive observation and lonely disinterestedness. The Adams trait they shared was a scientific turn of mind with a clear history for four generations—and something beyond that, an obscure love of cosmic necessity that seems to reach into the Calvinist Puritan past with its central, compelling interest in the providence of an inscrutable, omnipotent God.[47]

To be sure, Henry no longer believed in the Puritan God, but he surely held to the Puritan cast of mind, try though he did to use it to fathom the inscrutable.

That Adams should develop an interest in Darwinism in the years following the Civil War is hardly surprising. Darwinism was a rather loose body of ideas that swept the English-speaking world, particularly in the popularized form offered by Herbert Spencer and, in the United States, by William Graham Sumner. More often than not put to deeply conservative purposes as a defense of the allegedly fittest who had survived the rigors of laissez-faire competition, it could also be used by reformers to support cooperative action on behalf of the victims of unrestrained competition.[48] Adams, however, was not particularly interested in either political use. He was too critical of postwar capitalism to join with the conservatives, and his reformist sensibilities did not run in the direction of cooperative social and economic reform.

Indeed, his first response to evolutionary theory seems to have been simple curiosity: "Unbroken Evolution under uniform conditions pleased everyone—except curates and bishops; it was the very best substitute for religion; a safe, conservative, practical, thoroughly Common-Law deity. Such a working system for the universe suited a young man who had just helped to waste five or ten thousand million dollars and a million lives, more or less, to enforce unity and uniformity on people who objected; the idea was only too seductive in its perfection; it had the charm of art."[49] Thus, evolution attracted Adams as a possible way to reach his lifelong goal of unity, as well as providing a cosmic basis for moral intention, since Darwinism has a tendency to moralize force and necessity. But Darwinism proved not to be the answer, and he was not to reach the goal of theoretical unity by this or any other means.

Technical discussions of Adams's views on evolution need not detain us here.[50] The political and historical lessons he drew are of interest, however. On the level of scientific evidence, his brief explorations into the fossil record were not of much value to him. *Terebratula*, a kind of mollusk, proved to be uniform from the beginning of geological time, so there was no evidence of development through natural selection. Then he considered *Pteraspis*, a fish and a very early vertebrate. But he could detect no connection between *Pteraspis* and other higher vertebrates. He was untroubled by the idea that *Pteraspis* and sharks were "his cousins, great-uncles, or grandfathers." What did trouble him was that he could see no evidence of evolution from lower to higher species. "He could detect no more evolution in life since the *Pteraspis* than he could detect it in architecture since the Abbey. All he could prove was change."[51]

He elaborates this theme:

> Behind the lesson of the day, he was conscious that, in geology as in theology, he could prove only Evolution that did not evolve; Uniformity that was not uniform; and Selection that did not select. To other Darwinians—except Darwin—Natural Selection seemed a dogma to be put in the place of the Athanasian Creed; it was a form of religious hope; a promise of ultimate perfection . . . . [But Adams] felt he had no Faith; that whenever the next new hobby should be brought out, he should surely drop off from Darwinism like a monkey from a perch; that the idea of one Form, Law, Order, or Sequence had no more value for him than the idea of none; that what he valued most was Motion, and that what attracted his mind was Change.[52]

And then, shockingly for an Adams, "Henry Adams was the first in an infinite series to discover and admit to himself that he really did not care whether truth was, or was not, true. He did not even care that it should be proved true, unless the process were new and amusing. He was a Darwinian for fun."[53] This takes being playful with ideas to a considerable extreme.

But Adams fought against accepting this dangerous new thought. "From the beginning of history, this attitude had been branded as criminal—worse than crime—sacrilege. Society punished it ferociously and justly, in self-defense." This sort of relativism was a belief that annoyed his father, but it annoyed Henry no less; he had no thought of falling victim to Hamletian doubts. He wanted the dominant current of his time to be his current. "He insisted on maintaining his absolute standards; on aiming at ultimate Unity."[54]

There is a certain defiance of reason here. His mind tells him that truth is an illusion, but he vows to cling to the illusion because it is socially useful, as when Socrates propagates the myth of the metals in the *Republic,* but with this difference: Socrates remains undeceived. He knows that the myth is a myth or, in some interpretations, an outright lie. In the case of Adams, he too is a Socratic figure, but one trying as hard as he can to believe what his mind tells him is no longer valid. The tension between the New England heritage and the disruptions of modern thought and life is beginning to become extreme.

In any case, it is clear to Adams that while change is the law of life, there is no guarantee that the direction of change will be positive. In the optimistic nineteenth century, belief in progress was widespread, but of course, Adams believed, as we know, that the history of the presidency from Washington to Grant was enough to disrupt any fantasies about inevitable progress. As Levenson says, "Instead of having to deduce George Washington from the sum of all wickedness . . . he now faced the up-to-date, inductive question of explaining" presidential and, more generally, political decline.[55]

But other, more personal, more serious events were to create further problems, further education for Adams's developing perceptions. As we have seen, he thought that the country was in a constitutional crisis, a crisis brought about by sheer drift, his common term to describe the policies of the Grant administration but affecting the reformers as well. Political chaos could be seen in the pervasive corruption he documented in his journalism. To the reformer, it seemed that "the country might outlive it, but not he. The worst scandals of the eighteenth century were relatively harmless by the side of this, which smirched executive, judiciary, banks, corporate systems, professions, and people, all the great active forces of society, in one dirty cesspool of vulgar corruption."[56]

The last lesson of education, as he called it at the time, came in 1870, when he was called from London to his sister's bedside in Bagni di Lucca, Italy. She had been thrown from a cab and injured. Tetanus set in. Here, genuine chaos struck the family. Before, Adams had never really seen nature—only the "sugar-coating that she shows to youth." He remarks, "One had heard and read a great deal about death, and even seen a little of it, and knew by heart the thousand commonplaces of religion and poetry which seemed to deaden one's senses and veil the horror. Society being immortal, could put on immortality at will. Adams being mortal, felt only the mortality."[57]

He was deeply shaken. Gone are the usual cynical mannerisms, gone are all traces of superciliousness. Instead, he emits a cry of pure existential rage against the universe: "The usual anodynes of social medicine became evident artifice. Stoicism was perhaps the best; religion was the most human; but the idea that any personal deity could find pleasure or profit in torturing a poor woman, by accident, with a fiendish cruelty known to man only in perverted and insane temperaments, could not be held for a moment. For pure blasphemy, it made pure atheism a comfort. God might be, as the Church said, a Substance, but He could not be a Person."[58]

Reading these words, it is hard to see *Mont-Saint-Michel and Chartres* as a religious book. At most, it is a picture—highly partial, to be sure—of a beautiful society inspired by what, given the outburst precipitated by Catherine's death, Adams might well have thought to be a delusion. As Levenson says, while the earlier book confirmed the reality of the Virgin, "the other confirmed doubt." After quoting Adams's outburst, he continues, "instead of being about the works of love which defy reality, the *Education* is concerned with the ultimate reality of the real world. Yet the terrifying negation in this climax, it must be emphasized, is a turning point and not an end."[59] This is true enough, I think, for Adams had a mind too restless to ever come to a complete stop. But once again, the New England verities were shaken, and one can see in this statement the themes of Adams's later years beginning to take shape, affecting the still-to-be-written *History*, where even men conventionally called great become the mere playthings of forces beyond their control. Drift leading to chaos begins to be a central theme in Adams's thought. Again, Levenson is on the mark when he comments, "The discontinuities of experience, which made Adams repeat so often that he had a new world to learn, attained their ultimate form."[60]

One can see these ideas at work during Adams's brief tenure as a Harvard University history professor. As a result of President Eliot's famous reforms, this Harvard was much improved over the Harvard College Adams had attended and scorned. The problem he saw as a teacher was this: "A teacher must either treat history as a catalogue, a record, a romance, or as an evolution; and whether he affirms or denies evolution, he falls into all the burning faggots of the pit. He makes of his scholars priests or atheists, plutocrats or socialists, judges or anarchists, almost in spite of himself. In essence incoherent or immoral, history had either to be taught as such—or falsified."

Adams wanted to do neither. He had no theory of evolution to teach, and could not make the facts fit one. He had no fancy for telling agreeable tales to amuse sluggish-minded boys, in order to publish them afterwards as lectures. He could still less compel his students to learn the Anglo-Saxon Chronicle and the Venerable Bede by heart. He saw no relation whatever between his students and the Middle Ages unless it were the Church, and there the ground was particularly dangerous. He knew better than though he were a professional historian that the man who should solve the riddle of the Middle Ages and bring them into the line of evolution from past to present, would be a greater man than Lamarck or Linnaeus; but history had nowhere broken down so pitiably, or avowed itself so hopelessly bankrupt, as there. Since Gibbon, the spectacle was almost a scandal. History had lost even the sense of shame. It was a hundred years behind the experimental sciences. For all serious purposes, it was less instructive than Walter Scott and Alexandre Dumas.[61]

This is a stern indictment, though anyone teaching today can certainly recognize the problem inherent in engaging students with events in the distant past, particularly at a time when a generation seems like infinity. Having repudiated the lecture system, Adams introduced the German seminar to Harvard. Characteristically, Adams certified his years at Harvard as a failure. But his own words belie him. He found the students "excellent company. Cast more or less in the same mould, without violent emotions or sentiment, and, except for the veneer of American habits, ignorant of all that man had ever thought or hoped, their minds burst open like flowers at the sunlight of a suggestion."[62] Surely in this picture there is hope for democracy. For a professor, this is not failure but success. Adams should have taken his own words to heart. "A teacher affects eternity; he can never tell where his influence stops."[63]

Twenty Years After (1892)

Here there occurs a huge break in Adams's narrative and the start of what he often referred to as his posthumous life. The break, as I have mentioned, was occasioned by Adams's inability to write about the years of his marriage to Marian Adams, who committed suicide in 1885. We largely lose any further reflections he may have had on the political and social developments in these twenty years or any thoughts supplementing his writings, including, in particular, the *History*, but also the novels so close to his heart. And also, more important from our point of view, there is a change in his concerns, not immediate but nonetheless real. Adams does not lose interest in American politics; indeed, he has a considerable fascination with the Populist movement of the 1890s. But closely connected to this, he develops a growing interest in international capitalism, particularly in its banking dimensions; he is deeply interested in geopolitics; he displays an intensifying concern with the development of technology and an equally intensifying search for a source of unity in a world whose principal attribute is multiplicity. This last, in particular, leads him into deep, if often quixotic, reflections on the philosophy of history. The consequence of this is that much of the last third of the *Education* operates on a very high level of abstraction, making it necessary to refer more often to his correspondence to establish the context for his theorizing. But in no sense does he give up his intellectual quest. His ever-active mind pursues a general theory of history and politics to the end.

It is best to begin with the politics and economics, which are closely linked in his thought. As of 1892, when the narrative of the *Education* resumes, Adams is indifferent to party; politicians are graded according to whether they are friends or enemies of reform. In either case, as he wryly puts it, his views of politics and politicians "lacked enthusiasm."[64] But, as is already abundantly clear, to banks and to the rigid orthodox adherence to the gold standard, "he was fated to make his last resistance behind the silver standard." His own interests as an investor were with gold, but, he tells us, he was more interested in the "moral standard" than in the gold standard.[65]

Then came the panic of 1893, and Adams, incorrectly fearing that he was now a beggar, returned from Switzerland to help save the family fortune.[66] Though the situation proved to be less dire than initially thought, it did set Henry thinking, partly under the influence of his younger brother Brooks, about the nefarious role of banking in politics and society. And this process lessened his faith, already shaky, in the status of orthodox economics. As Ernest Samuels says, "The Panic of 1893 opened his eyes to the larger economic and social movement. The sacred laws of laissez-faire economics no longer supplied a clear guide to political morality, especially if they meant enriching one's enemies. Perhaps the power of government should be used after all when the laws of economics no longer served one's purposes. Perhaps their political philosophy had been wrong from the start."[67] On the political side, this meant that Adams allied himself, loosely, tentatively, and temporarily, with some of the more radical forces in American politics, the aggrieved farmers from the South and Midwest. It also brought him together with Brooks, who was developing the ideas that became his major contribution to the interpretation of history, *The Law of Civilization and Decay*. Finally, and very unfortunately, it tapped into a previously buried vein of anti-Semitism, based on his association of banking with Jews. The last result of his trip home for the family emergency was a visit to the Chicago Exposition, where he was particularly fascinated by the display of dynamos, which were to play a large part in his general theory of history and the forces that made it move.[68] Chicago raised serious questions about where the nation was going; Adams professed not to know the national destination and doubted that his fellow citizens did either. But Washington raised fewer questions. Already the decision had clearly been made for a system of centralized industrial capitalism, which Adams opposed, without elaboration, to simple industrialism standing alone. In 1893, when the decision turned on the gold standard, the choice was decisively for the new capitalism and all that it entailed, the very system Adams liked least. This result, as Russell Hanson and Richard Merriman argue, certainly precluded any revival of a civic republican tradition via a return to first principles of the political system.[69] Those principles had simply been superseded. And, even granted Adams's distinction between industrialism and capitalist industrialism, it was clearly too late to return to the earlier "precapitalist" form of organization.

Though Adams comments on how easily he and his silver friends adapted to the gold standard, in fact, the fight continued into the presidential election of 1896. Adams says very little in the *Education* about his temporary flirtation with the Populists. One suspects that he considered it an unfit subject for public discussion. But Adams misdates the final triumph of the gold system, which occurred not in 1893, as his chronology suggests, but with the presidential election of 1896. A brief look into his letters suggests the complexities of Adams's position. "Although I—very doubtfully—hold that on the whole the election of McKinley will do more mischief than that of Bryan, and, as a conservative anarchist, am therefore inclined to hope for McKinley's success, while I help Bryan all I can, certainly I cannot make so very complicated a program intelligible to any party." Unexpectedly, given the huge differences between his sensibility and the Democratic candidate's, he says, "I rather like Bryan—I mean politically—and go near going over to him." This was especially true if Europe were to go politically, socially, and financially bankrupt within the next five years, in which case he would definitely support Bryan, because that would "cut us free" at once. But then he lapses into his anti-Semitic obsession. If the "Jew regime" were going to continue for ten or twenty years, so that "all the world is to be owned by Lombard Street," then McKinley would be preferable, because the tariff would be more important than free silver, which could be useful for barely ten years as a weapon against Europe.[70] This, of course, rests on the crazed assumption that the international banking system was under Jewish control and centered in London, hence the reference to Lombard Street. For a time, this notion has a place in Adams's thought, and we will have to explore it further. But for now, the politics is of particular interest.

The statement about helping Bryan refers to the fact that, at the urging of his brother Brooks, and through him as an intermediary, Adams donated money to Bryan's campaign. He seems to have thought the money well spent. Again writing to Mrs. Cameron, Adams comments, "Bryan has made quite a wonderful fight, whether beaten or not, and poor McKinley seems a very sad jellyfish beside him. But the Major has never been regarded as serious by anyone—except himself—and me."[71] Thus, as I have mentioned, crusty old Henry Adams aligned himself temporarily, using what must be called bizarre reasoning, with some of the most radical forces in American politics.[72] But Adams lacked the courage of his peculiar convictions and in the end came round to McKinley, going home in October, as he put it, "with everyone else, to elect McKinley President and to start the world anew."[73]

Adams must certainly have had mixed feelings about this new world. It is true that John Hay, his closest friend, became ambassador to Britain and later secretary of state, so that Adams stood closer to the halls of power than he had ever been. At the same time, it is even clearer now than it was in 1906 that the election of William McKinley established a new regime in American politics that was to last until the New Deal. It was a regime of corporate domination and declining voter participation in elections, as well as a decline in the importance of political parties. Bryan had no appeal for the urban working class, and his capture of the Democratic Party narrowed the options for voters, a trend partially reversed by the New Deal, but now again one of the deepest dilemmas for American democracy. As Walter Dean Burnhan writes: "The ultimate democratic purpose of issue formulation in a campaign is to give the people at large the power to choose their and their agents' options. Moreover, so far as is known, the blunt alternative to party government is the concentration of political power in the hands of those who already possess concentrated economic power." Given the weakness of parties, we are thrown back on "image" and "personality" voting.[74]

The existence of such a system posed serious problems for Adams. He hated corporate capitalist domination, but he hated political parties as well. A lifetime of heterodox independence left him without the institutional means to fight back. We do not know in any detail what he thought of Theodore Roosevelt's attempts to regulate the trusts, though we do know that in general terms he was contemptuous of TR. Perhaps if his serious practical interest in the domestic scene had lasted longer, he would have continued his flirtation with radicals such as Bryan. But even in 1896, his attention was turning toward geopolitics and the philosophy of history. And of course, his interest was always more in diagnosis than in treatment, so he was an unlikely candidate to become an activist, no matter how much he despised the status quo.

When his thinking on international developments is considered, it is also important to take note of his intellectual relationship to his brother Brooks. "Brooks Adams had taught him [Henry] that the relation between nations was that of trade."[75] Of course, this implies a need for markets, and although Henry emphatically rejected territorial empire, he certainly favored keeping international markets open as a means to the end of American economic development. Henry pithily sums up Brooks's central thesis:

> All Civilization is Centralization.
> All Centralization is Economy.
> Therefore all Civilization is the survival of the most economical (cheapest).[76]

But Adams does not think that capitalism can continue indefinitely. One possibility that intrigues him comes from his brother. "Among other general rules he laid down the paradox that, in the social disequilibrium between capital and labor, the logical outcome was not collectivism, but anarchism," a point he marks for study.[77] But more immediately, he sees something else. Writing in 1898, he saw Hungary as a "child of State-Socialism in a most intelligent and practical form. In principle there is no apparent limit to its application." It is a form of society that deserves attention, "especially in connection with Russia." It is a future he says he wants nothing to do with. Nevertheless, he writes, "To me it seems to demonstrate the axiom of what we are civil enough to call progress, has got to be:—All monopolies will be assumed by the state; as a corollary to the proposition that the common interest is supreme over the individual." Then Adams goes on to urge Brooks to drop the free silver campaign and move on to socialism. He adds, in a peculiarly Hegelian fashion:

> Not that I love Socialism any better than I do Capitalism, or any other Ism, but I know only one law of political or historical morality, and that is that the form of Society which survives is always in the Right; and therefore a statesman is obliged to follow it, unless he leads. . . . Socialism is merely a new application of Economy, which must go on until Competition puts an end to further Economies, or the whole world becomes one Socialist society and rots out. One need not love Socialism in order to point out the logical necessity for Society to march that way; and the wisdom of doing it intelligently if it is to do it at all.[78]

This is a striking commentary, and not completely characteristic of Adams's thinking. Here, "Adams momentarily envisioned an ideal socialism which transcended nationality and was consistent with individual energy, but a mere glimpse could not revive youthful hope or generate a practical belief in a utopia he might help to build. . . . Intellectual curiosity was more important than humane sentiment in determining the meaning of this vision. What lasted from this phase of his peregrinations was the insistence that a real choice could be made between intelligence and drift."[79] This important point should be remembered as the fatalistic theories of his last years emerge after 1910.

Along this line, as Levenson suggests, the 1898 letter to his brother shows that he had not completely given in to determinism; intelligent leadership still had a role to play. Adams's position is very much like Joseph Schumpeter's thirty-six years later. Schumpeter, too, believed that capitalism would not survive if it continued along its present developmental path, which he saw threatened by the New Deal. However, unlike Adams, he was distressed by the thought, since he was an admirer of the capitalist system. Still, he saw a movement much like the one Adams suggests. In the long run, the difference between capitalism and socialism would not prove to be great, he thought; however, he hoped that the dire trends he saw could be halted in time. And though he did not much care, he thought that democracy would survive under capitalism, contrary to the ideas of some free-market liberals, though it would still be what he called "more of a sham than capitalist democracy ever was."[80]

Of course, Adams too was troubled by democracy under capitalism. But he saw more grounds for hope than did Schumpeter. He believed deeply in the need for a governing elite and felt that the need to manage the new socialist system would provide the Adamses a way back into power. R. P. Blackmur neatly sums up the implications of his analysis of the dynamics of capitalism.

> Henry Adams in making out his rough socialist position was making out, as much as anything, a case for the only possible vitalization of the governing class that he could see. Every other position constituted a more or less abject surrender to the money power; a surrender upon which every president since Lincoln had battened, just as the money power had battened on presidents. Socialism as framed was meant precisely to control the money power through absorption. So far, Socialism was the only means of control that went further than compromise. No government that was at the conspicuous mercy of the bankers, as Grant's had been, and Cleveland's, and Roosevelt's, could fairly be said to govern. . . . There was, in short, no such thing as political independence at home or abroad, unless there was financial independence.[81]

This is an extreme statement of Adams's position, though it is certainly not an illogical extension of it. In fact, however, his stance on socialism fluctuated frequently. As is so often the case, there is a tension in his thought. Reflecting this, he wrote in the *Education,* "By rights, he should . . . have been a Marxist, but some narrow trait of the New England nature seemed to blight socialism, and he tried in vain to make himself a convert. He did the next best thing; he became a Comteist, within the limits of evolution."[82] But he continued to forecast the eventual triumph of socialism in spite of his distrust, though in his view, as in Schumpeter's theory, capitalism and socialism would become virtually indistinguishable forms dominated by large-scale organizations.

Money, Markets, and Anti-Semitism

Throughout his career, Adams had always been interested in the subject of money, from early writings on British financial policy to his pieces "The Legal Tender Act" and "The New York Gold Conspiracy." But, at least partially under the influence of Brooks, foreign exchange, gold, and trade became of obsessive interest to him. This phase in Adams's thought lasted from the mid-1890s until 1906, at which point he regained some sense of proportion. But in this obsessional stage, Adams fell victim to delusions that resulted in a vicious anti-Semitism. This does not assume a large role in *Chartres* or the *Education*, but it is certainly there, even if not central to his theories. As Levenson says, his anti-Semitism "disfigures, albeit inessentially, his late masterpieces—pockmarks of a disease that can be fatal."[83] Certainly Adams had no idea of the horrors that were to come. "As a chapter of engineered cruelty, the genocidal programs that would come in consequence of the nineteenth century's discourse of hate far exceeded Adams's worst expectations of the twentieth century."[84] However, his letters are filled with a poisonous anti-Semitism. Jews, bankers, goldbugs, and usurers are mentioned more or less interchangeably, all as synonyms of something hateful. The attitudes spill over from monetary questions into such celebrated cases as the Dreyfus affair. Adams saw Dreyfus as a "howling Jew" and became a bitter anti-Dreyfusard.[85] And, bizarrely, he identified the British campaign against the Boers with the legal campaign for Dreyfus. "Both of them are Jew wars, and I don't like Jew wars."[86] For whatever reason, he does not take up this theme in the *Education*, and, as Samuels says, "Happily, in suppressing it he suppressed most other phases of his morbid anti-Semitism."[87]

But Adams did not always hold this ugly view of the world. When younger, he did not hesitate to chide Thomas Jefferson for an anti-Jewish remark, and in spite of occasional use of common stereotypes, "he had a genuine liberal's distaste for either scorn or pride of race."[88] During the years of his marriage to Marian Adams, the couple had many Jewish friends, and his much-loved sister was married to a Jew.[89] As late as 1880, as Barbara Miller Solomon writes, Jews appeared in his novel *Democracy* "as upper class Americans with no ethnic stigma."[90] In the *History*, he is almost rhapsodic about immigration to the United States and its relation to democracy, a position that seems to cover Jewish as well as other immigrants. There is no trace of ethnocentrism here: "[The Americans] said to the rich as to the poor, 'Come and share our limitless riches! Come and help us bring to light these unimaginable stores of wealth and power!' The poor came, and from them were seldom heard complaints of deception or disillusion. Within a moment, by the mere contact of a moral atmosphere, they saw the gold and jewels, the summer cornfields, and the glowing continent. The rich for a long time stood aloof,—they were timid and narrow-minded; but this was not all,—between them and the American democrat was a gulf." Adams continues on an even more exalted, less material plane. "Every American," except for a few Federalists, "seemed to nourish the idea that he was doing what he could to overthrow the tyranny which the past had fastened on the human mind." It was easy for the sophisticated or the cynical to fail to see in this "its nobler side, to feel the beatings of a heart underneath the sordid surface of a gross humanity." Europeans could not see this nobility. They found only cause for complaint "in the remark that the American democrat believed himself to be working for the overthrow of tyranny, aristocracy, hereditary privilege, and priesthood, wherever they existed."[91]

What happened to this Adams? Digby Baltzell points out that the first mention of the word "Jew" in Adams's letters occurs in 1896.[92] Until then, there is no sign of serious derangement in his thought. But in the 1890s, the leadership positions of the upper class were threatened; the old establishment could no longer claim unquestioned authority, nor could it count on winning positions of power as a matter of right. The upper classes tended to respond by turning an aristocracy, which Baltzell thinks of as open to the talented, into a closed caste, walling itself as a matter of self-protection. Privilege without power breeds resentment and leads to the creation of a caste system, thus depriving the nation of the services of an open-ended, upper-class elite.[93] This sense of having been displaced from positions of power can also be explained by Richard Hofstadter's well-known theory of status anxiety. Both theories clearly apply to the Adamses and are abundantly evident in the pages of the *Education*.

Combined with this was the nationwide emergence of patterns of deep-seated, nativist, anti-immigration sentiment, which included but was not limited to Jews.[94] As Samuels writes, "All the antiforeignism and racism of the time against the south European immigrant and the Oriental came to a head in the Jew as the master image of the enemy to Anglo-Saxon supremacy."[95] This sentiment tapped a powerful stain of ascriptive prejudice buried in the American national character and challenging the "official" liberal ideology so well reflected in Adams's *History*.[96] The anti-Semitic version of ascriptivism was widespread and could be found in virtually all segments of American life and culture. The Jewish stereotype did not appear until the 1870s and after that spread throughout the culture. In addition to Adams it can be found in such literary luminaries as Theodore Dreiser,

Willa Cather, Edith Wharton, Thomas Wolfe, and William Faulkner, not to mention the later and more egregious cases of T. S. Eliot and Ezra Pound.[97] The anti-Semitism of many of these writers was essentially cultural, with the Jew symbolizing liberal capitalist modernity without the saving grace of a Christian aristocracy that could dilute the vulgarity of capitalist society. It is also worth noting that the Jewish stereotype is based on Jews' success as immigrants to the American culture,[98] which occurred at a time when Adams saw himself as a failure, at least by the exalted standards of his family. Thus, in one of the few outbursts in the *Education* displaying his psychic disorder—one can hardly call it less—Adams cries out: "he twisted about in vain to recover his starting point; he could no longer see his own trail; he had become an estray; a flotsam or jetsam of wreckage. . . . His world was dead. Not a Polish Jew fresh from Warsaw or Cracow—not a furtive Jacoob or Ysaac still reeking of the Ghetto, snarling a weird Yiddish to the officers of the customs—but had a keener instinct, an intenser energy, and a freer hand than he—American of Americans, with Heaven knows how many Puritans and Patriots behind him, and an education that had cost a civil war."[99]

This is certainly part of what drove Henry Adams; he simply did not like the way his America had turned out and was looking for someone to blame. Carey McWilliams writes, "Although he regarded the new dispensation as inevitable, he could not accept it because he was too deeply immersed in the older democratic culture."[100] This sense of displacement and the decline of an earlier form of democracy would still be evident, even if we leave aside the anti-Semitic excrescences. Jews serve as a scapegoat for his more general rage against the widespread corruption of American society and politics.

All these factors no doubt played a part in the eruption of Adams's irrational anti-Semitism. But one other important factor needs to be taken into account—his detestation of capitalism. It is clear from his journalism that he saw an intimate connection between capitalism and the corruption of the political system that was so destructive to his idea of democracy. But where does the anti-Semitism come from? He despised capitalism before the emergence of the Jewish stereotype in the 1870s. Of course, anti-Semitism in general has an ancient and dishonorable pedigree. But the connection between Judaism and capitalism goes back before Adams; in fact, none other than Karl Marx—an example of that peculiar creature,

the anti-Semitic Jew—gives an early statement of the theme in his 1843
pamphlet *On the Jewish Question*. Writes Marx: "What is the profane base
of Judaism? *Practical* need, *self-interest*. What is the worldly cult of the
Jew? *Huckstering*. What is his worldly god? *Money*."[101] Almost immediately
he goes on, "In the final analysis, the emancipation of the Jews is the *emancipation* of mankind from *Judaism*." And then, sounding very like Adams
lamenting the presumed international power of Jews, he adds, quoting
Bruno Bauer, "'The Jew, who is merely tolerated in Vienna, for example,
determines the fate of the whole Empire by his financial power.'"[102]

Though it is extremely doubtful that Adams could have known these
early works of Marx, they have the tone he was to adopt, a tone that became
widespread in American culture and in other cultures as well. There is
the same paranoid distrust of bankers and the same tendency to list a set
of disparaging terms associated with the word *Jew:* in the case of Marx,
self-interest, huckster, and the like. And yet, as already mentioned, Adams
did not turn his disgust with capitalism into anti-Semitism until the 1890s.
Perhaps this cannot be adequately explained short of psychoanalysis. There
simply may be no fully rational explanation for the irrational. It can be said
that the anti-Semitic stereotype was not available to Adams when he began
his biting critique of capitalism. But in 1893, when the Adamses' financial
fortunes took a downturn, perhaps the new vocabulary seemed plausible to
him. It is also important to remember the political aspects of McWilliams's
interpretation. Deep down, what may have bothered Adams the most was
the decline of the democratic forms he believed in and their subversion by
capitalism.

The anti-Semitism never entirely disappeared, but the obsession with
markets and money did, and with it, the virulence of his ethnic hatred declined also. In 1906, probably reflecting the final stages of his work on the
Education, he wrote to Brooks, "But please give up the profoundly unscien-
tific jabber of the newspapers about MONEY in capital letters. What I see
is POWER in capitals also. You may abolish money and all its machinery,
the Power will still be there, and you will still have to trapeze after it in
the future just as the world has always done in the past. On the whole, our
generation has suffered least of any. The next can run its own machine."[103]
Certainly Adams was fully aware of money as a major source of power, so he
could not have meant to deny that. But by that time, technology was on his
mind as a force to be reckoned with, as was mass democracy. Just possibly,

there may have been hopeful moments in which he believed that, in a better world, democratic public opinion might regain some degree of power and become a force for positive change. Commenting on Theodore Roosevelt's approach to the trusts, he said that the problem was that "the public had no idea what practical system it could aim at, or what sort of men could manage it. The single problem before it was not so much to control the Trusts as to create the society that could manage the trusts." The new American must be either the child of the new forces or a sport of nature.[104] He must adapt to the new realities of the modern political economy and all that went with it. The import of this is not altogether clear. The distinction between control and management is muddy, to say the least. As someone who feared centralization, perhaps he hoped that society would replace centralized control with a revolutionary change in the public perception of the trusts. This would, as McWilliams suggests,[105] involve a transformation of values of major dimensions. Did Adams have any real hope that such a thing could happen? Probably not, but today we might, though there are certainly no particular grounds for optimism.

The Problem of Technology

When he visited Chicago for the Exposition of 1893, Adams was forcefully struck both by the city and by the power of technology. Putting aside his usual scorn for the Midwest, Adams was almost rhapsodic, though also quizzical. "The Exposition itself defied philosophy. One might find fault till the last gate closed, one could still explain nothing that needed explanation. As a scenic display, Paris had never approached it, but the inconceivable scenic display consisted in its being there at all—more surprising, as it was, than anything else on the continent."[106] Unlike Niagara Falls and the Yellowstone geysers, these were man-made creations, which made them especially remarkable. It seemed as if the Parisian school of the beaux arts had been transferred to the shore of Lake Michigan. Was it possible that it "could be made to seem at home there? Was the American made to seem at home in it? Honestly, he had the air of enjoying it as though it were all his own; he felt it was good; he was proud of it." And he goes on: "For the moment he [Adams] seemed to have leaped directly from Corinth and Syracuse and Venice, over the heads of London and New York, to impose classical standards on plastic Chicago. . . . All trader's taste smelt of bric-abrac; Chicago tried at least to give her taste a look of unity."[107] Could this be real, Adams wonders, saying that his own personal universe depended on the answer, "for if the rupture was real and the new American world could take this sharp and conscious twist towards ideals, one's personal friends would come in as winners in the great American chariot-race for fame." Artists and architects like Hunt, Richardson, St. Gaudens, McKim, and Standford White would be talked about when their "politicians and millionaires were otherwise forgotten." The artists themselves were not optimistic, but perhaps there was hope.[108] For Adams, this is a remarkable statement. It suggests a degree of optimism—cultural, in this case—a note not often heard in his late writings and one that ought to be remembered amidst the general gloom about the direction of his country, its culture, and indeed all of world history.

But of course what intrigued Adams even more than the architectural wonders of Chicago was the technology on display at the exposition. This is the force that began to move to the center of his thinking about the dynamics of history and that sent his historical imagination into overdrive. "One lingered long among the dynamos," he tells us, "and they gave to history a new phase."[109] Combined with his amazement at the fact of Chicago itself, the new technology posed vast problems for him to consider:

> Chicago asked in 1893 for the first time the question whether the American people knew where they were driving. Adams answered, for one, that he did not know, but would try to find out. On reflecting sufficiently deeply, . . . he decided that the American people probably knew no more than he did; but that they might still be driving or drifting unconsciously toward some point in thought; as their solar system was said to be drifting toward some point in space; and that, possibly, if relations enough could be observed, this point might be fixed. Chicago was the first expression of American thought as a unity; one must start there.[110]

Washington was another expression of American unity, and here the picture is much less attractive. At this point, Adams launches into the lament, already discussed, that in 1893 the American majority decisively declared itself in favor of capitalism, thus joining forces with the banks and creating the form of society and government that Adams liked least. Thus, says Adams, at this point, "education in domestic politics stopped."[111]

Unfortunately, this is largely true, though Adams continues to speculate on the domestic scene in his letters. We are left, it seems to me, with cultural hope in Chicago, though not without some uncertainty, and political gloom regarding Washington. Though he was well placed to do so, Adams has little to say about the efforts of the Progressive movement, however inadequate, to come to grips with the corporate capitalism he detested. Perhaps his distaste for Theodore Roosevelt held him back. In any case, he does nothing to explore his suggestion that what was needed was a society that could manage the trusts rather than a government that could control them. Instead, he largely leaves the American scene aside in order to explore the dynamics of world history.

At this point, we return to the world of the Virgin of Chartres. The year 1900 found Adams at an exposition again, this time the Great Exposition in Paris. He continues to mull over education, saying that nothing in it is "so astonishing as the amount of ignorance it accumulates in the form of mere facts." He had seen most of the art collected in the museums of the world but could not understand the art in Paris, and he had assiduously studied Marx and found his lessons inapplicable to Paris.[112] What *was* of interest were the giant electric motors. As he grew accustomed to the gallery of machines, he began to feel them as a moral force, much as the early Christians saw the cross. By the end, he began to pray to them.[113] To him, they were like an occult mechanism. "Between the dynamo in the gallery of machines and the engine-house outside, the break of continuity amounted to abysmal fracture for a historian's objects." At the same time, he sees, quite presciently, the force revealed by the discovery of radium: "The force," Adams notes, "was wholly new."[114]

Thinking about the nature of these new forces and technologies, Adams began to reconsider the nature of history, both as a substantive analysis of what had happened in the past and as a mode of disciplined inquiry. He tells us, "Historians undertake to arrange sequences,—called stories, or histories—assuming in silence a relation of cause and effect. These assumptions, hidden in the depths of dusty libraries, have been astounding, but commonly unconscious and childlike; so much so that if any captious critic were to drag them to light, historians would probably reply, with one voice, that they had never supposed themselves to know what they were talking about." Looking back on his own work, Adams recalls that he had published a dozen volumes of American history just to satisfy himself that facts arranged in a rigorous way could establish a "necessary sequence of human movement."[115] One may doubt that this was the reason, or at least the primary reason, for writing the history of the Jefferson and Madison administrations, but Adams still expressed dissatisfaction with the result, pointing out that when he presented his sequence, others saw something quite different. Of course, that others saw the same facts differently does not disprove Adams. These critics may only have looked at the facts from a different perspective. But, as Susan Haack has pointed out: "Truth is not relative to perspective; and there can't be incompatible truths. . . . But there are many different truths—different but compatible truths—which must somehow fit together." More importantly, Haack adds, "Although what is true is not relative to perspective, what is accepted as truth is; although incompatible statements cannot be jointly true, incompatible claims are frequently made."[116] And one might add, in good Millian fashion, that the conflict between differing perspectives can further the search for truth. Adams seems to have seen this; remember his suggestion to President Eliot of Harvard that he appoint Henry Cabot Lodge as a conservative counterbalance to his own radical democratic position. But still, Adams, for all his greatness as a historian, gives up too soon. The sequence of men leads to nothing, he concludes, and the sequence of society cannot go further, while the time sequence is artificial and the sequence of thought mere chaos. He therefore turns dramatically to the "sequence of force; and thus it happened that, after ten years' pursuit, he found himself lying in the Gallery of Machines at the Great Exposition of 1900, with his historical neck broken by the sudden irruption of forces totally new."[117]

This, he thought, was something very new. The discoveries of Copernicus and Galileo had broken professional necks in about 1600, and a hundred years before that, Columbus had turned the world upside down, "but the nearest approach to the revolution of 1900 was that of 310, when Constantine set up the Cross."[118] A totally new education was required to deal with this almost unprecedented situation. The comparisons that leaped to his mind are interesting and important in the context of his thought. "The force of the Virgin was still felt at Lourdes, and seemed to be as potent as X-rays; but in America neither Venus nor Virgin ever had value as force—at most as sentiment. No American had ever been truly afraid of either."[119]

Returning to a theme that goes as far back as his paper "The Primitive Rights of Women," Adams comments:

The Woman had once been supreme; in France she seemed potent, not merely as a sentiment but as a force. Why was she unknown in America? . . . When she was a true force she was ignorant of fig-leaves, but the monthly magazine-made American female had not a feature that would be recognized by Adam. The trait was notorious, and often humorous, but anyone brought up among Puritans knew that sex was sin. In any previous age, sex was strength. Neither art nor beauty was needed. Everyone, even among the Puritans, knew that neither Diana of the Ephesians nor any of the Oriental goddesses was worshiped for her beauty. She was a goddess because of her force; she was the animated dynamo; she was reproduction.[120]

The key here is clearly not sexual activity as such, but reproduction. It was the power to reproduce that made woman the central force in the family and thus the center of society as a whole. This was the source of woman's energy. Again returning to an earlier theme, this time from *Chartres,* he says: "On one side, at the Louvre and at Chartres, as he knew by the record of work actually done and still before his eyes, was the highest energy ever known to man, the creator of four-fifths of the noblest art, exercising vastly more attraction over the human mind than all the steam-engines and dynamos ever dreamed of; and yet this energy was unknown to the American mind. An American Virgin would never dare command; an American Venus would never dare exist."[121]

Here Adams steps back from the centrality of motherhood for a moment and asks questions about sex and its representation in American culture. Adams wants to know whether any American artist ever insisted on the power of sex, as the classics had always done. In general, the answer to the question was no. The major exception was Walt Whitman, who could hardly be more different from Adams. He also mentions Bret Harte, who wrote sympathetically of gamblers and prostitutes, and one or two unnamed painters.[122] For the rest, he says, sex was mere sentiment.

Adams is even critical of his friend, the sculptor Augustus St. Gaudens, claiming that as an American, his art was starved from birth, while Adams admits that his own instincts were "blighted from babyhood." For Adams, the Virgin of Amiens became a symbol of force, while for St. Gaudens, she was merely a model of taste. Even Adams began to feel the Virgin's force only in 1895, and even then, not everywhere. "At Chartres—perhaps at Lourdes—possibly at Cnidos if one could still find there the divinely naked Aphrodite of Praxiteles—but otherwise one must look for force to the goddesses of Indian mythology." Artists complained that the power of, say, a railroad train could never be captured. But Adams could see that "all the steam in the world could not, like the Virgin, build Chartres."[123] Adams therefore decided to pursue the mystery of this force, thus leading him to write *Mont-Saint-Michel and Chartres,* remarking wryly that the problem could scarcely be more complex than radium. The Virgin would be easier to handle, Adams thought, though he was later forced by his never-ending curiosity to consider radium and other aspects of the new science. And the specter of controlling force begins to be raised. "Forty-five years of study had proved to be quite futile for the pursuit of power; one controlled no more force in 1900 than in 1850, although the amount of force controlled by society had enormously increased."[124] The issue starts to become whether we can control the forces being unleashed by the new science and technology. The difficulty was that the world was growing more and more confusing and required more and more intellectual energy to cope with it. Looking at everyday life, he expresses his thought—his dilemma—with moving clarity:

> In all this futility, it was not the magnet or the rays or the microbes that troubled him, or even his helplessness before the forces. To that he was used from childhood. The magnet in its new relation staggered his new education by its evidence of growing complexity, and multiplicity, and even contradiction, in life. He could not escape it; politics or science, the lesson was the same, and at every step it blocked his path whichever way he turned. He found it in politics; he ran against it in science; he struck it in everyday life, as though he were still Adam in the Garden of Eden between God who was unity, and Satan who was complexity, *with no means of deciding which was truth.*[125]

Gone are the old New England certainties; this is a genuinely open and perplexed mind. This is no dogmatist, but rather a questing spirit casting doubt on the means of discovering truth and, by extension, truth itself. We may not like the results of the search, but we can only respect the intensity and tenacity with which it is carried out. Adams is not one to give in to despair, in spite of appearances. The search goes on.

And here his thoughts begin to turn again to politics, though on a very high level of abstraction. Politics and science begin to merge. "All one's life," Adams tells us, "one had struggled for unity, and unity had always

won. The National Government and the national unity had overcome every
resistance, and the Darwinian evolutionists were triumphant over all the
curates; yet the greater the unity and the momentum, the worse became
the complexity and the friction."[126] Adams has to deal with these complexities with no sure sense of the nature of truth. However much he loves the
image of the woman and the Virgin, deep down, Adams senses that it is too
late for them to be of much help. One can contrast the twentieth century
with the beauties of medieval France, all to the advantage of the latter, yet
Adams knows that he has no choice but to live in the very different world
of American modernity. Recall also that he lacks the faith so eloquently
portrayed in *Chartres*. And, to look ahead, it is by no means as clear as is
commonly believed that Adams completely rejects the modern American
world. He is always a divided and ambivalent thinker.

Another Try at Political Education

In 1901, Adams visited the Wagner Festival in Bayreuth, where, with the
dark strains of *Götterdämmerung* sounding in the background, he began
to explore his notion of conservative Christian anarchy. Though he does
not use the term there, the idea of a form of anarchism is explored earlier
in *Chartres;* if anything, there is more anarchy displayed there than in the
Education. Though he briefly cites Saint Thomas as one source, that seems
entirely implausible, but, given his probably heretical portrait of the Virgin,
she clearly qualifies for the label anarchist. In his image, Mary is distrustful of authority, is concerned with the victims of injustice, cares for the
poor, and is at home with ordinary people. In conventional modern terms,
however we may label Adams, his heroine is definitely positioned on the
Left. Adams cannot have been unaware of this. In the larger context of
his political thought, what does this mean? It is possible only to speculate,
because Adams gives us very little to go on. As I have already suggested, a
close reading of *Chartres* suggests more sympathy for modern complexity
or multiplicity than Adams usually allows. And, more speculatively, if my
reading of Adams on multiplicity is correct, his picture of the Virgin might
be a somewhat indirect way to introduce a critical leftist position into the
complex discussions of modern politics. This is, as I suggest, pure speculation; I know of no direct textual support, other than the guarded defense of
socialism he offers in his letter to his brother on Hungary, presenting it as

the best in an array of bad choices provided by modern politics. Of course, there is also the Virgin's disdain for authority and her tendency to support the underdog, both characteristic positions of the Left.

But, if this is not Adams's specific intent, are contemporary readers justified in using his work as a platform to explore such ideas anyway? I think the answer is yes, if they are cautious. Obviously, we are not entitled to make past political thinkers say any old thing we want them to say. Plato cannot be read as a modern democrat, and Marx is no partisan of capitalism beyond its "necessary" position along the road to socialism. But it is not uncommon or improper to discover hidden meanings in a text or to discern implications of a line of reasoning that the author may not have seen or intended or fully worked out. Once ideas reach the public, they take on a life of their own. If they are good and fruitful, they may stimulate others to take them beyond their initial boundaries. This is one way that traditions of thought grow. Perhaps it is possible to use Adams in this way,[127] though it is important not to claim that Adams read in this way is the historical Adams.

In any event, these implications are not so clear when Adams turns to conservative Christian anarchism. There he admits to having "played with anarchy; though not with socialism."[128] He tells us that his branch of the anarchist's party consists of two members, himself and Bay Lodge, the son of Henry Cabot Lodge. The role of each is to denounce the other as "unequal to his lofty task and inadequate to grasp it. Of course, no third member could be so much as considered, since this great principle of contradiction could be expressed only by opposition; and no agreement could be conceived, because anarchy, by definition, must be chaos and collision, as in the kinetic theory of a perfect gas." This law of contradiction was a kind of agreement, a limitation of personal liberty, but the continuous contradictions could lead to a still larger contradiction. "Thus the great end of all philosophy—the 'larger synthesis'—was attained, but the process was arduous, and while Adams, as the older member, assumed to declare the principle, Lodge necessarily denied both the assumption and the principle in order to assure its truth."[129] Of course, Adams is playing games with Hegel as well as with his readers, though one has to doubt that, given his aversion to metaphysics, he was seriously influenced by the great German. It is much more likely that what is at work here is his intellectual playfulness and his sheer contrariety.

But the game continues for a time, though I think that for Adams, it is more than just a game. What he calls the "last synthesis" is a recurrent theme in his late work, including the correspondence. The synthesis reached concludes that

> order and anarchy were one, but that unity was chaos. As anarchist, conserva-
> tive and Christian, he had no motive or duty but to attain the end; and, to
> hasten it, he was bound to accelerate progress; to concentrate energy; to ac-
> cumulate power; to multiply and intensify forces; to reduce friction, increase
> velocity and magnify momentum, partly because this was the mechanical law
> of the universe as science explained it; but partly also in order to get done
> with the present which artists and some others complained of, and finally—
> and chiefly—because a rigorous philosophy required it, in order to penetrate
> the beyond, and satisfy man's destiny by reaching the largest synthesis in its
> ultimate contradiction.[130]

The major conclusion is that order and unity are contradictory, that the paradoxical fact is that order and chaos are synonymous. Moreover, these conclusions are validated for Adams not by Hegel's dialectic but, more im-portantly, by the findings of modern science as they emerged in the early twentieth century. Finally, it is important to keep in mind the analysis of *Chartres*, in which the conclusion is that unity may not be superior to mul-tiplicity after all. With the exception of the last point, all these ideas become frequent motifs of Adams's thought, most notably in his late thinking about the nature of history. The prose may be playful, but the ideas are serious.

Adams is much too astute not to recognize the obvious objection to his formulations, namely, that they are neither conservative nor Christian nor anarchic. On the face of it, it seems like not a bad objection to say that the whole notion appears self-contradictory, but Adams is rather airily dismissive of this response. The "untaught critic," he says, should begin his education "in any infant school in order to learn that anarchy which should be logical would cease to be anarchic."[131] Prevailing anarchist doctrines were either innocent, sentimental derivations from Russian culture, such as those of Kropotkin, or the ideals of French workers "diluted with absinthe," leading to a bourgeois "dream of order and inertia." Both doctrines had simply inherited their conceptions of the universe from "the priestly class to which their minds obviously belonged." A mind that followed nature, as Adams's did, had no more in common with them than with socialists, com-munists, and collectivists. They all needed to go back to the twelfth century, where their ideas had enjoyed a reign of a thousand years. The conservative

Christian anarchist must rest on "the nature of nature" itself. This hardly even needed proof, he says. "Only the self-evident truth that no philosophy of order—except the Church—had ever satisfied the philosopher reconciled the conservative Christian anarchist to prove his own."[132]

Blackmur offers an analysis of Adams's rather murky conservative Christian anarchism that is interesting and without Adams's flippancy. He admits that Adams gives us only a "primitive and ambiguous sketch." But, he suggests, "We can say that the point of view behind it is *conservative* because it holds hard to what survives in man's mind, *Christian* because it must encompass in a single piety even the most contradictory of the values which survive, and *anarchic* because all the values and every act of encompassment are products of an order of forces that are beyond the scope of the mind to control and that are perhaps alien and ultimately destructive to it."[133] This is a reasonable interpretation, though I think only the comment on anarchism is wholly plausible. The interpretation of "conservative" is fairly close to the mark, though what survives in man's mind is by no means beyond debate, and one must ask whether encompassing contradictory values is particularly Christian; one might even say that Christianity often tries to exclude contradictory values. Still, this is an interesting effort that captures a sense of Adams's attempt to contain enormous turbulence within the framework of a deeply challenged tradition.

J. C. Levenson offers a simpler reading of conservative Christian anarchism. He considers it a term born from confusion that means the same thing as the conservative anarchism Adams mentioned in 1896. Here the term refers to someone who resists centralization "but anticipates (often with morbid glee) his own defeat with a general cataclysm to follow." Levenson sees this meaning as essentially frivolous, leading to Adams's facetious party of two. To find a serious meaning, we must go back to *Chartres*. Recall the formulation there in which Adams states that absolute liberty is the absence of restraint but that responsibility equals restraint, so that in an ideally free world, the individual is responsible to himself. Levenson reads this to mean that Adams is willing to accept that this is a world in which religion and society no longer control individual conduct. "Within that world he chose, on his own responsibility, to conserve the liberal values among which he had lived for as long as he could remember and, ultimately, the Christian values of which he had acquired a personal memory after great pains."[134]

This reading is, I think, closer to the mark than Blackmur's. It accommodates the point I made that Adams's formulation skips over the liberal theory of responsibility and substitutes anarchism for it. The case for Adams's anarchism, and for the Virgin's, is compelling, though Adams goes much beyond the conception of anarchy advanced by Levenson. Further, the idea of conserving liberalism is central to the American political tradition of which Adams is a part.[135] It is also important to remember that Adams's self-identification is as a liberal. However, it needs to be stressed that Adams's "Christianity" is entirely secular, paradoxical though that may be. The discussion of Christianity may have helped him recall a Protestant, Puritan code of conduct that supported his moral sense. His Christianity is certainly not Catholic. Adams, even if he had wished it, was not ready or able to embrace Roman Catholicism, as Levenson is well aware. As Adams wrote in 1915, referring to a priest with whom he was in correspondence: "Father Fay is no bore—far from it, but I think he has an idea that I want conversion, for he directs his talk much to me, and instructs me. Bless the genial sinner! He had best look out that I don't convert him, for his old church is really too childless for a hell in this year of grace."[136] On this, Levenson comments, "Except as his historical imagination carried him back to the high Middle Ages, he remained a stoic: God existed for him in the realm of essence and historical existence, perhaps, but not in the realm of present reality."[137] This is an odd sort of Christianity, I think.

Adams drops his arrogant tone almost immediately, admitting that, at the time, there was deep darkness. He could not even affirm, he says, that the "larger synthesis" would definitely turn out to be chaos, since contrarian to the end, "he would equally be obliged to deny the chaos." The rapid growth of industrial power and technology "drowned rhyme and reason." At least the conservative Christian anarchists saw light in the darkness.[138]

The political party that Adams describes is a strange sort of institution. Of course, it is not a party at all, except in a metaphorical sense, but rather a facet of Adams's philosophy of history. He is disturbed by the pace of social change. As he writes to Brooks, "Either our society must stop or bust." And in the same letter he says: "I rather incline to think that the situation is new, not contemplated by nature, as hitherto constituted on this planet, and that God Almighty couldn't guess what will or won't happen. This being my view of it, I am not disposed to put my fingers into the machinery. Today, no doubt, this sounds rather mad. Ten years hence, who knows? . . . *We know so little, and our power is so great.*"[139] One might read this as an expression of a conservative temperament distrustful of all efforts toward institutional reform. But I think the matter is more complex. By the time Adams wrote the *Education*, he clearly thought that nature was deeply involved in the dynamic of social change and that an adequate theory of history needed to take that fact into account. However, the other themes persist. He continues to believe in the absolute newness of the situation, and he continues to adopt a rather passive, let-nature-take-its-course position. There is a deep-seated pessimism in his thought, though it is important to keep in mind the occasions when a glimmer of hope rises to the surface. The pessimism is evident in a letter to the poet Bay Lodge, where he writes with perhaps a little more than his usual acerbity: "Also you know that Conservative Christian Anarchy, since Cain's time, has seemed somewhat to lack popular approval. Although Christ came personally down from God the Father to set things straight, he seems to have failed, like most other poets."[140]

And yet, amidst the gloom, there are outbursts of hope, not least about America, which he continues to see, for better or worse, as being well in advance of all other nations. To Americans' great advantage is this fact: "In America all were conservative Christian anarchists; the faith was national, racial, geographic. The true American had never seen such supreme virtue in any of the innumerable shades between social anarchy and social order as to mark it for exclusively human and his own. He never had known a complete union either in Church or State or Thought, and had never seen any need for it. The freedom gave him courage to meet any contradiction, and intelligence enough to ignore it."[141]

Here and elsewhere, it seems that at least as late as 1907, Adams was not ready to give up on America, whose saving grace seems to be an almost Whitmanesque ability to contain multitudes. What is troubling is his unwillingness to turn his mind toward meaningful reforms. This is not so much conservatism as an inclination to a passive determinism fostered by his understanding of science, sometimes tinctured by hope, but that proved, I argue later, to be a limiting factor on his political theory. And, of course, his flippant remarks about throwing his weight to whatever side would hasten the collapse of the system he loathed are totally irresponsible and potentially dangerous if acted upon. To see the danger, one need only consider the fate of the German communists who failed to confront the Nazis, thinking that the triumph of Hitler would lead to a rapid collapse, after which the Left would pick up the pieces.

In spite of this unwillingness to resuscitate his interest in reform, Adams remained an interested and interesting observer of politics.[142] Foreign policy was a matter of great concern to him, and he used his connection with John Hay to influence it as much as possible. But he was not always successful, and he opposed the sudden emergence of the American empire. Still, at the time in his life when, on the surface, he should or could have been very influential, he was not. He did not like what he called McKinleyism. Washington was needed to control the new power in the land, but, though, "amusing," the capital was interesting mainly for its distance from New York. "The movement of New York had become planetary—beyond control—while the task of Washington, in 1900 as in 1800, was to control it. The success of Washington in the past century promised ill for its success in the next."[143] After the death of McKinley, Adams might have tried to use his influence with his friends President Theodore Roosevelt and Henry Cabot Lodge, now a senior and very influential senator from Massachusetts. However, the young president was a problem rather than a solution. The trouble with Roosevelt was a basic character flaw. "Power when wielded by abnormal energy is the most serious of facts, and all Roosevelt's friends know that his restless and combative energy was more than abnormal." Wryly, Adams compares himself with Seneca, saying that Seneca "must have remained in some shade of doubt what advantage he should get from the power of his friend and pupil Nero Claudius, until, as a gentleman past sixty, he received Nero's filial invitation to kill himself. Seneca closed the vast circle of his knowledge by learning that a friend in power was a friend lost."[144] An instinct of self-preservation kept him from the White House. "Power is poison," he reflected.

> Its effect on Presidents had been always tragic; chiefly as an almost insane excitement at first, and a worse reaction afterwards; but also because no mind is so well balanced as to bear the strain of seizing unlimited force without habit or knowledge of it . . . . Roosevelt enjoyed a singularly direct nature and honest intent, but he lived naturally in restless agitation that would have worn out most tempers in a month, and his first year of Presidency showed chronic excitement that made a friend tremble. The effect of unlimited power on lim-

ited mind is worth noting in Presidents because it must represent the same process in society, and the power of self-control must have limit somewhere in face of the control of the infinite.[145]

More might have been expected from Hay and Lodge than from Roosevelt, but if Adams had expected it, he was disappointed. Hay was tired and sick, and Lodge was in an impossible position. "He could not help himself, for his position as the President's friend and independent statesman at once was false, and he must be unsure in both relations." But beyond this, Adams thought that Massachusetts was an impossible state to represent, a state with a fragmented political culture that Adams knew would emerge everywhere. Already in Massachusetts there were simply too many forces at work: State Street and the banks; the Congregational clergy; Harvard; immigrants, especially the Irish; and even a new socialist class. In another of his startlingly prescient analyses, Adams comments: "New power was disintegrating society, and setting independent centers of force to work, until money had all it could do to hold the machine together. No one could represent it faithfully as a whole."[146]

Given such leadership, it would not be surprising for Adams to despair of his hope of creating a society that would not merely control the trusts but manage them. As McWilliams says, for that to work, it would be necessary to place values ahead of programs.[147] Since ideally, programs are based on values, this would doubtless be healthy. A transformation of values obviously implies a need for fresh thought, a theme that runs throughout the late work of Adams. However, what that new thought might entail is left more than a little unclear. Still, there may be a hint in a letter from Adams to Brooks. Theodore Roosevelt's famous distinction between good and bad trusts is useless, Adams says. "*It gives away our contention that they have no right to exist.*" But this does not really take us anywhere, because "our society has chosen its path beyond recall." It is too late for reform. All that can be done is to "vapor like Theodore" about honesty, law, and decency. Adams damns all this as useless. The result is that all we can do is "make the machine run without total collapse in a catastrophe" until it suffers its inevitable breakdown.[148] Thus, by 1910, the hope extended in the *Education* seems to have been lost in a fit of despair, though the point that the trusts had no right to exist is a clue to his deeper feelings.

This does not imply that the failure to produce a society with the values and programs Adams would have preferred leads him to abandon democracy as a hope, even if it is not a reality. Nor are his concerns limited to the United States. When the Roosevelt administration privately negotiates a Far Eastern peace settlement, he complains: "About five hundred million people were waiting with their lives and money at stake, to hear what these two jackasses said, and nobody ever suggested that the 500,000,000 should be anyhow consulted. I'm going to die, soon—thank God."[149] But aside from this generalized and perhaps atypical concern, Adams continues to have faith in the ultimate good sense of the American people, in spite of his disgust with Theodore Roosevelt. As late as 1905, he writes: "As yet nothing is broken. Our people are quick and practical and have not yet lost their heads."[150]

It is not hard to understand why Adams was disturbed by the politics of his time. After all, it was much like our own. There is a certain symmetry between the beginning of the twentieth century and the beginning of the twenty-first. There *was* a great deal of corruption. Capital *did* at times seem out of control. And while Theodore Roosevelt was a better president than Adams thought, there was good reason to fear his volatile temperament. Of course, the problems were structural and institutional, not just products of the president's flamboyant personality. And in spite of his worries, through all this, Adams maintained faith in the American people. Just as in the War of 1812, he saw that the problems of the nation were much more the fault of the political and economic leadership than of the people. Adams did not subscribe to a theory of the "degradation of the democratic dogma." This is the title his brother Brooks gave to the posthumous collection of his papers aimed at a scientific theory of history. Indeed, Brooks probably read his own views into the title. Characteristically, "Brooks, when President Eliot mildly observed to him after an address at the Law School that he apparently did not overcherish democracy, responded abruptly in his harsh, full-carrying voice: 'Do you think I'm a damned fool?'"[151] This is not Henry's style. It is worth noting that when the scientific essays were reissued ten years after their first appearance, they were shorn of Brooks's title and his lengthy introduction as well. The new title was *The Tendency of History*, a much more suitable label.[152] As for Henry, while it is abundantly clear that he was not some precursor of the participatory democracy of the 1960s, he was still committed to the theory and practice of representative democracy. President Eliot of Harvard was quite mistaken, I think, when he said after reading the *Education*: "I should like to be saved from loss of faith in democracy as I grow old and foolish. I should be very sorry to wind up as the three Adamses did. I shall not unless I lose my mind." It is equally mistaken for Samuels to follow this point by suggesting that Adams repudiated democracy in his late work.[153] But it is also clear that democracy as well as much else was threatened by corporate capitalism, by the dramatic growth of technological power, and by the science that made technological power possible.

Notes

Originally appeared in James P. Young, *Henry Adams: The Historian as Political Theorist* (Lawrence: University Press of Kansas, 2001). Reprinted with the permission of the University Press of Kansas. © 2001 by the University Press of Kansas.

1. I want to use the *Education* much less as a clue to the life of Henry Adams than as a source of ideas on his political and social thought. Like most such books, Adams tells us what he wants us to know about his life with relatively little regard for the actual events. Nevertheless, we can learn something about the period itself, as well as his philosophy, from his observations.

2. Colacurcio argues, "The work which seems to be a history turns out to be a good deal more personal than the one which seems to be an autobiography" (Michael Colacurcio, "The Dynamo and the Angelic Doctor: The Bias of Henry Adams' Medievalism," *American Quarterly* [Winter 1965]: 697). Robert Manes agrees (*Henry Adams on the Road to Chartes* [Cambridge: Harvard University Press, 1971], 238).

3. Andrew Delbanco, "Henry Adams and the End of the World," in *Required Reading* (New York: Farrar, Straus, and Giroux, 1997), 98. I disagree with Delbanco's argument that Adams's corrosive irony was meant to dissolve the self. However, this is a fine essay.

4. Michael Rogin, "Christian v. Cannibal," *London Review of Books* (April 1, 1999), 19.

5. Alfred Kazin, *An American Procession* (New York: Vintage Books, 1985), 278; see also 294. One is reminded of the famous quip about Winston Churchill's history of World War I: "Winston has written a three volume work about himself and called it *The World Crisis.*"

6. J. C. Levenson, *The Mind and Art of Henry Adams* (Stanford, Calif.: Stanford University Press, 1957), 289.

7. For a somewhat overinterpreted account of the publishing history of the book, see Edward Chalfant, "Lies, Silence, and Truth in the Writings of Henry

Adams," in *Henry Adams and His World*, ed. David R. Contosta and Robert Muc-cigrosso (Philadelphia: American Philosophical Society, 1993), 8–22. The Samuels edition of the *Education* contains a useful editorial selection from Adams's letters bearing on his intentions as the author (507–18).

8. Alfred Kazin. *An American Procession* (New York: Vintage Books, 1985), 146.

9. *The Education of Henry Adams*, ed. Ernest Samuels and Jayne Samuels (Boston: Houghton Mifflin, 1973), 3–4.

10. Ibid., 7.

11. Ibid., 15–16.

12. Ibid., 32–33.

13. Ibid., 12.

14. Ibid., 38.

15. Ibid., 47–48.

16. Ibid., 48–49.

17. Ibid., 54–58; quote at 57–58.

18. Ibid., 60, 560, editor's nn.9, 10. Adams had a copy of the Marx dated 1887.

19. Ernest Samuels. *The Young Henry Adams* (Cambridge: Harvard University Press, 1948), 17; William Jordy, *Henry Adams: Scientific Historian* (New Haven: Yale University Press, 1952), 91, 179 n.51. Or, as Samuels puts it, "Henry continued to subordinate science to conventional metaphysics as did Agassiz himself" (*Young Henry Adams*, 165).

20. *Education*, 63.

21. Ibid., 70–97.

22. For Henry's detailed contemporaneous account, see the title essay in *Great Secession Winter.*

23. *Education*, 99.

24. Ibid., 100–101.

25. Ibid., 102.

26. Ibid., 104–5.

27. Ibid., 107.

28. Adams made belated amends to his slighting of Lincoln when he con-tributed an introduction to the letters and selections from the diary of John Hay, prepared with Mrs. Hay. In international politics, Adams wrote, "the hand is the hand of Hay, but the temper, the tone, the wit and genius bear the birthmark of Abraham Lincoln." As Samuels remarks, this comes with "sudden grace," while it also suggests reservations about Hay's achievements (Ernest Samuels, *Henry Ad-ams: The Major Phase* [Cambridge: Harvard University Press, 1964], 408). Herbert Croly recalled to Edmund Wilson a meeting with Adams to discuss the possibility of his writing a biography of Hay. "By the time he left Adams' presence, Croly

had been made to feel that he would not for anything in the world undertake the biography of Hay. Though Adams' ostensible role had been that of a friend of the family who was trying to provide a memorial for an old and valued friend, he had constantly betrayed this purpose by intimating in backhanded but unmistakable fashion his conviction that Hay was a mediocre person, that it would be impossible to write truthfully about him, and to satisfy the family at the same time, and that no self-respecting writer ought to think of taking on the job" (Edmund Wilson, introduction to Henry Adams, *The Life of George Cabot Lodge,* in *The Shock of Recognition,* ed. Edmund Wilson [New York: Modern Library, 1955], 743–44). This runs very much counter to the opinion of Hay expressed in the *Education.*

29. *Education,* 109; emphasis added.

30. On Socratic ignorance in this instance, see *Education,* 574, editor's n. 21. Samuels also comments on the "widening embrace of the metaphor of 'education.' Education becomes an omnibus term for knowledge of cause and effect in every area of human experience, especially history and politics." Adams, Samuels also notes, felt that he could assume that they knew less than he because they were unaware of *their* ignorance. One must doubt that this was the case with Lincoln. Finally, Samuels suggests that Adams implies that soldiers on the battlefield would teach their leaders what was at stake and what needed to be done. Perhaps. One might add that if so, there is a certain similarity to Tolstoy's *War and Peace* here. This is true, I think, in other aspects of Adams's work, though it seems less clear here.

31. There is no clue as to how close to the inside Henry got in his post or whether he participated as an adviser in the decision-making process. There is the precedent of his grandfather John Quincy Adams, who held responsible positions as a teenager. Henry was twenty-three when he went to London.

32. *Education,* 114–15.

33. Ibid., 116.

34. Ibid., 128, 132, 133.

35. Ibid., 135.

36. Ibid., 148.

37. Ibid., 149, 151.

38. Ibid., 153–54.

39. Ibid., 155. In fairness to Gladstone, it should be noted that his communication to Palmerston was dated before the news from Antietam, so that on this point, he looks less foolish than Adams suggests. However, Gladstone was soon to give Adams more ammunition after he was in full possession of the facts.

40. William Gladstone quoted in *Education,* 156.

41. Ibid., 156–59.

42. Ibid., 163–65.

43. Ibid., 161–62. Gladstone's notes are bizarre and are clearly designed to make both Russell and Palmerston look bad.

44. George F. Kennan, *Soviet-American Relations, 1917–1920, I, Russia Leaves the War* (Princeton, N.J.: Princeton University Press, 1956), viii. It is interesting to reflect on the similarities between Adams and Kennan. The latter, while not of Adams's class background, was still anxious to serve his country and was sometimes vilified for his pains. He can be highly critical and at the same time movingly patriotic in the best sense of the word, that is, by trying to serve and reserving the right to criticize.

45. Much of Brooks Adams's long introduction to his brother's posthumously published collection of essays directed toward a "science" of history is devoted to John Quincy Adams. See "The Heritage of Henry Adams," in *The Degradation of the Democratic Dogma*, ed. Charles Hirschfeld, with an introduction by Brooks Adams (New York: Harper Torchbooks, 1969), 1–122.

46. John Adams, *Discourses on Davila*, quoted in Levenson, *Mind and Art*, 27.

47. Levenson, *Mind and Art*, 27, citing Yvor Winters.

48. After more than fifty years, the outstanding work on the subject is still Richard Hofstadter, *Social Darwinism in American Thought*, rev. ed. (1944; Boston: Beacon Press, 1955). For a brief summary, see also James P. Young, *Reconsidering American Liberalism* (Boulder, Colo.: Westview Press, 1996), 127–36, and the literature cited there.

49. *Education*, 225–26.

50. For those interested in a more technical discussion, see Jordy, *Scientific Historian*, esp. 172–88; and Samuels, *Young Henry Adams*, 161–67. Jordy and Samuels disagree on some of the technical aspects of Adams's writing on evolution, particularly his review of Sir Charles Lyell's *Principles of Geology* (see Jordy, *Scientific Historian*, 178–79 n. 51).

51. *Education*, 230.

52. Ibid., 231.

53. Ibid., 231–32.

54. Ibid., 232.

55. Levenson, *Mind and Art*, 319.

56. *Education*, 271–72.

57. Ibid., 287–88.

58. Ibid., 288–89.

59. Levenson, *Mind and Art*, 323.

60. Ibid., 321. Yet, as Levenson points out, in *Chartres*, Adams tells us that we may choose between Saint Francis's embrace of death and the complexities of Saint Thomas. This, he says, is as close as Adams came to saying, with Dylan Thomas, "Do not go gentle into that good night." Adams, "fully conscious of how

fragile were the works of man, chose the less simple solution" (ibid., 324; for *Chartres*, see 661).

61. *Education*, 300–301.

62. Ibid., 301.

63. Ibid., 300. Adams was doubtless right that he could teach students nothing (ibid., 306). Students really teach themselves, but they can be guided, and by all accounts, Adams was brilliant in that role.

64. Ibid., 321, 325.

65. Ibid., 335, 336.

66. As it turned out, Adams, being a more prudent investor, was in less danger than his brothers Brooks and Charles. As Brooks says, "Henry was not the least affected by our indiscretions" ("The Heritage of Henry Adams," in *Degradation*, 90).

67. Samuels, *Major Phase*, 124.

68. *Education*, 342.

69. Russell L. Hanson and W. Richard Merriman, "Henry Adams and the Decline of the Republican Tradition," *American Transcendental Quarterly* (September 1990): 175. They suggest that since one way to return to first principles to revive civic virtue is to write history, this may explain Adams's abandonment of traditional history. Perhaps this is so, though it is just as possible that Adams, with his interest in sweeping generalizations, merely wanted to expand his horizons. Recall that he wrote that between them, he and John Hay had written most of the American history worth writing. Hanson and Merriman are certainly right that at this point in the nineteenth century, a return to republican principles was too late.

70. Henry Adams to Elizabeth Cameron, July 27, 1896, in *Letters*, 4:404, 406.

71. Henry Adams to Elizabeth Cameron, October 19, 1896, ibid., 433.

72. Brooks Adams was also delighted by Bryan's performance, particularly since he had refused to be bought off by Wall Street money. However, he feared that the moneyed interests would seize the government if Bryan won (Samuels, *Major Phase*, 169).

73. *Education*, 355. It should be remembered that since he resided in the District of Columbia, Adams could not vote there. Moreover, he did not maintain a Massachusetts voting address. Perhaps he felt that, given the state of the parties, there was no point in voting.

74. Walter Dean Burnham, "The Changing Shape of the American Political Universe," in *The Current Crisis in American Politics* (New York: Oxford University Press, 1982), 51, 25–55. This is an important article for understanding the crisis of both Adams's time and our own; indeed, the two are part of the same movement.

75. *Education*, 360. On Brooks Adams and his relation to Henry, I found the following to be helpful: Charles A. Beard, introduction to Brooks Adams, *The Law*

of Civilization and Decay (1896; reprint, New York: Alfred A. Knopf, 1943), 3–53; Daniel Aaron, *Men of Good Hope* (New York: Oxford University Press, 1951), 252–80; Samuels, *Major Phase*, 17–155; and, above all, R. P. Blackmur, "Henry and Brooks Adams: Parallels to Two Generations," *Southern Review* (Autumn 1939): 308–34.

76. Henry Adams to Brooks Adams, April 2, 1898, in *Letters*, 4:557. Adams goes on to add a second formula to the effect that, given centralization, Asia is cheaper than Europe, so that Asia tends to survive and Europe to perish (ibid., 558).

77. *Education*, 339.

78. Henry Adams to Brooks Adams, May 7, 1898, in *Letters*, 4:586–87.

79. Levenson, *Mind and Art*, 292–93.

80. Joseph A. Schumpeter, *Capitalism, Socialism, and Democracy*, 3rd ed. (New York: Oxford University Press, 1950), esp. 64–163; quote at 302.

81. Blackmur, "Henry and Brooks Adams," 321–22.

82. *Education*, 225. Adams did follow developments in Marxist theory. Brooks sent him a copy of the German edition of Eduard Bernstein's *Evolutionary Socialism*. Saying that he took Marxism to be the foundation of Brooks's ideas, Henry added, "The assertion of the law of economy as the law of history is the only contribution that the socialists have made to my library of ideas, and I am curious to get their best statement" (Henry Adams to Brooks Adams, October 31, 1899, in *Letters*, 5:54–55). A few days later, he responded in more detail. After noting that Bernstein is Jewish and that his writing style is impossible, Adams states: "He seems to prove that he is very much in my intellectual condition. He throws up the sponge in the whole socialist fight. Absolutely nothing is left of Karl Marx except his economical theory of history in its crudest form. . . . Bernstein not only argues, but proves, that the Marxian theory of a social cataclysm has been abandoned, and that the socialist has no choice but to make himself a petit bourgeois, with all the capitalistic machinery and methods. He preaches the bankruptcy of the only idea that our time has produced." He adds that the capitalists have abandoned their teachers and principles and that there is no reason why the capitalist "should not become a socialist functionary" (Henry Adams to Brooks Adams, November 5, 1899, ibid., 56). This is an early statement of the convergence theory so much discussed two to three decades ago. The influence of Comte is most clear in an essay called "The Rule of Phase Applied to History."

83. Levenson, *Mind and Art*, 226.

84. William Merrill Decker, *The Literary Vocation of Henry Adams* (Chapel Hill: University of North Carolina Press, 1990), 98.

85. Henry Adams to Elizabeth Cameron, January 13, 1898, in *Letters*, 4:522–25; Henry Adams to Elizabeth Cameron, September 5, 1899, in *Letters*, 5:26.

86. Levenson, *Mind and Art*, 223–24; Henry Adams to Elizabeth Cameron, September 5, 1899, in *Letters*, 5:26. Levenson notes that Adams's virulence tapered off when the Dreyfus affair came to an end and he turned to more constructive work. "The latter explanation is the one hopeful aspect of a story which is disagreeable in itself and necessarily alarming to a world that has witnessed antisemitism as a catastrophic social event rather than as, in Adams's case, a datum of personal psychology like insomnia or an addiction to privacy. One consequence of the episode is the occasional use of the word 'Jew' which disfigures, albeit inessentially, his late masterpieces—pockmarks of a disease that can be fatal" (*Mind and Art*, 226).

87. Samuels, *Major Phase*, 358.

88. Levenson, *Mind and Art*, 224. Samuels is comprehensive in his coverage of Adams's anti-Semitism; see *Major Phase*, esp., 129–30, 356–58.

89. Eugenia Kaledin, *The Education of Mrs. Henry Adams* (Amherst: University of Massachusetts Press, 1994), 121–22.

90. Barbara Miller Solomon quoted in E. Digby Baltzell, *The Protestant Establishment: Aristocracy and Caste in America* (New York: Vintage Books, 1964), 91.

91. *History I*, 119–20. Levenson comments that this indicates a profound commitment to American democracy. "The scion of presidents, not the first of his family to be accused of blood-pride, made steerage immigrants, malarial frontiersmen, and lower-class inventors his heroes alongside the Virginia aristocrat to whom he gave his qualified allegiance" (*Mind and Art*, 148).

92. E. Digby Baltzell, *Protestant Establishment: Asitrocracy and Class in America* (Glencoe, Ill.: Free Press, 1958), 91. This date might be subject to correction if one searched the now standard Harvard edition of the letters, which was not available to Baltzell when he wrote. He used the Cater edition. However, the date is surely approximately correct.

93. Ibid., 93. For Baltzell's more general theory, see 7–10.

94. The classic study of this subject is John Higham, *Strangers in the Land* (New York: Atheneum, 1963).

95. Samuels, *Major Phase*, 357.

96. See the massive study by Rogers Smith, *Civic Ideals* (New Haven, Conn.: Yale University Press, 1997). Smith is mainly interested in the problems of African Americans and women. Somewhat strangely, there is no index entry for Jews or antiethnic prejudice generally. Henry Adams is quoted briefly without reference to the subject.

97. Carey McWilliams, *A Mask for Privilege* (Boston: Little, Brown, 1948), 179–81.

98. Ibid., 164.

99. *Education*, 238.

100. McWilliams, *Mask for Privilege*, 70. In spite of this observation, Adams, in an excess of self-pity combined with a seeming failure of self-knowledge, claims that he "found no fault with his time" and that he was no worse off than the buffalo or the Indians, but he did insist that "he himself was not at fault" (*Education*, 238).

101. Karl Marx, *On the Jewish Question*, in *The Marx-Engels Reader*, 2nd ed., ed. Robert C. Tucker (New York: W. W. Norton, 1978), 48; emphasis in original.

102. Ibid., 49; emphasis in original. It is interesting to note that at the time, the German word *Judentum* had, as its secondary meaning, commerce (ibid., 50, editorial note).

103. Henry Adams to Brooks Adams, April 12, 1906, in *Letters*, 6:13.

104. *Education*, 500–501. Cf. Carey McWilliams, *The Education of Carey McWilliams* (New York: Simon and Schuster, 1979), 323.

105. McWilliams, *Education of McWilliams*, 323.

106. *Education*, 339.

107. Ibid., 340.

108. Ibid., 340–41.

109. Ibid., 342.

110. Ibid., 343. To this day, Chicago seems the quintessentially American city that Adams suggests it is, as well as an architectural marvel.

111. Ibid., 344.

112. Ibid., 379.

113. In fact, Adams wrote a prayer to the dynamo in the form of a poem included in a longer prayer to the Virgin of Chartres. One verse seems to hint at the possibility that he sees technology as a neutral force:

> We know not whether you are kind
> Or cruel in your fiercer mood;
> But be you Matter, be you Mind,
> We think we know that you are blind,
> And we alone are good.

"Prayer to the Dynamo," in *Novels, Mont-Saint-Michel and Chartres, The Education of Henry Adams*, ed. Ernest Samuels (New York: Library of America, 1986), 1204. See also David E. Noble, *The Religion of Technology: The Divinity of Man and the Spirit of Invention* (New York: Alfred A. Knopf, 1997).

114. *Education*, 380–81.

115. Ibid., 382.

116. Susan Haack, "Staying for an Answer: The Untidy Process of Groping for the Truth," *Times Literary Supplement* (July 9, 1999), 13.

117. *Education*, 382. The comment about Adams giving up too soon on con-

ventional history does nothing to undermine the importance of his work pursuant to the impact of the dynamos.

118. Ibid., 383.

119. Ibid. Notice the parallel between the force of the Virgin and the power of X-rays, as Adams tries to assimilate the latest science to his thinking.

120. Ibid., 384.

121. Ibid., 384–85.

122. For a discussion of Whitman and Adams, see William H. Jordy, "Henry Adams and Walt Whitman," *South Atlantic Quarterly* (April 1941): 132–45.

123. *Education*, 387–88.

124. Ibid., 389.

125. Ibid., 397; emphasis added.

126. Ibid., 398.

127. The closest approach to such a reading is Martin J. Sklar, "Disaffected with Development: Henry Adams and the 1960's 'New Left,'" in *The United States as a Developing Country* (Cambridge: Cambridge University Press, 1992), 197–208. Sklar calls himself an *"extremely* old leftist" who believes in the Enlightenment and nineteenth-century rationalism, humanism, and evolutionism. Sklar sees the 1960s radicals as miniature Adamses, caught in a period of transition between capitalist industrialism and socialism—a socialism that does not look very different from the capitalism it is trying to supplant.

128. *Education*, 405. Note that this is eight years after his speculations on Hungarian socialism in his letter to Brooks Adams.

129. Ibid., 406.

130. Ibid., 406–7.

131. Ibid., 407.

132. Ibid.

133. R. P. Blackmur, *Henry Adams*, ed. Veronica A. Makowsky, foreword by Denis Donoghue (New York: Harcourt Brace, 1980), 154.

134. Levenson, *Mind and Art*, 296. Perhaps the point is not as frivolous as Levenson claims. Wilson Carey McWilliams suggests to me that Adams's teaching is not unlike Matthew Arnold's "Dover Beach," where "ignorant armies clash by night."

135. Louis Hartz, *The Liberal Tradition in America* (New York: Harcourt Brace, 1955).

136. Henry Adams to Elizabeth Cameron, January 22, 1915, in *Letters*, 6:681.

137. Levenson, *Mind and Art*, 271.

138. *Education*, 408. However, in his late "Letter to American Teachers of History," he succumbs to chaos.

139. Henry Adams to Brooks Adams, May 7, 1901, in *Letters*, 5:251; emphasis added.

140. Henry Adams to Bay Lodge, December 1, 1904, in *Letters*, 5:616. Note that Bay Lodge had just written a poem about Cain.

141. *Education*, 408.

142. In working through the complexities of Adams's thought on politics early in this century, particularly as expressed in his letters, I relied heavily on Levenson, *Mind and Art*, esp. 289–304.

143. *Education*, 436.

144. Ibid., 417.

145. Ibid., 418. It is no wonder that Roosevelt was not enthusiastic about the *Education*. Adams's comments there are mild compared with his abuse of Roosevelt in his private correspondence.

146. Ibid., 418–19. In time, Adams came to be disdainful of Lodge. In 1900 he wrote: "Cabot more and more makes me sea-sick. His senatorial atmosphere has become unendurable" (Henry Adams to Elizabeth Cameron, April 16, 1900, in *Letters*, 5:121). Earlier the same year, he wrote: "As usual, the Senate makes trouble; and you know that to me the Senate means practically Cabot; and you know Cabot; and you don't know that Cabot is ten times more *cabotin* than ever. The word was made to describe him, and it fits as though it were a Sargent portrait" (Henry Adams to Elizabeth Cameron, February 19, 1900, ibid., 94). According to an editorial note, *cabotin* means a "second-rate strolling actor; hence, political showman."

147. McWilliams, *Education of McWilliams*, 323.

148. Henry Adams to Brooks Adams, September 20, 1910, in *Letters*, 6:369; emphasis added. As I suggest later, 1910 marked a crucial turning point for Adams, and not a turning point for the better.

149. Henry Adams to Elizabeth Cameron, August 27, 1905, in *Letters*, 5:710.

150. Henry Adams to Elizabeth Cameron, ibid., 486. Earlier in the same letter, in one of his moods where he seems to hope that catastrophe will usher in a dramatically different system, Adams says, "Only I fear that, with their confounded practical common-sense, our people will soon realize [what is happening], and invent some practical working system" (485).

151. Blackmur, "Henry and Brooks Adams," 316. Blackmur observes that Henry's sophistication overrode his candor and that Brooks's candor sometimes triumphed over his sophistication. During World War I, Brooks was elected to the Massachusetts constitutional convention, where he astonished the delegates with his "totalitarian proposals to save society." He believed that democracy would perish without draconian measures. In spite of this, he attacked what he saw as Wilson's "dictatorial methods," saying that they were not "the right foundation for an authoritarian society." His hatred for the president was so great that "in an agony of frustration he wildly exhorted Lodge, 'Kill Wilson!'" While Henry was

by this time as critical of the failures of democracy as Brooks, "he was as skeptical of the prescriptions of the radical Right as of those of the radical Left—and, for that matter, of every other point of the political compass" (Samuels, *Major Phase,* 567–68).

152. See Charles Hirschfeld, introduction to *Degradation*, vii.

153. Charles William Eliot quoted in Samuels, *Major Phase,* 369. For Samuels's view, see ibid. It is true that after his final published work, Adams was bitterly critical of democracy in his letters, but his published work held, sometimes tenuously, to his belief.

CHAPTER 10

Henry Adams and the "Burden of History": Intimations of Fraternity amidst the Ravages of Nature Conquered

Wilson Carey McWilliams
edited by Patrick J. Deneen

WILSON CAREY MCWILLIAMS (1933–2005) was a dean of American political thought, author of the magisterial and sweeping study *The Idea of Fraternity in America* (1973) and of countless essays on American thought, religion, and politics. *The Idea of Fraternity in America* explores America's less dominant, but essential, "alternative" tradition to that of classical liberalism, identifying a long-standing and persistent theme in American political thought that emphasized fraternity, community, self-sacrifice, and even love as a main object and purpose of human politics. The "alternative" tradition in American political thought is a necessary antidote to liberalism's false promises of individual autonomy and human mastery over nature. Human beings' efforts to realize these promises ends in alienated, undignified lives. McWilliams traces the theme of fraternity from the thought of the Puritan founders of America, through its greatest literary figures, and in the thought of a number of America's figures outside the mainstream, such as the Anti-Federalists, the populists, and the literary voices of America's black novelists such as Baldwin and Ellison. *The Idea of Fraternity in America* was based on McWilliams's dissertation, which was written at the University of California at Berkeley under the direction of Sheldon Wolin. This essay on the thought of Henry Adams, found among McWilliams's papers, was one of a number of chapters in the original dissertation that explored some defenders of fraternity. In this essay, McWilliams examines the integrity and interconnections of Adams's thought among his many works in various genres, finding there a robust defense of fraternity that was ardently commended in a time of the ascent of the human mastery of nature. Although it can't be known if and how McWilliams would have revised the essay for publication in this venue, it is almost certain that he would have wanted to contribute to a treatment of Adams's political thought. McWilliams continued throughout his entire career to teach *The Education of Henry Adams* as a constitutive text in his core course on American political thought, and he considered Adams to be among the most important thinkers in the American tradition. As this essay evinces, Adams represented for McWilliams a remarkable voice of dissent from the dominant liberal tradition of American political thought and thus a great resource for and defender of the idea of fraternity in America.

❖

Henry Adams has been an annoying, as well as perplexing, figure in American thought and letters. Adams had the advantages that any critic might wish for himself: good birth and high status, independent financial means, and a brilliant and subtle intelligence. Moreover, at virtually everything he attempted, Adams attained at least a modicum of success. Teacher, historian, journalist, novelist, aesthetician: in all his roles, he achieved some degree of notoriety and historical importance. Yet Adams persisted in pronouncing himself a failure.

The literal-minded among his critics have been sent scurrying in search of some "failure" in Adams's life, some unrealized ambition like the dream of political power. Such an analysis may have its points, but these are very limited. Adams himself, of course, identified his failure with the paradoxical term "education." The connection is not hard to seek: at least at one level, Adams learned that life itself, on its own terms, is a "failure," inadequate to the demands of the spirit of man.[1] Yet, at a second level, the literal-minded critic is closer to the truth. Adams did sense himself as a failure even within the limits of human existence. In that sense, it may be said that Adams believed that he had failed to realize some promise of potential within himself, been unable to translate *potentia* into *potestas*.[2]

The two "failures" of Henry Adams reflect his own basic understanding of the nature and condition of man. Dualism was the underlying theme of that understanding: man is divided between desires for affection, emotional gratification, and freedom from responsibility on the one hand, and his reason, his imagination, his sense of choice and desire for purpose on the other. Those two aspects of man Adams recognized in the deities of *Mont-Saint-Michel and Chartres*: God and the Virgin, judgment and innocence, purpose and affection.[3]

Adams was reared in the Enlightenment tradition (which his brothers never discarded),[4] and it was natural for him to make an early identification of purpose with the natural order: to see in the movement of matter and the logic of process the signs of an evolving purpose, and of historical progress. Yet the "education" of Henry Adams led him to doubt his faith in history, to recognize the power of the contingent in natural process, to discern unique facts that the process of events seemed unable to explain. Certainly, the comfortable faith of his ancestors lapsed: if there was purpose and intention in the process of events, it was mysterious and unknown, still to be discovered by man.[5]

Man, in Adams's view, became a wanderer, estranged from a knowledge of God and purpose, destined to seek Him—in vain—in the universe of natural things. Lived in isolation, man's life is a history of failure, guilt, and self-reproach. Nor will man long bear that state of self-guilt with equanimity: he will seek to turn his mind from the quest for purpose to the conquest of nature, the struggle to impose his own order on process, to command nature to conform to his overfragmentary understanding. Yet such an effort is folly; it is self-defeating and destructive of the nature of man. Nonetheless, it testifies to the fact that life as man perceived it, as a "drift toward death, is not enough"; man will seek to impose purpose *in* it if he lacks the courage to seek purpose *beyond* it.[6]

It is, of course, love, the affection of person for person, that satisfies the need of man for meaning-in-nature, and provides him with the courage to continue his wandering. Yet "love" is not, for Adams, simply a sentimentalist's resolution of the human dilemma. Not all love is admirable; certainly, physical attraction and gratification are hardly sufficient on their own terms. Hence, both Henry Adams's heroines reject the "love" they are offered since it is devoid of what hallows love—a common purpose and "object" of love that draws men together. The male figures in *Democracy* and *Esther* are, in one sense, identical: they are guided by egotism, by a theatrical desire for reputation and fame, or by the cynical pursuit of wealth and power. Neither can acknowledge ignorance, weakness, and failure, the dependence that is a prerequisite of any genuine interpersonal affection. Their objects of love are still themselves, and the demand of the heroines an adoration of that illusionary self rather than affection for the real man. Adams often used "male" and "female" as moral archetypes: God and the Virgin, the wanderer and the affection-giver. Yet it is important to realize that Adams did not imagine that these ideal types corresponded to actuality. His own heroines are the seekers, needing affection yet unwilling to endure the moral pretense of men; Adams wrote his second novel under a feminine pseudonym, suggesting perhaps his own desire to give and receive affection. Indeed, it is their "maleness," their entrapment in a social role that requires an inhuman strength and independence, that fatally isolates Adams's leading male characters and destines them to the effort to "conquer" or to gain fame as a means to affection, an end they fear to acknowledge. Mankind is the same in spirit, regardless of sex, yet affection is the sine qua non of the quest for purpose. Hence, for Adams, woman is closer to the path of human development. Her social role allows her the affectionality which that of man is inclined to deny; neither role, however, is complete in itself.[7]

The two roles, however, like the two deities, create roles that form the basis of Adams's historical theory. "Decline" or "progress," the terms that Adams contrasted in his famous essay, are far too simple to explain the facts and development of human history. If, in some sense, Adams felt more inclined to "decay," it was because that term spoke more meaningfully to the conditions of the modern age. The historical theory that Adams developed from his dualistic analysis may be summarized as follows:

The Development of Purpose
The Stage of Militancy
The Stage of Physical Success and Psychological Failure
The Quest for Innocence and Affection

For example, the Middle Ages, based on the high purpose of Christianity, began with the militant age of Normanry that Adams illustrates in *Mont-Saint-Michel and Chartres.* The Normans overcame the sense of estrangement from God in the effort to conquer nature and the infidel;

estranging themselves from nature, they could believe that they had grown closer to the Divine. Yet the very success of the Middle Ages in achieving political order and a modicum of prosperity, in pacifying and taming the world, drew men back into the nature they had never really left. Their involvement with the world left them with a terrifying sense of their distance from the God of Judgment, their shortcomings and failures. Hence, in the later Middle Ages, the cult of the Virgin came to dominate men's religious thought. Purpose was succeeded by a desire for forgiveness, for love and affection, for freedom from the terrible burdens of failure that high purpose lays on men.

The cycle completed, however, reasserts itself. Calvinism, the high school of the Protestant revolt, sought once again to separate God from nature to restore the sense of human imperfection. It laid a burden of "self-mortification" on man that man himself could not endure. Hence, Calvinism yielded logically to a new age of militancy: the effort to conquer nature, to share the world in the image of the ideal. Man, believing himself the instrument of purpose, might escape the burden of guilt.[8]

Yet the new cycle is an imperfect analogue of the pattern of the Middle Ages. The Church Militant sought to make man the instrument of a purpose *beyond* nature. Science, the basis of the new faith (Adams was always careful to note that scientificity depends on predispositions and commitments no less than more orthodox faiths), reduces man to the instrument of *natural* purpose. The triumph of science, the expansion of the scale and power of human society, is achieved only by reducing man to a force, a mass of beings independent but weak, and, in their weakness subject to prediction on the basis of the laws of atomic physics. Technology and science come to appear as supersensual, metahuman powers with the qualities man once attributed to the Divine. The new age has lost meaning for the individual, yet it is not such as to be able to compel him to feel guilt. He feels, rather, only the weakness and meaninglessness of his condition. Resentful, he is yet unwilling to seek either. He retains an independence of action that the things of nature lack. If he lacks humanity, he may yet turn the weapons of his tormentors back on them. In an astonishingly accurate prediction, Adams forecast that the end cataclysm of the scientific age was likely to begin in 1932, by which time he judged the wrecking and the arming of man would have reached its crisis point.[9]

Any escape from the cycle of history demands fraternity. Men must have communion if they are to face judgment and seek purpose, to accept the humbling of their pride. So sovereign did this requirement seem to Adams (especially in an age of individualism) that he was not without a tendency to romanticize community, to see redemption in that perennial tempting ground of the New England Puritan, the South Sea Isles. Yet such temptations did not change Adams's basic understanding that pure affect without purpose is not enough. He could call, for example, for a "school" of writers in America, united by personal relations and the common quest for purpose, able to avoid the "random and insulated work" for "temporary and personal" aims that characterized the American intellectual. Indeed, a mere minimal solution would prove acceptable: he called for a "party of two" who could criticize American life and society without the desperate desire of the isolated critic for recognition and admiration that leads him either to suppress his criticism or to offer a criticism so extreme as to be "disloyal" and blind to the virtues of the state.[10]

Notably, such a conception, while "aristocratic," is based on political and civic responsibility. The intellectual must criticize, but he must always retain his "loyalty," his sense of obligation to his fellows and to the political order. Indeed, fraternity among intellectuals, while necessary to intellectual excellence, was also the prerequisite of political redemption in Adams's eyes.

Man, if he is to develop humanity, needs political society and civic fraternity. Adams's early quasi-Federalist reverence for the great "machine" of the Constitution yielded with the passing of time. The virtues of the United States, he came to believe, were more dependent on accident than design, and certainly independent of the constitutional mechanism. Jefferson and Gallatin, and their Republican allies, had been wrong to trust the individual—especially the uneducated individual—as generally as they had. Yet they had been right in seeking to base the state on the people; civic virtues and fraternity were the true foundation of political excellence. The great constitutional design, the effort to make self-interest and the public good identical mechanisms of competition, had failed. Only by strengthening the personal devotion of the individual citizen to the public good could republican government be attained.[11]

Such civic virtue, however, required the small state and decentralized government, in which the emotional support of his fellow citizens, and his own sense of personal importance, combined to hold the citizen to the civic ideal. The United States had been, for a time, blessed with isolation from war, been able to avoid the development of a centralized regime. However, Adams noted, the decentralized government of the Union had been turned to a perverted end: the defense of slavery. Neither humanity nor republican principles could tolerate slavery, and hence, given the resistance of the South, centralized government became necessary to overcome the obstruction of local regimes. Adams saw the origins of southern perversity in the hyperindividualism inculcated in the slaveholder. All political institutions were, in such hands, perverted into an instrument of political will rather than fraternity.

The resulting political order in America conformed to Adams's model of mass society. The vast social universe of America had lost any connection to the emotions of the individual: as a result, it had ceased to be able to ennoble him. Sensing only their own weakness, men became the prisoners of natural drift, able to pursue no end more exalted than abundance and material prosperity. Even the ostensible "managers" of the system, the business elites, were capable of no real direction and no higher end. The natural result, then, was the "wreckage" forecast by Adams's historical theory.[12]

Yet Adams's view of men was never entirely fatalistic. The "scientific scandal," man might end in disaster, but he might also be won from the decay of modern life. The raising of the average man to the heights of human nobility, that high goal for which Jefferson and his fellows had discarded the dictates of political prudence—the need for small societies, religion, and hierarchy—was, of course, "improbable" of realization. Yet, Adams argued, it remains the "only experiment worth making," for the process of that experiment alone could avert the coming disaster. Americans must be taught to accept the "burden of humanity" redirected to the perennial purpose and goals of man and their inevitable burden of guilt. Moreover, they must be taught to lessons of the past, and the need for community. Only by such means could Americans escape the cycle in which the idea of war as a "duty" (imposed by purpose) yields to the craven sense of peace as a "passion" (which results from the flight from purpose). America was not a new departure from humanity, a "chosen nation": militancy and the despair following material success were alike a delusion and a snare.[13]

Yet, of course, this educational ideal was at best an improbable one, a political frustration to add to the inevitable frustrations of the intellectual. Those twin frustrations made an intellectual fraternity the more necessary, added a note of desperation to the tones of irony and resignation that play in his writings. Adams's theory left him little to hope for if that fraternity were to be lacking. Intellectual isolation, lived at best as "two lives"—one hidden behind a permanent mask—would be the likely result, along with the eventual poisoning of the spirit by its own need for affection and the resulting attempt to conquer and impose order on the world.[14]

Adams was often accurate as a prophet, and nowhere more so than concerning himself. Man, and especially the man Henry Adams, will not rest with fatalism. In the absence of the fraternity he demanded (and which was all too lacking in his brothers), he felt the temptations of messianism. If creative action, the construction of political fraternity, could not avert the coming disaster, might it not be better to hasten the end? The destruction of the scientific age, with its perversion of man, might be perilous indeed. Yet Adams, with his conviction that—however mysterious—there was a purpose at work in the process of nature, could see that destruction as the condition for the opening of a new cycle, a reborn possibility.

Conscious that war merely provided men with the illusion of control over events, and the shadow of fraternity—the old delusion of militancy— he could refer to the Spanish-American War as a "god-sent call to duty," somehow ennobling America. Indeed, he could treat even Cabot Lodge to lectures on patriotism. Conflict with the foe and the enemy, the Jew or the German, could come to be viewed as redemptive, enabling man to escape the impasse of the age of science. War alone could close the gap between the ideal and the actual, the dream of fraternity and man in the scientific age. That conviction, which his brother Brooks was to feel so much more strongly, might type Henry Adams with the most unfavorable of sobriquets: the precursor of American fascism.

Such a reference, however, would be undeserved. Adams had qualities that made his surrender to the messianic temptation no more than an aberration in his life. The first was his irony, and his ability to be amused even with himself. The second, from which the first derived, was his faith, never deeply hidden, in a unity and purpose beyond nature. That faith might convict Adams of failure, but it imposed also a certain tolerance that moderated Adams's rage at himself, and at a society that failed him and failed men, and failing both, betrayed its own promise and its best heritage.

Notes

1. The words "man" and "woman" have not been changed to gender-neutral language. The distinction between the sexes is important to the argument of *The Idea of Fraternity in America*. For a thoughtful consideration of Professor McWilliams's use of gender-specific language, see Susan McWilliams, "The Brotherhood of Man(liness)," *Perspectives on Political Science* 35, no. 210 (Fall 2006).

2. Henry S. Kariel, "The Limits of Social Science: Henry Adams' Quest for Order," *American Political Science Review* 50 (1956): 1074–92; Yvor Winters, *In Defense of Reason* (New York: Swallow and Morrow, 1947), 495.

3. *Mont-Saint-Michel and Chartres* (New York: Doubleday, 1959), esp. 290, 307, 305–422.

4. Charles Francis Adams, for example, was almost the pure case of the "reform liberal," and Brooks Adams, while more critical of the eighteenth century, always adulated the "liberation" of Massachusetts from religious orthodoxy and could laud the effort of John Quincy Adams to lay science to establish the "ideal" doctrine of liberty, equality, and fraternity for all mankind. See W. C. Ford, ed., *A Cycle of Adams Letters* (Boston and New York: Houghton Mifflin, 1920), 2:90; E. Greifer, "The Conservative Base in America: The Adamses Search for a Pre-Liberal Past," *Western Editorial Quarterly* 15 (1962): 7–8; *The Degradation of the Democratic Dogma* (New York: Capricorn, 1958), 3, 7–36, 53, 74; Brooks Adams, in the *North American Review*, no. 243 (1874): 446; and *The Emancipation of Massachusetts* (Boston and New York: Houghton Mifflin, 1962).

5. George Hochfield, *Henry Adams* (New York: Barnes and Noble, 1962), 3, 91, 122–24; E. Samuels, *The Young Henry Adams* (Cambridge: Harvard University Press, 1942); William Jordy, *Henry Adams: Scientific Historian* (New Haven: Yale University Press, 1958); James Truslow Adams, "Henry Adams and the New Physics: Its Effect on His Theory of History," *Yale Review* 19 (1929): 283–302; Adams, "The Cost of Embargo," in *History of the United States* (New York: Scribner's, 1889–91), vol. 4.

6. *Degradation*, 222–26, 239–43; J. C. Levenson, *The Mind and Art of Henry Adams* (Boston: Houghton Mifflin, 1957), 323; Hochfield, *Henry Adams*, 100–103, 112.

7. *Degradation*, 3–4, 112, 118; Adams, *Democracy* (New York: Holt, 1880); Adams, *Esther* (New York: Holt, 1884); Winters, *In Defense of Reason*, 399; Hochfield, *Henry Adams*, 29–33, 44–54, 100–103, 112.

8. *Mont-Saint-Michel and Chartres*, passim; *Degradation*, 12; Winters, *In Defense of Reason*, 405; Van Wyck Brooks, *New England's Indian Summer* (New York: Dutton, 1940), 481–82. Certainly the best discussion of Adams's conception of history is Ralph Henry Gabriel, *The Course of American Democratic Thought*

(New York: Ronals, 1940), 251–68. See also Jordy, *Henry Adams: Scientific Historian*; and Nathalia Wright, "Henry Adams' Theory of History: A Puritan Defense," *New England Quarterly* 18 (1945): 204–10.

9. *The Education of Henry Adams* (Boston Massachusetts Historical Society, 1918), 34, 265, 443–51, 458–61, 485–88, 494–96; W. C. Ford, ed., *The Letters of Henry Adams* (Boston and New York: Houghton Mifflin, 1930–38), 1:123, 2:244; Gabriel, *The Course of American Democratic Thought*, 264–68; Levenson, *The Mind and Art of Henry Adams*, 209, 302–3; *History*, 9:224–25; Hochfield, *Henry Adams*, 123–24; M. F. Neufield, "The Crisis in Prospect," *American Scholar* 4 (1935): 397–408.

10. *Education*, 19, 343–44, 386–87; *Letters*, 1:46, 177, 308, 418, 439; 2:414; Levenson, *The Mind and Art of Henry Adams*, 202–3; Griefer, "The Conservative Base in America," 13; Dixon Wecter, "Harvard Exiles," *Virginia Quarterly* 10 (1934): 244–57; *Tahiti: Memoirs of Arii Taimai* (New York: R. Spiller, 1947).

11. *History*, 1:55–60, 72–73, 76, 86–87, 114–16, 158–59, 200; 3:348; 9:237; *Degradation*, 78–79, 85; *Democracy*, 75, 77; *The Life of Albert Gallatin* (Boston, 1879), 4–5, 492, 653; *John Randolph* (Boston: Houghton Mifflin, 1882), 58–59; Levenson, *The Mind and Art of Henry Adams*, 60.

12. *Education*, 265, 267, 328, 344, 406–8, 421–22; *History*, 1:116, 170–74, 212; 9:222–24, 241–42; *Degradation*, 109, 207, 231, 257–58; *Letters*, 1:111, 123; 2:177–78, 248; *Democracy*, 10, 72–73, 86–88, 129–30, 340; *John Randolph*, passim; *Essays in Anglo-Saxon Law* (Boston, 1876), 4, 19–25, 36–38, 54; Hochfield, *Henry Adams*, 6–10, 20–22, 36, 58, 98–99; Levenson, *The Mind and Art of Henry Adams*, 60.

13. *Cycle*, 2:96–97; *Education*, 34, 83–91, 420; *History*, 4:289; 9:242; *Democracy*, 75, 77; Levenson, *The Mind and Art of Henry Adams*, 60.

14. *Letters*, 2:251–52; *Degradation*, 99.

Selected Bibliography

Works by Henry Adams

The Degradation of the Democratic Dogma. Edited by Charles Hirschfeld, with an introduction by Brooks Adams. New York: Harper Torchbooks, 1969.

Democracy: An American Novel. In *Novels, Mont-Saint-Michel and Chartres, The Education of Henry Adams,* edited by Ernest Samuels. New York: Library of America, 1986.

The Education of Henry Adams. In *Novels, Mont-Saint-Michel and Chartres, The Education of Henry Adams,* edited by Ernest Samuels. New York: Library of America, 1986.

The Great Secession Winter of 1860–61 and Other Essays. Edited by George Hochfield. New York: Sagamore Press, 1958.

History of the United States during the Administrations of Thomas Jefferson and James Madison. Edited by Earl N. Harbert. New York: Library of America, 1986.

John Randolph. Edited by Robert McColley. Armonk, N.Y.: M. E. Sharpe, 1996.

Letters of Henry Adams. Vols. 1–3. Edited by J. C. Levenson, Ernest Samuels, Charles Vandersee, and Viola Hopkins Winner. Cambridge: Harvard University Press, 1982.

Letters of Henry Adams. Vols. 4–6. Edited by J. C. Levenson, Ernest Samuels, Charles Vandersee, and Viola Hopkins Winner. Cambridge: Harvard University Press, 1988.

The Life of Albert Gallatin. New York: J. B. Lippincott, 1879.

Mont-Saint-Michel and Chartres. In *Novels, Mont-Saint-Michel and Chartres, The Education of Henry Adams,* edited by Ernest Samuels. New York: Library of America, 1986.

Biographies of Adams

Brookhiser, Richard. *America's Dynasty: The Adamses, 1735–1918.* New York: Free Press, 2002.

O'Toole, Patricia. *The Five of Hearts: An Intimate Portrait of Henry Adams and His Friends 1880–1918.* New York: Simon and Schuster, 1990.

Samuels, Ernest. *The Young Henry Adams.* Cambridge: Harvard University Press, 1948.

———. *Henry Adams: The Middle Years.* Cambridge: Harvard University Press, 1958.

———. *Henry Adams: The Major Phase.* Cambridge: Harvard University Press, 1964.

Secondary Sources

Barber, David S. "Henry Adams' Esther: The Nature of Individuality and Immortality." *New England Quarterly* 45, no. 2 (1972): 227–40.

Bell, Millicent. "Adams' *Esther:* The Morality of Taste." *New England Quarterly* 15 (1962): 147–61.

Brooks, Van Wyck. *New England: Indian Summer.* New York: E. P. Dutton, 1940.

Colacurcio, Michael. "The Dynamo and the Angelic Doctor: The Bias of Henry Adams' Medievalism." *American Quarterly* 17, no. 4 (1965): 696–712.

Contosta, David R., and Robert Muccigrosso. *Henry Adams and His World.* Philadelphia: American Philosophical Society, 1993.

Decker, William Merrill. *The Literary Vocation of Henry Adams.* Chapel Hill: University of North Carolina Press, 1990.

Decker, William Merrill, and Earl N. Harbert. *Henry Adams and the Need to Know.* Boston: Massachusetts Historical Society, 2005.

Diggins, John Patrick. "'Who Bore the Failure of Light': Henry Adams and the Crisis of Authority." *New England Quarterly* 58 (1985): 165–92.

Donoghue, Denis. "Henry Adams's Novels." *Nineteenth-Century Fiction* 39, no. 2 (1984): 186–201.

Edwards, Herbert. "Henry Adams: Political Statesman." *New England Quarterly* 22, no. 1 (1949): 49–60.

Ernest, John. "Henry Adams' Double: Recreating the Philosophical Statesman." *Journal of American Culture* 14, no. 1 (1991): 25–35.

Fuehrer, Natalie. "The Landscape of *Democracy.*" *Legal Studies Forum* 22, no. 4 (1998): 627–39.

Harbert, Earl N. *The Force So Much Closer to Home: Henry Adams and the Adams Family.* New York: New York University Press, 1977.

————. *Critical Essays on Henry Adams*. Boston: G. K. Hall, 1981.

Jordy, William. *Henry Adams: Scientific Historian*. New Haven: Yale University Press, 1952.

Kariel, Henry S. "The Limits of Social Science: Henry Adams' Quest for Order." *American Political Science Review* 50 (1956): 1074–92.

Kentleton, John. "Henry Adams and *Democracy*: Public Morality vs. Private Integrity?" *Halcyon* 9 (1987): 21–34.

Lears, T. J. Jackson. *No Place for Grace*. Chicago: University of Chicago Press, 1981.

Levenson, J. C. *The Mind and Art of Henry Adams*. Stanford, Calif.: Stanford University Press, 1957.

McIntyre, John P. "Henry Adams and the Unity of Chartres." *Twentieth Century Literature* 50, no. 4 (1962): 159–71.

O'Brien, Michael. *Henry Adams and the Southern Question*. Athens: University of Georgia Press, 2005.

Rubin, Charles T. "Shoreless Ocean, Sunless Sea: Henry Adams's *Democracy*." In *Challenges to the American Founding: Slavery, Historicism, and Progressivism in the Nineteenth Century*, edited by Ronald J. Pestritto and Thomas G. West. Lanham, Md.: Lexington Books, 2005.

Samuelson, Richard. "The Real Education of Henry Adams." *Public Interest* 147 (2002): 86–102.

Saveth, E. N. "The Heroines of Henry Adams." *American Quarterly* 8 (1956): 234–42.

Shklar, Judith N. "*The Education of Henry Adams* by Henry Adams." In *Redeeming American Political Thought*, edited by Stanley Hoffman and Dennis F. Thompson. Chicago: University of Chicago Press, 1981.

Sommer, Robert F. "The Feminine Perspectives of Henry Adams' *Esther*." *Studies in American Fiction* 18, no. 2 (1990): 131–44.

Wills, Gary. *Henry Adams and the Making of America*. New York: Houghton Mifflin, 2005.

Wolfe, Patrick. "The Revealing Fiction of Henry Adams." *New England Quarterly* 49, no. 3 (1976): 399–426.

Young, James P. *Henry Adams: The Historian as Political Theorist*. Lawrence: University Press of Kansas, 2001.

Contributors

Michael Colacurio is Distinguished Professor of English at UCLA. His publications include *The Province of Piety*; *Doctrine and Difference*; *Godly Letters*; and a number of seminal essays and reviews in the field of American literature and intellectual history.

Henry Steele Commager was professor of history at Columbia University and professor emeritus of history at Amherst College, where he last taught in 1992. He was the author of numerous books on American history, including *The Growth of the American Republic*; *The Study of History*; and *Jefferson, Nationalism, and the Enlightenment*.

Patrick J. Deneen is the Markos and Eleni Tsakopoulos-Kounalakis Associate Professor of Government at Georgetown University. He is the author of *The Odyssey of Political Theory* and *Democratic Faith*, and the coeditor of *Democracy's Literature*. He has published widely on ancient political thought, American political thought, literature and politics, and religion and politics.

Denise Dutton serves as assistant provost at the University of Tulsa, where she directs the Honors Program and the Henneke Center for Academic Fulfillment. Her research engages the challenges of, and impediments to, democratic citizenship that arise with the disenchantment of the late modern world.

B. H. Gilley retired from Louisiana Tech University in 1996. In addition to being a teacher and scholar, Professor Gilley has also served as president of the Louisiana Historical Association.

Russell L. Hanson is professor of political science at Indiana University. He is the author of *The Democratic Imagination in America*; editor of *Governing Partners*; and coeditor of *Political Innovation and Conceptual Change; Reconsidering the Democratic Public;* and *Politics in the American States.*

Wilson Carey McWilliams was professor of political science at Rutgers University. He wrote on a range of topics including religion and politics, contemporary electoral politics, and American political thought. He is most often remembered for his sweeping work *The Idea of Fraternity in America.*

W. Richard Merriman is president of Southwestern College in Winfield, Kansas, and coauthor of *Rights and the Constitution* for the Jefferson Foundation, as well as scholarly articles on tolerance and race-based government policy.

Richard Samuelson is assistant professor of history, California State University, San Bernardino, and the 2009–2010 Garwood Visiting Fellow, James Madison Program, Princeton University. He completed work on this essay while serving as the Henry Salvatori Visiting Scholar in the American Founding at Claremont McKenna College. He has published articles on the political thought of John Adams, John Quincy Adams, and Henry Adams, and on American constitutional thought in general.

Natalie Fuehrer Taylor is associate professor of government at Skidmore College. She is the author of "The Landscape of *Democracy*," an essay on Henry Adams's novel, and of *The Rights of Woman as Chimera: The Political Philosophy of Mary Wollstonecraft.*

James P. Young is professor of political science emeritus at Binghamton University and Visiting Scholar at the University of Michigan. He is the author *of Reconsidering American Liberalism: The Troubled Odyssey of the Liberal Idea;* and *Henry Adams: The Historian as Political Theorist.* He specializes in American political thought, both historical and contemporary.

Index